A Common Theory of Law

Rustam Atadjanov

A Common Theory of Law

Textbook on New Legal Approaches for Post-Soviet States

ASSER PRESS

Springer

Rustam Atadjanov
School of Law
KIMEP University
Almaty, Kazakhstan

ISBN 978-94-6265-710-6 ISBN 978-94-6265-711-3 (eBook)
https://doi.org/10.1007/978-94-6265-711-3

Published by T.M.C. ASSER PRESS, The Hague, The Netherlands www.asserpress.nl
Produced and distributed for T.M.C. ASSER PRESS by Springer-Verlag Berlin Heidelberg

This T.M.C. ASSER PRESS imprint is published by the registered company Springer-Verlag GmbH, DE, part of Springer Nature.
The registered company address is: Heidelberger Platz 3, 14197 Berlin, Germany

Foreword

It was 2008, and I still remember that my first class in law school was a subject described as the foundation for all the courses I was about to take: *Theory of State and Law*. Like in other countries shaped by the Soviet tradition of law, in Ukraine it was also a tapestry of the post-Soviet political science, the *Rechtsstaat* doctrine, and other sophisticated legal theories, served with a generous sauce of *étatisme*. It was no secret that most students despised this class.

However, times have changed. In many law schools, "Theory of *State* and Law" slowly evolved into "Theory of *Law* and State", and eventually became "*Theory of Law*". It was not merely a transformation of a discipline's title; such an onomastic "revolution" reflected the social and political shifts in many post-Soviet countries, as well as changes in academic approaches to the study of law.

It is, therefore, a rare privilege to introduce the monumental work "A Common Theory of Law" by Dr. Rustam Atadjanov, a researcher from Central Asia. Dr. Atadjanov has undertaken a truly Herculean task: to summarise the existing post-Soviet legal theory and present it in a language that offers a different perception of legal realities.

As a scholar of public law and a long-time colleague of the author, I have witnessed his firsthand dedication and intellectual rigor with which this textbook has been developed. This work fills a critical void in legal education within the post-Soviet region, offering an innovative and comprehensive exploration of the theory of law as an autonomous and unifying discipline. I must say that it is, without exaggeration, a landmark contribution to the region's legal academic literature.

Since the dissolution of the Soviet Union, the post-Soviet states have faced significant challenges in reconstructing their legal and educational systems. Legal thought in these countries has often been confined to the dualistic framework of the abovementioned "Theory of State and Law", dominated by statist and positivist paradigms. This approach, rooted in the Soviet legacy, prioritizes the state as the central axis of legal theory while neglecting the broader societal, individualistic and humanistic dimensions of law. Dr. Atadjanov's textbook boldly breaks away from this tradition, presenting a refreshingly holistic and anti-statist perspective that views law not merely as an instrument of state power but as a much wider societal phenomenon, a means of regulation, and a value in its own right.

This textbook is the first of its kind to be written in English, a decision that carries profound significance for legal education in the post-Soviet region. English, increasingly the lingua franca of global academia, serves as a bridge for connecting regional legal thought to the broader international discourse. By situating the theory of law within a global context while addressing the specific challenges and realities of post-Soviet states, Dr. Atadjanov has created a work that is both locally relevant and internationally significant. The textbook promises to be an indispensable tool for professors, instructors, scholars, and students of public law, as well as for legal practitioners and experts who engage with the theory of law in their work.

What sets this book apart is its comprehensive and inclusive approach. It meticulously examines a wide range of legal theories, from classical and positivist traditions to alternative schools of thought such as natural law, libertarian theory, and psychological theory. By doing so, it provides readers with a balanced and nuanced understanding of the diverse intellectual currents that have shaped the development of legal theory. The book also addresses the practical implications of these theories, demonstrating their relevance to contemporary legal and societal challenges in the post-Soviet region. This integration of theory and practice is a testament to the author's commitment to making legal education both meaningful and applicable.

Another commendable feature of this textbook is its innovative methodology. Dr. Atadjanov employs a pluralistic approach, combining historical, analytical, and comparative perspectives to provide a rich and multi-dimensional exploration of legal concepts. He emphasizes the dynamic interplay between law, society, and the state, challenging the rigid and often reductive frameworks that have dominated the region's legal scholarship. By treating the state as one of several key legal concepts—alongside society, power, human will, and regulation—the book repositions the theory of law as a discipline that transcends narrow doctrinal boundaries.

The textbook's structure is thoughtfully designed to guide readers through a logical progression of topics, from the foundational principles of legal theory to its application in specific legal systems and practices. Each chapter is a self-contained unit, yet they collectively form a cohesive narrative that underscores the unifying theme of law as a public good and a societal value. The inclusion of cross-disciplinary insights further enriches the text, making it relevant not only to legal scholars but also to those in related fields such as political science, sociology, and philosophy.

For the post-Soviet region, this book is more than a textbook—it is a manifesto for rethinking legal education and scholarship. It challenges entrenched paradigms and calls for a more open, critical, and innovative approach to understanding the role of law in society. At a time when many countries in the region are grappling with issues of legal nihilism, low legal culture, and the over-instrumentalization of law, this work serves as a beacon of hope and a source of inspiration. It underscores the potential of law to promote not only state interests but also individual rights, societal well-being, and the ideals of justice and constitutionalism.

As someone who has had the honor of knowing (and befriending) Dr. Atadjanov for over a decade, I can attest to his passion for advancing legal scholarship and education in the region. Since 2016, our professional collaboration has been marked by mutual trust, respect, and a shared commitment to the transformative power of law. This textbook is a culmination of his years of academic rigor, practical experience, and unwavering dedication to the field of law.

In conclusion, "A Common Theory of Law" is a groundbreaking contribution that will undoubtedly shape the future of legal education and scholarship in the region. It is a must-read for anyone engaged in the study, teaching, or practice of law, and it deserves a place on the desk of every legal scholar, instructor, and practitioner. I have no doubt that this book will become a foundational text for generations to come, inspiring new approaches to understanding and teaching the theory of law. And I believe students will find studying the theory of law much more engaging with this handbook.

Dr. Atadjanov's work stands as a testament to the power of inclusive ideas to transcend borders and paradigms. It is a privilege for me to recommend this book to readers, and I am confident that it will have a lasting impact on the legal academic landscape of the post-Soviet region and beyond.

Kharkiv, Ukraine
July 2025

Dr. Oleksandr Marusiak
Senior Research Fellow
Scientific Research Institute of State Building and Local Government of National Academy of Law Sciences of Ukraine

Preface

This book is the culmination of years of contemplation, teaching and research into the profound and multifaceted relationship between law and society, particularly in the unique context of the post-Soviet region. Its primary aim is to offer a comprehensive theoretical framework that transcends the conventional and state-centric approaches to legal theory. Instead of viewing law as a mere instrument of state power, this book proposes a more holistic perspective, positioning law as a societal phenomenon and a value in its own right—essential (without exaggeration) for human civilization to thrive and endure.

The need for such a work, I feel, stems from persistent challenges faced by legal education and practice in the post-Soviet states. Despite the passage of decades since the dissolution of the Soviet Union, many of these countries continue to grapple with legal nihilism, underdeveloped legal awareness, and a tendency to reduce law to a tool for serving state interests. By addressing these gaps, this book seeks to provide students, educators, and practitioners with a richer understanding of law as an integral part of societal life, capable of promoting justice, cohesion, and the rule of law.

At its core, this textbook is intended to hopefully and "well-wishingly" fill a critical void in legal education by presenting a unified theory of law that bridges theoretical abstraction and practical application. It draws on diverse traditions and methodologies, ensuring its relevance for a wide range of readers, from undergraduate students to seasoned legal professionals. The book is written in English, recognizing its growing importance as a medium for instruction and academic discourse in the region, and aiming to make its insights accessible to a broader audience.

The guiding principle of this work is the conviction that law is not only a mechanism for regulating behavior but also a cornerstone of human civilization itself. The survival and flourishing of societies depend on their ability to institutionalize and respect the rule of law. In an era of increasing populism and a declining regard for critical thinking, this message resonates more urgently than ever.

It is my sincere hope that this textbook will serve as a meaningful resource for students, scholars, and practitioners alike, fostering a deeper appreciation of legal values and inspiring new approaches to the challenges facing the legal systems of the post-Soviet states. Through a more nuanced understanding of law, I believe we can contribute to building a more just and equitable society.

Almaty, Kazakhstan
July 2025

Rustam Atadjanov

Contents

Chapter 1
Introduction

Contents

Abstract This introductory chapter lays the groundwork for a reimagined legal theory tailored to the post-Soviet states, a region still grappling with the legacy of statist, positivist legal traditions. The author critiques the long-standing Soviet-era framework that conflates law with the interests of the state, arguing for a departure from this approach toward a concept of law as an autonomous, societal phenomenon. The chapter introduces the "common theory of law" as a foundational shift, emphasizing law's role not just in governance but in shaping and reflecting broader societal values. The author frames this textbook as a timely response to persistent issues like legal nihilism, the erosion of critical thinking, and the lack of high-quality legal materials in English for the region. It outlines the book's structure and pedagogical goals, aiming to present law as a value-driven public good that promotes justice, integration, and societal development. This new perspective seeks to equip students, scholars, and practitioners with tools for meaningful legal reform and engagement in post-Soviet contexts.

Keywords Post-Soviet legal theory · Common theory of law · Legal positivism and statism · Legal education reform · Legal nihilism · Law and society · Rule of law in transition · Legal culture in Post-Soviet states

1.1 Introduction

As has regularly been observed—and contemplated by this author, the countries of the post-Soviet region currently find themselves in a crucial phase of societal and legal transformation. In the decades since gaining independence at the beginning of 1990s, these nations have faced the dual challenge of distancing themselves from the legacy of Soviet legal and governance systems while attempting to construct frameworks

R. Atadjanov, *A Common Theory of Law*, https://doi.org/10.1007/978-94-6265-711-3_1

that address their specific historical, cultural, and societal contexts. Despite some progress, the region continues to grapple with issues[1] stemming from the statist and positivist approaches to law, which prioritize state authority and governance over broader societal values and human-centric perspectives. This textbook is designed to offer a fresh, alternative framework for understanding and teaching law in this region as ambitious as it may sound and seem.

The present book introduces and develops the concept of the "common theory of law", which views law as an autonomous, unifying phenomenon within society rather than a mere tool of the state. It aims to dismantle the rigid dualism of the so-called "Theory of State and Law" that has dominated legal education in the region (Central Asia, Caucasus, and Northern Black Sea region[2]), a framework that tends to conflate the legal and state apparatus and subordinates law to state interests. Instead, this textbook positions law as an integral component of society, a mechanism for regulation, and an instrument for addressing complex societal challenges. The objective is to present law as a value and a public good, capable of fostering integration, justice, and social development.

1.2 Background to the Book

The textbook comes, as I believe, particularly timely given the current state of legal culture and awareness in the post-Soviet region. Many countries in the region suffer from pervasive legal nihilism, characterized by a distrust of the population towards legal institutions and norms, as well as a widespread lack of faith in the potential of law to bring about societal change.[3] This has been compounded by rising populism and increasing disregard for critical thinking,[4] both of which undermine efforts to strengthen legal frameworks and promote rule-of-law principles. Against this backdrop and despite possible accusations in excessive alarmism (on the author's side), the need for a renewed focus on legal values and the proper instrumentalization of law is more urgent than ever. By presenting a hopefully comprehensive, structured theory of law, this textbook seeks to enhance legal awareness, contribute to improving the legal culture, and equip readers with the tools necessary to address those pressing issues.

One of the central goals this author attaches to the textbook is to redefine how legal theory is taught and understood across the post-Soviet region. Historically—and it is difficult to deny, legal education in these countries has been heavily influenced by Soviet-era approaches, which emphasized the instrumental role of law in upholding state authority. This perspective has often led to a lack of critical engagement with legal concepts, fostering a view of law as rigid, dry, and inaccessible. The current

[1] Which is understandable given the complexity of the task.

[2] Which includes Belarus, Moldova, Russia, and Ukraine.

[3] See Chap. 5 for more on that point.

[4] A worrying trend that may be observed even among law students.

work challenges this legacy by offering a pluralistic and inclusive approach to legal theory, one that encourages readers to view law not only as a set of rules but also as a dynamic and evolving but also fascinating societal phenomenon necessary for the society to prosper and for the people to lead a civilized life.

This book also addresses the absence of high-quality, English-language resources tailored to the legal systems and academic needs of the post-Soviet states. While Russian remains the dominant language of legal scholarship in the region, the growing importance of English in education, research, and professional practice makes the availability of English-language materials increasingly needed. By providing a comprehensive and accessible treatment of legal theory in English, my textbook seeks to bridge the gap between regional legal scholarship and global academic discourse, enabling students, educators, but also practitioners to engage more effectively with international perspectives.

1.3 Structure of the Book

The structure of the textbook reflects its commitment to providing a systematic and holistic understanding of legal theory, beginning with foundational concepts and gradually moving toward practical applications. The first chapter, i.e., this introduction, sets the stage by outlining the purposes and objectives of the book, explaining the rationale behind its approach, and offering an overview of its content, as the reader can see. Each subsequent chapter is designed to build on the insights of the previous one, creating a hopefully coherent and interconnected narrative that guides readers through the complexities of legal theory.

Chapter 2, titled "The Subject of Common Theory of Law", establishes the framework for the discipline. It defines the scope and methodology of common legal theory, describing its role as a foundational science that synthesizes diverse legal traditions and provides a unified framework for understanding legal phenomena. This chapter lays the groundwork for the rest of the textbook, offering readers a conceptual toolkit for analyzing the emergence, evolution, and societal significance of law. The approach presented in this chapter also emphasizes the interdisciplinary nature of legal theory, showing how insights from sociology, philosophy,[5] and political science can deepen our understanding of legal phenomena.

In Chap. 3, dealing with society as a legal phenomenon, the book explores the dynamic relationship between law and society. It examines how social norms and regulators influence human behavior and how legal norms, in turn, shape societal values and interactions. This chapter emphasizes the dual role of law as both a product of societal processes and an active agent in societal transformation, with a particular focus on the role of civil society in the post-Soviet context. It also highlights the importance of understanding society not merely as a backdrop for

[5] Despite the modern tendencies to dismiss philosophy as irrelevant and impractical.

legal processes but as a complex and evolving entity that both shapes and is shaped by legal frameworks.

Chapter 4, "Power and State", delves into the concept of power as a central element of legal theory, examining its various forms and manifestations within society. This chapter scrutinizes the nature of state power and its relationship with law, addressing historical and contemporary perspectives on the state's role in governance and regulation. It also critiques the statist approaches prevalent in the region, advocating for a more balanced understanding of the interplay between law, power, and state institutions. The analysis extends to the different types of power that operate within society—such as political, economic, and social power, and their influence on legal systems.

Chapter 5—"*Rechtsstaat* (State of Law) and Civil Society", addresses the principles of the rule of law, human rights, and the role of civil society in fostering democratic governance and societal progress. The chapter discusses the theoretical foundations and practical implications of these concepts, offering insights into their relevance for the legal and political systems of post-Soviet states. It emphasizes the need for legal frameworks that support accountability, transparency, as well as the protection of fundamental individual rights. By highlighting successful examples from other regions, this chapter offers practical recommendations for incorporating these principles into the legal and governance structures of post-Soviet countries.

Chapter 6, which reviews the notion of law as such, provides my detailed analysis of the nature, function, and defining characteristics of law. It examines law's role as a regulator of social behavior and introduces key legal concepts, including volition, interest, and the dichotomy of ius and lex. This chapter offers readers a nuanced understanding of law's societal significance, bridging the gap between theoretical abstraction and practical application.

Chapter 7, called "The Main Theories of the Origin and Nature of Law", provides a historical and analytical overview of influential legal theories. It examines the evolution of legal thought, beginning with mythological and religious conceptions of law and progressing through patriarchal, natural law, social contract, and positivist theories. The chapter also includes critical perspectives such as libertarian and psychological theories, highlighting their contributions to understanding law's development and purpose. This exploration provides readers with a broad intellectual foundation, essential for contextualizing legal concepts within historical and contemporary debates. The diversity of theories discussed underscores the richness of legal thought and its potential to address contemporary challenges.

Chapter 8, on the principles and functions of law, builds on this foundation by exploring the fundamental principles that underpin legal systems and the diverse functions that law serves in society. This chapter discusses the regulatory and protective roles of law, analyzing how these principles are implemented in practice and their implications for the development of legal systems in the post-Soviet region.

Chapter 9, titled "Sources of Law", offers a comprehensive overview of the origins and types of legal norms, from customary law and judicial precedents to normative legal acts and religious texts. This chapter highlights the diversity of legal sources in the region and their role in shaping the content and application of law, providing readers with a deeper understanding of the foundations of legal systems.

Chapter 10, denominated as "System and Structure of Law", examines the internal organization of legal systems, including the components and structure of law, such as legal norms, institutions, and branches. It addresses the distinction between the system of law and the system of legislation and explores the dynamics of law's operation within these frameworks.

Chapter 11, called "Interpretation of Law", focuses on the process of legal interpretation, discussing its object, subject, and various methodologies. This chapter underscores the importance of interpretation in ensuring the effective application of legal norms and resolving ambiguities within legal systems, particularly in contexts where legal traditions and societal norms intersect.

Chapter 12, "Lawful Behavior and Legal Responsibility", investigates the concepts of lawful and unlawful behavior and the principles of legal responsibility. This chapter provides a theoretical framework for understanding these ideas and their practical significance, addressing issues such as the enforcement of legal norms and the promotion of compliance within society.

The penultimate chapter, Chap. 13, which concentrates on major contemporary legal systems, situates the post-Soviet legal experience within a global context. It provides a comparative analysis of major legal systems, including continental law, common law, socialist law, and others, highlighting both the shared principles and unique features of these systems. This part of the book serves as a capstone to the textbook, demonstrating the potential for integrating post-Soviet legal approaches into broader global frameworks.

Finally, Chap. 14 contains the book's conclusion, synthesizes the key insights and arguments presented throughout the textbook. It reflects on the implications of the proposed common theory of law for the region and beyond, offering recommendations for the future development of legal theory and practice. This chapter ties together the threads of the book, providing readers with a clear sense of its overarching contributions and objectives.

Chapter 2
The Subject of the Common Theory of Law

Contents

Abstract This chapter defines the core subject and methodology of the Common Theory of Law, positioning it as both a legal and social science that investigates the universal patterns, origins, and evolution of legal phenomena. It explains the discipline's role in identifying the systemic nature of law within society, distinct from narrower sectoral legal sciences. The chapter outlines its essential functions—cognitive, heuristic, and prognostic—and details the methodological principles that guide its research, including historicism, objectivity, concreteness, and pluralism. Logical tools such as induction, deduction, synthesis, and hypothesis formulation are highlighted as mechanisms for scientific inquiry and theory building. Furthermore, the chapter explores the Common Theory's integrative function within the legal sciences, providing the conceptual foundation for both theoretical-historical and sectoral disciplines. Finally, it critically evaluates the challenges in legal education across post-Soviet states, especially the lingering dominance of statist-positivist frameworks. It calls for a shift toward value-based, pluralistic, and interdisciplinary teaching to build a healthier legal culture and promote critical engagement with legal theory.

Keywords Common theory of law · Legal methodology · Legal science system · Post-Soviet legal education · Legal positivism vs. pluralism · Rule of law culture · Legal theory curriculum · Interdisciplinary legal analysis

R. Atadjanov, *A Common Theory of Law*, https://doi.org/10.1007/978-94-6265-711-3_2

2.1 The Subject and Methodology of the Common Theory of Law

The common theory of law constitutes a scientific discipline dedicated to the study of legal phenomena within the broader framework of social life. As with any science, it possesses a distinct subject of research, encompassing a clearly defined set of phenomena, elements, and the regularities that govern them. The subject matter of the common theory of law pertains to the fundamental and universal patterns underlying the emergence, functioning, as well as evolution of law. This scientific field examines the origins of law, its diverse manifestations, and typological classifications, as well as the foundational principles governing the structure of legal systems and their undeniable functional influence on society. The specificity of the subject matter of the common theory of law as a science is reflected in its two key aspects. First, it addresses legal superstructure in its entirety, synthesizing the accumulated experience of legal development across different historical epochs. Second, the focus of its inquiry is not on particular or isolated legal phenomena, but on the fundamental and universal regularities of law, through which its intrinsic nature and social significance are revealed.[1]

From the nature of its subject matter, it follows that the common theory of law constitutes a **social science**, insofar as it investigates legal phenomena as integral components of broader social structures, including society and the state. At the same time, it is a **legal science**, given that its domain of inquiry is confined to the juridical dimension of social reality. Furthermore, it qualifies as a general theoretical science, since it seeks to identify and elucidate the universal principles underlying the development of law as a systemic phenomenon.[2]

The common theory of law studies the universal patterns, origins, and development of law within its social and systemic contexts

Like all scientific disciplines, the common theory of law fulfills a range of essential functions that define its theoretical and practical significance for the progressive transformation of social life. Its **cognitive** function manifests in the explanation of legal phenomena and processes, offering a comprehensive understanding of the legal superstructure in a generalized form. Beyond mere description, it elucidates the objective mechanisms governing the evolution of legal institutions, identifies the regularities underlying their transformation, and determines their substantive essence. The **heuristic** function extends beyond the mere recognition of known legal

[1] While Khropanyuk utilizes the old traditional misnomer of "theory of state and law", I took the liberty of applying his reasoning and explanation of the subject and methodology to my "common theory of law" as their rationale can be fully applied to the latter without having to maintain the notorious dualism of "state and law". Khropanyuk 2019, at 23.

[2] Ibid., at 24.

regularities by probing deeper into their tendencies, interrelations, and linkages with broader social processes. In doing so, it facilitates the discovery of new patterns governing the legal life of society. The **prognostic** function, in turn, enables the common theory of law not only to establish the existence of emerging legal trends but also to identify the stable trajectories of their future development. By formulating scientific hypotheses regarding the prospective evolution of law, this function ensures that theoretical insights are grounded in an objective reflection of legal regularities, with the veracity of these hypotheses ultimately subjected to empirical verification through practical application.[3]

The carrying out of these functions by common theory of law is closely tied to the specificity of its methodological approach. In fulfilling its explanatory and predictive roles, it not only relies on its own theoretical findings but also synthesizes insights from other legal sciences. What distinguishes its methodological framework is the reliance on general theoretical reasoning, which systematically unveils the causal and functional interdependencies of legal phenomena. This analytical approach enables the identification of universal legal principles in a form abstracted from contingent historical fluctuations and extraneous influences.[4]

While the subject matter of the common theory of law delineates the scope of its inquiry, its methodology addresses the question of how legal phenomena are examined. The method of any science comprises the systematic procedures and conceptual foundations upon which its investigative framework is built. In the case of the common theory of law as presented and explained in this very textbook, methodological approaches are employed to study legal reality through principles that ensure a comprehensive and objective understanding of law's inherent dynamics.[5]

The methodology of the common theory of law involves the application of a system of theoretical principles, logical techniques, and specialized methods aimed at studying the fundamental and universal patterns underlying the emergence and development of legal phenomena. The most essential principles guiding the theoretical study of law encompass several key approaches. The principle of **historicism** necessitates the examination of legal phenomena within the context of their historical evolution and interconnection. A comprehensive study of law requires identifying the conditions and factors that led to its emergence, tracing its principal developmental stages, and, based on this historical perspective, providing a scientifically grounded assessment of contemporary legal structures. The principle of **objectivity** demands an accurate and truthful reflection of legal reality in scientific inquiry. Theoretical analysis must define legal concepts in a manner that reveals their essence, articulating general patterns of their operation that correspond to objective social reality. The principle of **concreteness** emphasizes the necessity of considering the specific conditions under which legal phenomena exist. This approach requires identifying

---

[3] Ibid.

[4] Khropanyuk 2019, at 24–25. Khropanyuk's principles, which can apply to the common theory of law, were sifted out and re-analyzed, to be applied to the common theory of law laid out in this textbook.

[5] Ibid., at 25.

the primary and essential properties, connections, and developmental trends of law. Ultimately, practice serves as the decisive criterion for verifying the validity of scientific knowledge, as the truth of theoretical propositions is confirmed only when they successfully replicate, model, or generate phenomena corresponding to them. The principle of **pluralism** underscores the necessity of a multifaceted approach to legal research. A scientific inquiry that focuses exclusively on select aspects or properties of a legal phenomenon while disregarding others risks reaching one-dimensional conclusions. Pluralism in scientific knowledge ensures comprehensiveness by incorporating diverse perspectives on the origin, essence, social function, structural organization, and developmental trajectory of law. By embracing this methodological pluralism, the common theory of law constructs an optimal system of knowledge that faithfully reflects objective reality, while avoiding the limitations of a unilinear approach, which invariably leads to partial and inadequate conclusions that fail to capture the full complexity and practical significance of legal phenomena.[6]

The common theory of law employs principles like historicism, objectivity, and pluralism to analyze the evolution, structure, and functioning of legal phenomena

To comprehend and elucidate the fundamental patterns governing legal phenomena, the common theory of law employs a range of logical techniques that facilitate the transition of theoretical principles from abstraction into the domain of empirical reality, thereby rendering them operational within the framework of scientific theory.[7] The development of legal concepts relies on various logical mechanisms, including analysis and synthesis, induction and deduction, analogy, and hypothesis formulation. These methodological tools serve as the operative mechanisms by which the truth and objectivity of theoretical propositions are substantiated and verified.

Analysis, as a method of scientific inquiry, serves to dissect the structure of law, delineate its constituent elements, and establish the nature of their interrelationships. A crucial tool for the logical analysis of the legal superstructure is the method of formalization, which enables the identification of logical connections and relationships between the fundamental components of law by abstracting from its secondary properties. Through formalization, the systematization, clarification, and methodological refinement of the content of the common theory of law become possible, allowing for a more precise articulation of its theoretical premises, the clarification of conceptual relationships, and the identification of unresolved scientific problems.[8]

Synthesis, in contrast, operates as a method of integrating the results obtained through analytical investigation. Within the framework of the common theory of law, synthesis facilitates the unification of analytical knowledge concerning individual

[6] Khropanyuk 2019, at 25–26.

[7] These approaches and techniques are well known in the science of logics.

[8] Khropanyuk 2019, at 26–27.

elements of legal phenomena, thereby generating a holistic conceptualization of law.[9]

Induction, as a logical method, proceeds from the particular to the general. The process of legal inquiry often begins with the examination of individual aspects or properties of the state and legal institutions, from which broader generalizations are subsequently derived at various levels of abstraction.[10]

Deduction, conversely, operates through logical reasoning that moves from the general to the particular. By deriving specific conclusions from general premises, deduction enables the identification of overarching legal patterns and principles. These general insights are then systematically classified into distinct categories, formations, or analytical units, whereupon they are subjected to scientific evaluation and precise definition. This deductive approach allows for a structured investigation of law that progresses from its most general characteristics and system-wide structure to the more specialized domains of legal branches, sub-branches, and institutions. Ultimately, this analytical process culminates in the study of the legal norm, which represents the fundamental structural element of the legal system as a whole.[11]

Now, finally, **hypothesis** is a scientifically formulated assumption proposed to explain a phenomenon, which must undergo empirical verification and theoretical substantiation before it can be established as a scientific theory. According to I. Kant, a hypothesis is not a mere conjecture but a reasoned assertion about the actual state of affairs, formulated under the rigorous guidance of rational inquiry.[12] The common theory of law is not confined to documenting and systematizing existing legal knowledge; its essential function lies in progressing from uncertainty to understanding by analyzing empirical data, uncovering the fundamental principles governing law, and identifying its distinctive characteristics and developmental tendencies.

The combination of these and other scientific methods and techniques constitutes the methodological foundation of the common theory of law as a discipline.

2.2 The Role of the Common Theory of Law Among Other Legal Sciences

The common theory of law occupies a central position within the system of legal sciences, which are collectively encompassed by the broader concept of jurisprudence. This system consists of a multitude of specialized legal disciplines, reflecting the complex and multifaceted nature of law as a phenomenon intrinsically linked to various dimensions of social life. Given the breadth and diversity of legal phenomena, their comprehensive study cannot be confined to a single discipline, necessitating the specialization of legal knowledge across different domains of legal activity.

---

[9] Ibid., at 27.

[10] Ibid.

[11] Ibid.

[12] Khropanyuk 2019, at 27.

Consequently, legal sciences are classified into distinct branches of knowledge, each addressing specific aspects of law.[13]

The system of legal sciences can be categorized into three principal groups: theoretical and historical, sectoral, and special sciences. *Theoretical and historical sciences* include the common theory of law, the history of law, and the history of political and legal doctrines. *Sectoral sciences* encompass disciplines such as constitutional law, administrative law, financial law, civil law, labor law, and criminal law, among others. *Special legal sciences* include forensic science, forensic medicine, forensic psychology, forensic psychiatry, and forensic accounting.[14]

The relationship between the common theory of law and theoretical and historical sciences reveals both unity and distinction. The shared objective of the common theory of law and theoretical and historical sciences lies in their holistic approach to studying law. They examine law as a comprehensive phenomenon, consider all historically existing legal systems, investigate the causes of the emergence of law, and identify the patterns underlying its development. However, their methodologies and focuses diverge. The history of law examines the historical evolution of legal forms within specific countries, following a chronological sequence. By contrast, the common theory of law abstracts and generalizes these historical processes, formulating theoretical conclusions about the patterns governing the origin, essence, and mechanisms of legal regulation.[15]

The interaction between the common theory of law and theoretical and historical sciences is reciprocal. On one hand, a thorough analysis and synthesis of historical material are indispensable for addressing theoretical legal questions and discerning the patterns of law's historical development. On the other hand, the history of law depends on the theoretical frameworks and generalizations provided by the common theory of law, which enhance its analytical depth and interpretative precision.[16]

This discipline provides the theoretical basis for specialized legal sciences and fosters their integration through universal principles of law

The common theory of law also maintains a significant relationship with the so-called sectoral legal sciences. While the common theory of law investigates the universal laws governing legal phenomena as a whole, irrespective of the specific contexts in which they manifest, sectoral sciences focus on particular components of the legal system. These include the functions of specific state organs—legislative, executive, and judicial—and the operation of distinct groups of legal norms within specific branches of law. For instance, administrative law examines the legal forms of

[13] This "branchification" is rather typical to and widespread in the legal systems of the post-Soviet countries, and is well-known among local lawyers.

[14] Khropanyuk 2019, at 29.

[15] Generally, ibid., at 29–30.

[16] Khropanyuk 2019, at 30.

executive and administrative activities, while labor law analyzes the legal regulation of relationships arising from labor activities.[17]

Despite their differences, the common theory of law does not supplant or merge with sectoral sciences. Each branch of legal science retains its own subject matter, studying the particular laws and distinctive characteristics of its domain. Within the framework of legal sciences, the common theory of law serves as a foundational and methodological discipline. It provides the theoretical basis for resolving specific problems within branch sciences and offers a unified conceptual framework from which sectoral theories are developed. The foundational concepts formulated by the common theory of law—such as those pertaining to the law, society, power, legal norms, legal relationships, and legal liability—constitute the essential groundwork upon which constitutional, administrative, civil, criminal, family, and other legal disciplines are built.[18]

The relationship between the common theory of law and branch sciences is characterized by a dynamic, bidirectional interaction. While the common theory of law supplies sectoral sciences with theoretical tools and methodological guidance, the branch sciences, in turn, enrich the common theory with empirical data and insights drawn from their specialized investigations. These contributions enable the common theory of law to refine its theoretical generalizations and advance its understanding of the broader patterns underlying legal phenomena.[19] This reciprocal relationship underscores the integrative role of the common theory of law within the system of legal sciences as a whole.

2.3 The Common Theory of Law as a Legal Discipline

The system of educational legal disciplines is typically structured to align with the system of legal sciences. The purpose of teaching these academic disciplines is to enable students to acquire a deep and comprehensive understanding of the knowledge developed within legal sciences while fostering the skills and abilities necessary for practical work in various domains of legal regulation. For instance, the study of the history of law provides students with systematic knowledge about the historical evolution of legal phenomena. Similarly, through sectoral and special legal disciplines, students gain expertise in current regulatory legal acts, the practice of their application, the drafting of legal documents, and the execution of specific legal tasks.

The legal profession intersects with diverse facets of public life, necessitating a broad spectrum of academic disciplines in legal education. However, the structure of these disciplines does not always mirror the system of legal sciences. The curriculum is often tailored to align with the profile of training, resulting in distinctions between academic disciplines and their corresponding legal sciences. Some

---

[17] Ibid.

[18] See ibid., at 31.

[19] Ibid.

legal disciplines include material drawn from a specific branch of legal science, such as copyright law as a component of civil law. Others incorporate content that spans multiple legal sciences, such as commercial law or transport law. Furthermore, legal educational institutions often include non-legal disciplines—such as accounting or basic computer technology—in their curricula to meet the practical demands of the profession.

Within the system of legal education, the common theory of law holds, or should hold, a central position. It provides students with an understanding of the most universal principles governing the legal life of society, laying the foundation for a broad legal culture, legal reasoning, and a scientifically grounded legal worldview. The common theory of law introduces students to fundamental legal concepts, which are indispensable for mastering sectoral and specialized legal disciplines. By engaging with the common theory of law, students cultivate the ability to evaluate complex legal phenomena from a rigorous scientific perspective, uncover their essential nature, and appreciate their societal role and function within the political system. This foundational knowledge enables future legal professionals to effectively address issues of legal regulation and contribute meaningfully to the development and application of the law.

The study of the common theory of law is organized according to a systematic framework, reflecting the logical arrangement of topics based on the objective structure and content of the subject matter. The curriculum typically begins with an examination of the relationship between society and the state, exploring the laws governing their origin and development. Students then progress to studying the common theory of law, where they are introduced to the essence of law and its fundamental unit—the rule of law. This includes examining the forms in which legal norms are expressed, the nature of laws, and their position within the system of normative legal acts. The course further addresses the role of law and normative regulation in contemporary public life, as well as the principles underpinning the organization and operation of the legal and legislative systems. Students also study the implementation of legal norms, focusing on the distinctive features of law enforcement activities by competent authorities.

Of particular practical importance is the study of methods for interpreting and elucidating the meaning of legal norms, which are crucial for ensuring the effective regulation of social relations. The course concludes with an exploration of the general laws governing legal relations, lawful behavior, offenses, legal liability, legality, and legal order. This comprehensive approach ensures that students are equipped not only with theoretical knowledge but also with the practical insights necessary for addressing the challenges of legal regulation and contributing to the broader legal system.

2.4 The Study and Teaching of Legal Theory in the Post-Soviet States

The teaching of legal theory in the post-Soviet states faces—and has been facing –, a complex set of challenges rooted in the region's historical, political, and educational contexts.[20] While the independence of these nations provided an opportunity to reshape their legal systems, many of the Soviet-era ideologies and methodologies persist, worryingly and particularly in legal education. Legal theory, often regarded as abstract or impractical,[21] is undervalued in curricula, and its improper or incomplete teaching undermines the quality of future legal professionals. This issue affects not only the technical competencies of lawyers but also the broader societal perceptions of law and its role as a foundational pillar of justice and governance.

One critical issue is the dominance of positivist and statist approaches in the teaching of legal theory. These perspectives, inherited from the Soviet legacy, treat law primarily as a tool of the state, emphasizing its instrumental function while neglecting its value as a mechanism for protecting rights and fostering social progress. The prioritization of "state" in "theory of state and law" is displayed in, for example, requirements from educational authorities (e.g., ministries of education and science) for universities and law schools to include in their respective curricula the course specifically named "theory of state and law" and not otherwise. As a result, legal education in these countries often produces lawyers who may excel in procedural and technical knowledge but unfortunately lack the ability to critically assess laws, understand their societal impact, or engage in normative reasoning. This positivist dominance also discourages exploration of alternative legal theories, such as natural law or human-rights / individual-rights-based approaches, which are critical for fostering a balanced legal culture.

In post-Soviet states, legal theory is undervalued, emphasizing technical over value-driven approaches, thereby limiting critical thinking and societal impact

The ideological framing of legal theory teaching further exacerbates the problem. In many post-Soviet states, legal education remains heavily influenced by authoritarian structures, limiting academic freedoms and discouraging open debate. This stifles intellectual curiosity and critical thinking among students, resulting in a legal education that prioritizes conformity over innovation. The lack of value-oriented teaching in legal theory, which should instill principles such as justice, fairness, and equality, diminishes the capacity of future lawyers to address societal issues meaningfully. Instead, legal education often reinforces a perception of law as rigid and

---

[20] See *passim*, e.g., Sokolova 2012, 639–643.

[21] I myself regularly encounter such opinions in my work coming from students, scholars and lawyers in general.

unchangeable, and even dry and boring, thus deepening legal nihilism and eroding public trust in legal norms and institutions.

The practical implications of this approach are—again unfortunately—profound. Lawyers trained under these conditions often struggle to adapt to the complexities of modern legal practice, particularly in areas requiring interdisciplinary knowledge or the ability to navigate ethical dilemmas. This gap between legal education and the demands of practice undermines the professional competence of lawyers, contributing to low levels of legal awareness and a deficient legal culture in society. In such an environment, legal practitioners are ill-equipped, it appears, to advocate for reforms, protect human rights, or foster a rule-of-law culture, perpetuating systemic weaknesses in governance and justice systems.

Another pressing concern is the insufficient integration of contemporary global perspectives into the teaching of legal theory. While some institutions have begun offering courses in English and incorporating international materials (for example, Kazakhstan, Uzbekistan, Ukraine), the majority of legal theory textbooks and teaching tools remain rooted in outdated or Soviet-era frameworks. This isolation from global legal discourse deprives students of exposure to comparative legal systems and modern methodologies, leaving them unprepared for the increasingly internationalized nature of legal practice.

Improving the teaching of legal theory in post-Soviet states requires a comprehensive reevaluation of curricula, methodologies, and ideological underpinnings, it goes without saying. A more pluralistic and interdisciplinary approach is essential, one that introduces students to diverse legal theories and emphasizes the role of law as a value-driven force for societal betterment; the value-based learning outcomes in the course syllabi on legal theory are therefore important. Integrating perspectives from sociology, philosophy, and political science (in a measured way) can enrich the understanding of legal phenomena and foster a deeper appreciation for the ethical dimensions of law.

Ultimately, the failure to adequately teach (and learn) legal theory has far-reaching consequences for legal professionalism, societal legal awareness, and the broader legal culture. It is difficult to argue against that. By neglecting the foundational principles of law and focusing narrowly on technical competence, post-Soviet legal education risks perpetuating a system where law is seen as only a tool of power rather than a mechanism for justice. Reforming the study and teaching of legal theory in these states is not merely an academic concern but a vital step toward strengthening the rule of law and promoting social progress.

Questions for Students

1. *What is the primary subject matter of the common theory of law, and how does it differ from sectoral legal sciences?*
2. *How do methodological principles like objectivity and pluralism enhance the study of legal phenomena?*

3. *In what ways does the common theory of law support and interact with other legal sciences?*
4. *What are the key challenges in teaching legal theory in post-Soviet states, and why do they undermine the development of a rule-of-law culture?*

References

Khropanyuk V (2019) Theory of State and Law (in Russian), 13th edn. Omega-L, Moscow

Sokolova A (2012) Legal Education in Post-Soviet Countries: Problems and Principles of Reform". 2(5) Int'l Lawyer 46

Chapter 3
Society as a Legal Phenomenon

Contents

Abstract This chapter explores the concept of society as a foundational legal phenomenon, emphasizing its central role in shaping, reflecting, and being shaped by legal norms. It begins by differentiating various definitions of society and argues for a legal interpretation that sees society as the structured and normative interaction of individuals and groups. This chapter asserts that understanding society from a legal standpoint is essential for comprehending how law emerges from, and functions within, social realities. It examines the distinction between society and civil society, critiques the overemphasis on the state in legal thinking, and promotes a society-centered approach aligned with integrative legal theory. The chapter also delves into the complex web of social norms—legal, moral, religious, customary, and explains how they regulate behavior. Legal norms are presented as the most formalized and enforceable category, but deeply interwoven with other social norms and traditions, particularly in post-Soviet contexts. The final section introduces the concept of social regulators, dividing them into normative and non-normative types. It highlights the importance of aligning legal norms with broader social values and regulatory mechanisms such as tradition, information, and directives, to ensure their effectiveness and legitimacy.

Keywords Society as a legal concept · Legal norms and social regulation · Post-Soviet legal culture · Social norms and traditions · Normative vs. non-normative regulators · Law and societal interaction · Civil society and legal development

R. Atadjanov, *A Common Theory of Law*, https://doi.org/10.1007/978-94-6265-711-3_3

3.1 What Is Society?

The Oxford English Dictionary online defines "society" as follows: "The aggregate of persons living together in a community, esp. one having shared customs, laws, and institutions".[1] In turn, the Cambridge Dictionary online provides the following definition: "a large group of people who live together in an organized way, making decisions about how to do things and sharing the work that needs to be done. All the people in a country, or in several similar countries, can be referred to as a society".[2] Yet another definition, *inter alia*, this time from the Merriam Webster Dictionary, consists in the following: "a community, nation, or broad grouping of people having common traditions, institutions, and collective activities and interests".[3] This diversity of definitions is only a tip of the iceberg and it demonstrates how difficult it is to properly define such a multifaceted and varied notion as "society".

However, defining "society" as a legal phenomenon represents both a theoretical challenge and a practical necessity. The diversity of definitions non-exhaustively outlined above reflects the multifaceted nature of society as a concept. From sociological, cultural, and philosophical perspectives, "society" encompasses the relationships, norms, and institutions that bind individuals into cohesive groups. But, from a legal perspective—which is what interests us here, the inquiry shifts toward how these elements interact with legal norms, shaping and/or being shaped by them. The complexity of defining society lies in its simultaneous embodiment of shared customs, organizational structures, and evolving dynamics that resist simple categorization. That turns out to be especially challenging for lawyers who are used to define concepts and apply the principle of legal certainty. Despite this, a legal exploration of society is indispensable if one wishes to understand properly the social foundations of law and the normative expectations law seeks to regulate.

Society operates through a complex interplay of social norms, values, and institutions. These components facilitate cooperation, regulate conflict, and promote collective goals. Legal systems emerge as formalized extensions of these mechanisms, codifying societal expectations into enforceable rules. The social nature of law means that it both reflects and influences the underlying structure of society. Understanding society as a legal phenomenon involves recognizing this bi-directional relationship, where laws draw legitimacy from societal norms while simultaneously shaping the behavior and identity of the society they govern ("law is created by people for the people"). This dynamic is particularly important in contexts where legal reforms are part of societal transformation, as seen in post-Soviet countries navigating the transition from authoritarianism to more pluralistic legal and political systems (which is still a very problematic process in this part of the world).

---

[1] Available at https://www.oed.com/search/dictionary/?scope=Entries&q=society (last accessed 8 April 2025).

[2] Available at https://dictionary.cambridge.org/dictionary/english/society (last accessed 8 April 2025).

[3] Available at https://www.merriam-webster.com/dictionary/society (last accessed 8 April 2025).

Society—as a legal concept—refers to the structured interaction of individuals and groups governed by legal norms that reflect and shape collective life

From a legal perspective, distinguishing society from civil society is crucial. While "society" refers broadly to the aggregate of people and their interactions, "civil society" denotes organized, voluntary associations operating independently of the state.[4] In many post-Soviet states including Central Asian contexts, the development of civil society remains a work in progress, hindered by historical legacies and contemporary political challenges. The broader concept of society, however, is omnipresent and it serves as the canvas upon which legal norms are articulated. By focusing on society as a whole, one can better understand the foundational role of law in structuring the behavior and organization of individuals and groups, irrespective of whether civil society institutions are robust or nascent.

One more significant point would be that it is even more important to look at society as a legal concept than the state because society represents the broader and more foundational framework within which legal norms originate and operate. While the **state** is a central institution of governance,[5] it is **ultimately a construct of society, deriving its authority and legitimacy from the collective will and values of the people it serves**. A society-centric approach aligns with the integrative theory of law,[6] which emphasizes law's organic relationship with social norms, culture, and human behavior, rather than reducing it to mere state-imposed coercive rules. By focusing on society, we highlight the cooperative and dialogical nature of law as a phenomenon that emerges from and adapts to the diverse needs and dynamics of human interaction, transcending the rigid confines of legalism and statist approaches. This perspective is crucial for understanding law as a tool for integration, cohesion, and justice, rather than a mere instrument of state power.

The diversity of societal configurations further underscores the importance of defining society as a legal phenomenon. Societies vary in their cultural, economic, and institutional frameworks, but all rely on legal mechanisms to mediate relationships and ensure cohesion. In this sense, **society as a legal phenomenon refers to the structured interaction of individuals and groups within a normative framework governed by law**. This perspective emphasizes the role of legal norms as not only reactive to societal needs but also proactive in shaping societal evolution. Laws are not merely tools for dispute or conflict resolution; they are instruments for constructing and maintaining the shared reality of society.

Society as a legal phenomenon can be defined, according to this author, as **the structured and normative interaction of individuals and groups within a shared framework of laws and institutions that both reflect and shape collective life**.

---

[4] See Chap. 5 for a more detailed treatment of the notion of "civil society" and its role within the State of Law.

[5] See Chap. 4 for the exploration of the nature of state and power.

[6] As explained in Chap. 6.

This definition captures the dual nature of law as a product of society's customs and a mechanism for its transformation. By approaching society through a legal lens, one gains insight into the ways legal norms serve as the architecture of social order, making the study of society indispensable to any comprehensive theory of law. This understanding is particularly relevant in post-Soviet contexts, where evolving societal structures and legal frameworks continue to redefine the relationship between law and society.

3.2 Social Norms and People's Behavior

It is a truism that no society can exist without mechanisms to regulate human behavior, known as social regulators. These regulators, embodied in the rules of community life or social norms, are essential for maintaining order and cohesion. Social norms define acceptable behaviors within a community, shaping individuals' interactions and attitudes toward others. Unlike personal self-imposed rules, **social norms inherently involve intersubjective relationships**; they are meaningful only when one person addresses another. Social norms may also extend to human interactions with the animal world. While animals themselves may not comprehend or act upon these norms, they can benefit from them, as exemplified by legal norms designed to protect animal welfare.[7] The primary object of regulation by social norms is the behavior of individuals and groups, manifesting in social relations.

Despite their diversity, social norms share several defining characteristics. First, they serve as *behavioral guidelines*, prescribing measures of acceptable and permissible conduct. Second, they are *general* in nature, applying not to specific individuals but to broad categories of people within a society. Third, social norms typically exhibit an element of *obligation*, though this does not necessarily equate to coercion. Mandatory compliance can manifest in varying degrees, depending on the type of norm. Importantly, *not all norms rely on coercive measures for their enforcement*. This is what the post-Soviet space's countries and societies as well as their legal communities are still struggling to understand. The system of social norms in any modern society encompasses a wide range of categories, including legal norms, moral norms, customs, and religious norms. These norms understandably differ in their methods of creation, expression, content, and enforcement mechanisms.

Social norms, including legal norms, regulate behavior and relationships within a society, serving as guidelines for acceptable conduct and maintaining social order

[7] For a comprehensive overview of animal law, see *passim* Dalpane and Baideldinova 2024.

The distinction between various types of social norms arises from their unique methods of establishment, forms of expression, and societal roles. **Legal norms**, for instance, are formally codified and enforceable through institutional mechanisms. In contrast, **moral norms** derive from shared values and are upheld by public opinion or individual conscience. **Political norms** regulate relationships within the political system and pertain to the exercise of state power. **Corporate norms** are established by organizations and enforced through internal measures, often outlined in charters or bylaws. **Customary norms** evolve organically within specific social environments, becoming habitual through repeated practice, while traditions embody practices and rules passed down across generations. In this author's experience, in post-Soviet societies, particularly in the Caucasian and Central Asian regions, traditions remain deeply influential, shaping community dynamics and individual behavior.

Traditions occupy a prominent role in post-Soviet societies, serving as a cornerstone of cultural and social life. In regions like the Caucasus and Central Asia, traditions often coexist with or even take precedence (in people's actual behavior, not in terms of legal validity (!)) over formal legal systems, particularly in matters of family, community, and ceremonial practices. These traditions are not static; they may evolve over time, somewhat adapting to changing social, economic, and political contexts. Yet, they retain their authority by virtue of their historical continuity and the respect they command within the community. This strong traditional foundation underscores the need for legal norms to be sensitive to and compatible with (read: contextual) deeply ingrained cultural practices to ensure their effective implementation and acceptance. However, this should not undermine the universal nature of many values the law aims at protecting and which are not endemic only for some selected societies but are globally relevant.[8]

The interplay between different types of social norms highlights their collective role in shaping societal behavior and maintaining order. While legal norms often receive the most formal attention, they exist within a broader framework of moral, political, corporate, and customary norms, all of which contribute to regulating human behavior and social relations. Understanding the diversity and interconnectedness of these norms is particularly important in societies with a rich tradition of cultural practices, such as those in the post-Soviet space. Recognizing the nuances of social norms allows for a more integrative and culturally attuned approach to law, ensuring that legal systems remain relevant and effective within their social contexts.

In contemporary society, traditions are increasingly understood as guiding principles for significant personal and communal celebrations, such as weddings, birthdays, and other milestone events. Within the realm of property relations, traditions often manifest as business customs or usages, which establish recognized practices in commercial interactions. It is important to distinguish customs from rituals and ceremonies: while customs set the normative framework for acceptable behavior, rituals represent the specific enactment of social relations, such as marriage or military ceremonies. Customs should also not be conflated with customary law. Customary law consists of state-sanctioned norms derived from traditional practices, reflecting

[8] For the discussion of some of those values, such as, e.g., human rights, see Chap. 5.

community interests and enforced through state authority. While customary law remains prevalent in regions like South America, Southeast Asia, and Africa, even in developed countries, customs often underpin state-recognized norms in areas such as marital and family relations or inheritance law.

Social norms encompass a broad spectrum, including religious rules, family traditions, norms of etiquette, rituals, and ethical principles. Customs are only one component of this diverse category, with each type of norm contributing to the regulation of social behavior in its own way. Legal norms, as a subset of social norms, deserve special attention due to their formalized and binding nature. While customs operate on the basis of habit and societal acceptance, legal norms derive their authority from formal codification and state enforcement. The interaction between these different forms of norms demonstrates the layered complexity of social regulation and the importance of understanding the distinctions between them.

Legal norms are distinct among social norms because they possess unique characteristics that elevate their role in regulating social relations.[9] Unlike customs, legal norms are **formally defined**, meaning they are documented in stable and authoritative sources that specify not only the rules of conduct but also the circumstances under which they apply, the consequences of violations, and the procedures for enforcement. This formal certainty ensures consistency and predictability in the application of legal norms, distinguishing them from more fluid and informal social norms.

A key feature of legal norms is their **enforceability** by the state or its equivalents. In cases of non-compliance, legal norms allow for the application of coercive measures, underscoring their mandatory nature. This state-backed enforcement mechanism sets legal norms (with a partial exception of international legal norms) apart from other social norms, which often rely on social consensus, moral persuasion, or religious sanction for compliance. Additionally, legal norms have a **dual character**: they confer rights upon individuals (representative aspect) while simultaneously imposing obligations on others (binding aspect). This reciprocal structure ensures a balance of responsibilities and protections within the legal framework.

While legal norms hold a unique and prominent position among social norms, they do not exist in isolation. They interact with and often incorporate elements of customs, traditions, and other social norms, reflecting the cultural and societal context within which they operate. Recognizing these interconnections enhances our understanding of law not just as a system of rules but as a dynamic framework deeply embedded in the fabric of society. This perspective is essential for appreciating the full scope of legal norms and their role in shaping and responding to the evolving needs of communities.

Among all categories of social norms, legal norms most effectively and efficiently influence human behavior due to their formal structure, enforceability, and logical coherence. Unlike customs or moral norms, which rely on tradition or subjective values, legal norms are explicitly codified and clearly articulated, providing individuals with unambiguous guidelines for acceptable behavior. This formal certainty ensures consistency and predictability, which are essential for fostering trust and

[9] See Chap. 10 for a more comprehensive and detailed description of legal norm and its system.

stability in social interactions. Additionally, legal norms are backed by the authority of the state, enabling enforcement mechanisms that ensure compliance and address violations, thus reinforcing their mandatory nature.[10] Their logical framework, which aligns rights with corresponding obligations, creates a balanced system of accountability, making legal norms a rational and adaptable tool for regulating behavior across diverse and complex societies. This combination of clarity, enforceability, and logical design enables legal norms to function as the most reliable and universal regulator of human conduct.

3.3 Social Regulators

Social norms and social regulators, while closely related, are distinct concepts. Social norms refer to established patterns of behavior or rules that dictate how individuals should act within a society. In contrast, social regulators encompass the **broader system of mechanisms—normative and non-normative—that influence and direct human behavior**. Regulators determine the methods by which social norms are enforced, providing the structure and tools necessary to guide human interactions and maintain social order. In the view of this author, such a distinction is important, as it highlights that norms are a subset of the regulatory framework, while regulators operate at a systemic level, shaping the very fabric of societal relations.

Social regulators, both normative (like laws and morals) and non-normative (like values and information), influence behavior and ensure societal cohesion through enforcement and incentives

In every society, a system of social regulators develops over time to guide the behavior of individuals and groups. Even in primitive societies, regulatory mechanisms existed in the form of mononorms, which governed essential aspects of clan life. Regulation involves defining behavior, giving it a specific direction, setting boundaries, and organizing it within established frameworks. In modern societies, including those of the post-Soviet region, social regulators may be categorized into **normative** and **non-normative** types. Normative regulators, such as legal, moral, political, and corporate norms, establish specific and clear behavioral standards, often backed by mechanisms of social coercion to ensure compliance.

Normative social regulators often employ coercion to enforce compliance and organize social relations effectively. This coercion can take various forms. State coercion is used to enforce legal norms through penalties and sanctions for violations. Moral coercion operates through public condemnation of actions that breach ethical or moral standards. Corporate coercion enforces adherence to the rules set out in

[10] But this is not to say, in any way, that legal norms bear a statist or a necessarily statist nature.

the charters and regulations of organizations. At an international level, violations of widely accepted principles of international law may invite coercion from the global community.[11] In addition to coercion, normative regulation often employs other tools, such as incentives, recommendations, and rewards, to achieve its goals. Together, these mechanisms help maintain the desired order in social relations.

In addition to normative regulators, societies including the post-Soviet societies, rely on **non-normative** regulators—**value**, **directive**, and **informational**—to influence behavior and social relations. **Value** regulators are rooted in the cultural and psychological fabric of society. They consist of historically established social values, behavioral stereotypes, and psychological attitudes, often embedded in the traditions, rituals, and symbols of specific ethnic groups, professions, or age demographics. **Directive** regulators, by contrast, exert influence through explicit instructions, orders, or directives aimed at achieving specific goals. For example, during the administrative-command era of the Soviet Union, directives of the Communist Party were central to shaping not only governance but also lawmaking and societal behavior.

Informational regulators affect social behavior through the dissemination of information, often via mass media. These regulators play a critical role in raising awareness of important societal issues, protecting human rights and freedoms, and mobilizing public opinion. Their effectiveness is closely tied to the principle of transparency, or *glasnost*, which ensures that the public is informed about and engaged in state affairs. However, informational regulators can also amplify, obstruct, or distort the effects of normative regulators. For instance, media campaigns can either enhance the acceptance of legal norms or undermine their legitimacy, depending on how information is framed and disseminated. In this context, the problem of propaganda comes to the fore.

The interplay between normative and non-normative regulators is complex, with each influencing the effectiveness of the other. *A legal norm may fail to achieve its intended purpose if it does not align with the value system of the society it seeks to regulate.* Value regulators, with their deep-rooted power of imitation and tradition, can undermine legal norms that disregard societal values. Similarly, directive and informational regulators can wield significant influence, as seen in the Soviet era, where non-compliance with party line directives could result in severe penalties and even repressions. Understanding the interaction of these regulators is crucial for identifying the factors that render certain legal norms inactive or ineffective. Ultimately, effective legal regulation requires harmonizing legal norms with the broader system of social regulators to reflect the values, traditions, and expectations of the society in which they operate.

---

[11] However, one should bear in mind that in international law there is no formal enforcement mechanism analogous to that of national (domestic or municipal) legal systems. This is one of the major differences between international and domestic law.

Questions for Students

1. *What distinguishes society as a legal phenomenon from its broader sociological definitions?*
2. *How do social norms differ from other categories of norms, such as customs or traditions?*
3. *What are the key characteristics of legal norms that make them distinct from other social norms?*
4. *How do normative and non-normative social regulators interact to influence behavior and maintain order in a society?*

Reference

Dalpane F, Baideldinova M (eds) (2024) Animal Law Worldwide: Key Issues and Main Trends Across 27 Jurisdictions. T.M.C. Asser Press, The Hague

Chapter 4
Power and State

Contents

Abstract This chapter examines the nature, structure, and functions of power and the state through a legal lens, situating them within the broader framework of societal organization and legal theory. The chapter opens by exploring various types of power in society—political, economic, religious, charismatic, legal, and introduces distinctions such as legal versus legitimate power and formal versus shadow power. It then turns to the state as the central wielder of public power, defining its unique features including sovereignty, universality, legislative monopoly, and its public and institutional character. The state is analyzed as both a political and legal organization, with emphasis on its role in upholding the rule of law, advancing public welfare, and mediating collective interests. The chapter provides a detailed overview of historical and contemporary theories of state formation, including classical Greek thought, Hegelian idealism, Marxist materialism, the civilizational approach, and the libertarian model. It presents various typologies of state such as ethnic, class-based, individual-political, and natural-positive, and outlines forms of governance (monarchy, republic), territorial structure (unitary, federal, confederal), and political regimes (liberal, authoritarian). The functions of the state are categorized as law-making, law-implementing, human rights protection, and external (international) functions, reinforcing the legal and moral obligations of statehood. Finally, the chapter addresses the structure and functioning of the state mechanism, highlighting its legal framework, challenges in post-Soviet contexts, and key strategies for reforming bureaucratic inefficiencies to build a rule-of-law-based, people-centered state.

R. Atadjanov, *A Common Theory of Law*, https://doi.org/10.1007/978-94-6265-711-3_4

Keywords State and public power · Sovereignty and legitimacy · Theories of state formation · Forms of governance and state structure · State functions and legal authority · Rule of law vs. statism · Post-Soviet state apparatus reform · Political regimes (liberal vs. authoritarian)

4.1 Types of Power in Society

Power as a legal concept refers to the **authority or capacity to make, enforce, and interpret rules that govern society, derived from legal norms and institutions**. In this context, public power in society signifies the structured ability of governmental or public entities to regulate behavior, allocate resources, and resolve conflicts in a manner deemed legitimate under the rule of law. This power is exercised through mechanisms such as legislation, administration, and adjudication, often bounded by constitutional frameworks, to ensure accountability, equity, and justice in maintaining societal order and advancing public welfare.

Power is a multifaceted phenomenon with diverse areas of operation, modes of expression, and types. These include clan power, tribal power, political power, state power, economic power, power within public associations, parental authority, religious (church) power, and more. Power is classified in various ways. Socially, it can be categorized based on levels of interaction: **(a)** *power operating on a societal scale*, **(b)** *power within social groups or communities*, and **(c)** *power in interpersonal relations*. One common distinction is between political and non-political power. Political power often encompasses class or group dominance, state authority, party power, and leadership power. Some scholars, such as Baitin,[1] equate political and state power, arguing that true political power is inherently state-based or functions through the state's direct or indirect involvement. Others, like Burlatsky and Keyzerov,[2] distinguish between the two, viewing political power more broadly as the influence exerted by all components of the political system, not merely the state.

Power can also be classified based on its organizational method as democratic or non-democratic. The sociologist Max Weber (1864–1920) famously identified three types of power: (a) **traditional power**, rooted in societal customs, rituals, and traditions that change slowly or persist over time; (b) **legal power**, founded on established laws and norms that regulate authority; and (c) **charismatic power**, arising from the extraordinary qualities of a leader perceived by their followers as capable of overcoming challenges and achieving visionary goals.[3]

[1] Baitin 1990.

[2] Burlatsky and Keyzerov 1989.

[3] Weber 1978.

Power in society includes political, state, economic, and other forms, and can be classified as traditional, legal, or charismatic based on its source and structure.

In addition to formal or legal power, there is also the so-called "shadow power", exercised by informal groups within the ruling elite, such as political factions or organized criminal networks (e.g., mafia groups). A distinction is also made between legal and legitimate power. While closely related, these concepts are not identical. Legal power derives from a lawful foundation, adhering to and operating within the boundaries of the law. Legitimate power, on the other hand, is based on public recognition and acceptance, reflecting the population's trust and willingness to comply. Power can be legal without being legitimate, as legality pertains to its conformity to law, whereas legitimacy involves its moral and social acceptance.

4.2 The State as a Wielder of Public Power: Definition and Nature

State power, as a specific type of social power, shares the general attributes of social power while possessing distinct characteristics unique to its nature. These characteristics include the following:

Implementation through state structures: State power is exercised through the state and its institutions. Uniquely, it is the only form of power with a coercive apparatus that applies to all individuals within the state's territory, without exception.

Public nature: State power is inherently public. Broadly speaking, this means it operates within and is visible to society, a trait it shares with all forms of social power. However, in the theory of state and law, "publicity" also refers to the professionalized and institutional nature of state power. It is distinct from society itself, executed by a specialized apparatus that is separate from the general population.

Sovereignty: State power is sovereign, characterized by supremacy and unity within its borders and independence externally. Its supremacy means no higher authority exists within the state, and all individuals and entities are subject to its rule. In democratic systems, however, state sovereignty is derived from and subordinate to popular sovereignty, emphasizing that the people are the ultimate source of authority. Externally, state sovereignty includes the discretion to enter or abstain from interstate unions, treaties, or agreements.

Universality: The authority of state power extends across the entire national territory and applies to the entirety of its population, making it comprehensive in scope.[4]

Legislative monopoly: State power has the exclusive authority to enact laws and other legally binding norms. This monopoly on legislation ensures its ability to make its directives universally obligatory, including upon itself. By issuing legal norms, the state binds its own actions to the framework of the law, reinforcing the rule of law.

Promotion of public interests: The state is entrusted with the responsibility to serve public interests, foster social cohesion, and protect human rights and freedoms. This consolidating role highlights the state's duty to prioritize collective well-being and uphold justice and individual liberties.

These features collectively define state power as a centralized, authoritative, and public mechanism essential for maintaining order, governance, and societal development.

State power is public, sovereign, and universal, with the authority to create and enforce laws for the benefit of society

While the state's legislative monopoly ensures uniformity and enforceability of laws, it is not without criticism. Critics argue that concentrating legislative authority solely in the state risks centralizing too much power, potentially leading to abuse or neglect of diverse societal needs. To mitigate this, many legal systems incorporate checks and balances, such as judicial review, public participation in lawmaking, and the recognition of customary or decentralized legal norms, to ensure that state power is neither absolute nor unaccountable. Importantly, and as this author firmly believes, the state's obligation to bind its actions within the framework of law underscores a foundational principle: *the state is subject to the rule of law, not its master*. This principle affirms that **the law, as an expression of justice, equality, and collective governance, stands above the state**. The legitimacy of state power, therefore, is derived from its adherence to the law, reinforcing the idea that no authority, including the state, is above the legal and moral order that governs society.

4.3 The State as a Political and Legal Organization

The state, as a political and legal organization, represents a pivotal construct in organizing public life and governance. It operates at the intersection of legal norms and political authority, serving as both a mechanism for structuring societal relations

[4] It is not universal in the global sense; the universality only applies to the state's territory and is limited by its jurisdiction and its official borders.

and an instrument for implementing collective decisions. Within the framework of **integrative legal theory**,[5] which emphasizes the harmony between law, morality, and social realities, the state is best understood not merely as a coercive apparatus but as **a territorial, structural, and institutional entity that facilitates the rule of law and advances public welfare**. This perspective aligns with liberal principles, positing that the state's legitimacy derives from its adherence to law, its embodiment of shared values, and its role in promoting inclusive governance rather than imposing arbitrary control.

At its core, the state is a **territorial and structural organization tasked with maintaining order, resolving conflicts, and advancing common interests within a defined geographical boundary**. This territorial dimension is foundational, as it demarcates the jurisdiction within which the state exercises its authority. However, the state's authority must be structured by and subordinate to the law, ensuring that its actions align with principles of justice and equity. The integrative theory rejects the notion of the state as a purely coercive entity, emphasizing instead its role as a **unifying force** that consolidates/should consolidate societal interests and channels them through legal norms and institutions, thus ensuring both stability and fairness.

The state functions as a territorial and institutional entity that balances governance, public welfare, and adherence to the rule of law

Historically, in many post-Soviet contexts, the state's role has been heavily statist, marked by centralized decision-making and a reliance on bureaucratic authority. This legacy often reflects an apparatus-centric view of governance, where power is concentrated in elites and decision-making prioritizes the interests of ruling classes over broader public participation. While such systems may have achieved certain organizational efficiencies, they often neglect the integrative role of the state as a mediator of public life and a *guarantor of rights*. Liberal and integrative perspectives challenge these remnants of illiberal governance by advocating for a state that is both legally constrained and morally attuned to societal needs.

A key tenet of the integrative approach is that the state must operate as a legal organization, meaning its structures and actions are grounded in the rule of law and are never in contradiction to it. This underscores the idea that t**he state is not above the law; rather, the law serves as the foundation for the state's legitimacy and authority**. Legal norms should reflect shared societal values, ensuring that the state functions as a servant of the public good rather than a self-perpetuating power structure. This principle is particularly crucial in societies transitioning from statist to more liberal frameworks, where the vestiges of authoritarianism often challenge efforts to institutionalize the supremacy of law over political expediency.

In line with the above, the state as a political and legal organization must be seen as an **enabler of public life** rather than a dominator of it. Its territorial and

---

[5] See Chap. 6, Sect. 6.1 for the explanation of the integrative, or synthetic theory of law.

structural dimensions are vital, but they must be animated by a commitment to law, equity, and inclusive governance. For post-Soviet societies, this vision entails a transformative shift from coercive and apparatus-driven models of statehood to integrative frameworks that prioritize the rule of law, human dignity, and collective well-being. Such a transformation not only aligns with liberal ideals but also fosters a more resilient, just, and progressive societal order, where the state serves as a cornerstone of public trust and a guardian of legal and moral coherence.

4.4 Major Theories of the Formation of States

Ancient philosophers such as **Socrates,**[6] **Plato,**[7] **Aristotle,**[8] and **Cicero**[9] classified forms of government into two categories: correct and incorrect. **Correct forms** of government were characterized by the exercise of power based on laws and aimed at serving the common good. In contrast, **incorrect forms** were defined by power that disregarded legal principles and prioritized the interests of the rulers. Plato, employing this framework, identified three correct forms of governance: **royal power** (legitimate monarchy, where one ruler governs according to laws), **aristocracy** (the legitimate rule of a few), and **lawful democracy** (the rule of the people based on laws). Correspondingly, he categorized **tyranny** (unlawful rule by one), **oligarchy** (unlawful rule by a few), and **illegal democracy** (popular rule that disregards laws) as the three incorrect forms.

Aristotle adopted a similar approach but offered a slightly modified classification. He identified royal power, aristocracy, and polity (the rule of the majority grounded in legal principles) as the correct forms of governance. Conversely, he regarded tyranny, oligarchy, and democracy (majority rule not grounded in law) as the incorrect forms. The central criterion for this typology was the distinction between legality and lawlessness, emphasizing the necessity of legal foundations for legitimate governance.

This distinction between lawful and unlawful rule provided a foundation for subsequent political and legal thought, influencing discussions on governance across centuries. The typology underscores the enduring significance of legality as a benchmark for evaluating the legitimacy of political systems. Even today, this ancient framework continues to resonate, informing modern debates on the relationship between law, authority, and the pursuit of the common good.

Hegel[10] approached the typology of states through the lens of the world-historical process, viewing it as the progressive development of the spirit of freedom and its realization in different forms of the state. He argued that "world history" is a necessary

[6] Socratic views as presented in Plato 1937a.

[7] Plato 1937b.

[8] Aristotle 1995.

[9] Cicero 1928.

[10] Hegel 2001.

manifestation of the concept of freedom, representing the unfolding of reason, self-consciousness, and the spirit's freedom. As he wrote, "World history is necessary only from the concept of freedom of the spirit, the development of moments of reason, and thus self-consciousness and freedom of the spirit—the interpretation and implementation of the universal spirit."

In Hegel's view, the realization of this universal spirit occurred through four "world-historical kingdoms": **the Eastern, Greek, Roman, and German kingdoms**. These kingdoms, he asserted, represent objective-historical formations or stages in the development of the world spirit, embodying the evolution of reason and freedom in world history. Each kingdom corresponded to specific forms of state and conceptions of freedom. The Eastern kingdom was associated with theocracy, characterized by the freedom of one—the supreme ruler. The Greek and Roman kingdoms were linked to democracy or aristocracy, representing the freedom of some, or a segment of the population. Finally, the German kingdom corresponded to the constitutional monarchy of the modern era, featuring a representative system and embodying the freedom of all.

Hegel emphasized this progression in his famous distinction: "The East knew and knows only that one is free, the Greek and Roman world knows that some are free, the German world knows that all are free." By the "German world", Hegel referred to the countries of northwestern Europe, which he regarded as the culmination of this historical development. The "monarchy" he described was not an absolute monarchy but a constitutional one, grounded in a system of representation and the separation of powers.

For Hegel, the typology of states was thus inextricably tied to the broader historical evolution of freedom and reason. The forms of governance in each world-historical stage reflected the spirit of the age, advancing from the limited recognition of freedom to its universal acknowledgment. This interpretation underscores the dynamic relationship between political forms and the philosophical ideas of liberty and rationality.

Hegel's framework, while shaped by his specific historical and cultural context, offers a profound lens through which to understand the interplay of law, governance, and freedom in history. It highlights the state as not merely a political institution but as a manifestation of deeper, evolving ideas, with the constitutional monarchy as the apex of a process that progressively realizes universal freedom.

The **Marxist doctrine** of socio-economic formations, developed by Karl Marx and Friedrich Engels from a materialist, proletarian-class, and communist perspective, forms the basis of the Marxist typology of state and law. According to Marxism, **the economic (production) relations within a society constitute its foundational basis, which in turn determines the corresponding superstructure, including the state and legal systems**. Based on this approach, Marxism divides human history into five socio-economic formations: **the primitive communal system, the slave system, the feudal system, the capitalist system, and the communist system.**[11]

[11] Marx and Engels 1976.

Within this framework, three class-antagonistic formations—slave, feudal, and capitalist—correspond to distinct types of state and law: the slave state and law, the feudal state and law, and the bourgeois (capitalist) state and law. Under the primitive communal system, there is no state or law, and under communism, Marxism posits that the state and law, as class-based phenomena, will ultimately "wither away". During the transitional phase of socialism (the first phase of communism), Marx envisioned the "dictatorship of the proletariat" and a system of bourgeois "equal law" to regulate labor and consumption.[12]

In Soviet Marxist literature, however, this theoretical framework underwent significant modifications. Diverging from the prognostic positions of Marx and Engels, Soviet theorists introduced the concept of a socialist type of state and law, revealing an inconsistency in the anticipated transition from socialism to full communism without a state or legal system. This reinterpretation highlighted the practical challenges of implementing the Marxist vision and exposed contradictions in the Marxist doctrine itself. While economic and class relations undeniably play a critical role in shaping the state and law, the Marxist overemphasis on these factors leads to a reductionist view, neglecting the multifaceted influences of cultural, spiritual, and social dynamics in the development of legal and political systems.

A key critique of Marxist theory lies in its fundamentally negative view of the state (and law, for that matter), which it portrays as mere instruments of class violence, domination, and oppression. This interpretation disregards the historical reality that freedom has evolved and expanded precisely within state-legal frameworks. Contrary to Marxist assertions, the historical development of states and legal systems—from early forms of governance to modern constitutional democracies—reflects not the perpetuation of violence and domination, but the progress of human liberty, the broadening of freedom, and the inclusion of larger portions of society in the realm of rights and equality.

Moreover, the Marxist typology of state and law inherently rejects the state and law as positive values or achievements in human culture. This anti-statist and anti-legal stance overlooks the essential role of the state and law in protecting rights, fostering societal cohesion, and advancing justice. By negating the intrinsic value of these institutions, Marxism diverges fundamentally from the principles of jurisprudence and the integrative theory of law, which emphasize the state and law as foundational to the realization of freedom and the rule of law.

Ultimately, the Marxist doctrine, with its class-reductive approach and hostility toward legal and state systems, fails to account for the complex, dynamic, and progressive role these institutions have played in human history. While Marxism sheds light on important socio-economic factors, its rejection of the positive functions of the state and law undermines its relevance to modern legal thought. Instead, the historical record demonstrates that state-legal forms have been indispensable in advancing human rights, freedom, and justice, aligning with the integrative understanding of law as a mediator of both societal and individual interests.

---

[12] Ibid.

In post-Soviet legal literature, references to the **civilizational approach** to the typology of state have gained significant attention. This approach draws on the theories of English historian Arnold J. Toynbee (1889–1975), who was heavily influenced by Oswald Spengler's ideas, particularly those articulated in "The Decline of the West".[13] Spengler rejected the notion of a single, universal human culture, instead proposing the **existence of multiple distinct, self-contained cultures**. According to Spengler, vibrant, creative cultures, when reaching their decline, transform into sterile, mechanical civilizations.[14] Toynbee expanded on this idea by identifying several dozen local, autonomous civilizations, each with its unique characteristics. He also dismissed the idea of civilizational unity in human history, emphasizing the uniqueness of each civilization's social, political, and legal structures, which he viewed as tailored "responses" to the unique "challenges" posed by their historical contexts.[15]

Toynbee's framework, while valuable for understanding the diversity of historical experiences, poses limitations when applied to the typology of state. By focusing on the autonomy and specificity of each civilization, his approach implicitly denies the possibility of a unified or integrative typology of state and law. At best, it can highlight the varied forms of power organization and normative regulation within individual civilizations, but it lacks the theoretical coherence necessary to construct a universal classification of states and legal systems. Even attempts to find analogies or recurring patterns across civilizations fall short of establishing a single, overarching criterion that encompasses all historical and cultural contexts.

If a universal civilizational criterion were possible, it would require acknowledging the existence of a shared human civilization—a notion Toynbee and his followers resist. Such a concept would position individual civilizations as components or contributors to a broader, unified human history. This integrative perspective, however, is absent in Toynbee's approach, which isolates civilizations and treats them as closed, self-contained entities. As a result, while the civilizational approach offers valuable insights into the diversity of state systems, it struggles to provide a cohesive or comprehensive framework for their classification.

Moreover, neither Toynbee nor Spengler delved deeply into the specific issues of state within their civilizational theories. This omission leaves their frameworks insufficient for developing a typology of state with theoretical or historical significance in the field of jurisprudence. Without a focused examination of how state forms emerge, evolve, and interact across civilizations, their approaches lack the analytical depth required for constructing a robust typological framework.

While the civilizational approach enriches our understanding of the diversity and uniqueness of human societies, it remains ill-suited for a systematic typology of state. Its emphasis on the fragmentation and specificity of civilizations precludes the identification of universal criteria necessary for a coherent legal and political theory. A more integrative perspective that bridges the unique with the universal would be

[13] Toynbee 1934; Spengler 1926.

[14] Spengler 1926.

[15] Toynbee 1934.

essential to address this gap, situating individual civilizations within the broader trajectory of human development while acknowledging their distinct contributions.

The libertarian legal concept views the types of state as the principal historical forms for recognizing and organizing human freedom, marking distinct stages in its evolution. From this perspective, **state is a necessary instrument for enabling freedom, with the individual understood as both a subject of law and a participant in state power**. The typology of state is thus fundamentally tied to the historical criteria by which individuals have been recognized as subjects of legal and political systems, reflecting the progress of freedom across different epochs.

In the states of the ancient world, the recognition of individuals as free persons and subjects of law and state was based on an ethnic criterion. For example, in Athens, only members of the Athenian demes (clans) could be citizens and subjects of Athenian law, while in Rome, only *quirites* (original Romans) were members of the *civitas* (civil community) and subjects of Roman law (*ius civile*). This ethnic type of state and law marked an early, necessary stage of organizing society, where freedom and legal subjectivity were restricted to specific ethnic groups, and the distinction between free and unfree was legally institutionalized. The free were subjects of law and state, while the unfree (slaves) were merely objects of law, their status defined by the ethnic exclusion that characterized ancient legal systems.

The transition from antiquity to the Middle Ages brought about the class-based state, representing a further stage in the progress of freedom. In this system, the ethnic criterion of freedom gave way to a class-based criterion. While slavery was largely eradicated, freedom became stratified by class, with different measures of legal and political rights allocated to different social classes. Under European feudalism, all individuals were considered free in the sense of no longer being slaves, but their freedom was shaped by the privileges and restrictions associated with their class. Legal and state subjectivity was tied to class membership, leading to intra-class equality but inter-class inequality, as legal and state status varied significantly across different classes.

The dissolution of feudalism in the modern era marked the emergence of an individualistic state and legal system. In this phase, the class-based system was replaced by one that recognized individuals as independent political actors, subjects of law and state not because of ethnic or class affiliation but by virtue of their status as individual citizens. This shift was facilitated by the separation of private and political life and the development of a non-political civil society distinct from the state. The individualization of legal and political subjectivity reflected the growing emphasis on universal rights and the decline of hierarchical social structures, establishing a more inclusive framework for freedom.

The modern liberal-democratic legal state, constitutionally formalized and historically the latest stage of development, represents a mixed type of law. It integrates natural law and positive law, blending humanitarian-individual principles with political-authoritarian elements into a cohesive legal system. This "natural-positive" or "humanitarian-political" type of law is characterized by the pragmatic coexistence of traditionally opposing principles, such as private individual rights and public political obligations. The modern state thus represents a synthesis of these principles, enshrining them within a unified legal framework that balances personal freedom with collective governance, embodying the highest realization of organized freedom to date.

The natural law or humanitarian component of the modern natural-positive type of law and state introduces a significant innovation: the formal recognition and authoritative affirmation of certain natural rights and freedoms as inherent to all individuals. These natural rights, constitutionally enshrined, are endowed with legal force, taking precedence over other sources within the unified system of positive law. This priority underscores the legal obligation of the state to uphold these rights, making them foundational to the character of both the state and its legal system. However, within this framework, natural law's scope is tempered by the inclusion of other sources of positive law that define specific rights and obligations tied to citizenship, distinguishing the rights of individuals as private persons from their rights as members of the political community.

This distinction reflects a dual conceptualization of rights. Human rights, derived from natural law, pertain to individuals as private persons, while citizen rights encompass the public-political rights and duties granted exclusively to members of a specific state. A citizen, therefore, is simultaneously a subject of universal natural rights and the holder of particular rights tied to their membership in a given political-legal community. These citizen rights often translate into privileges in relation to non-citizens, such as foreigners or stateless persons, emphasizing the unique relationship between individuals and the state to which they belong. This differentiation also highlights the individuality of each state and its legal system, rooted in the historical and political identity of its community, and underscores the sovereignty of the state in internal and external affairs.

According to libertarians, the modern natural-positive type of law and state represents a compromise between natural law (jus naturalism) and positive law (legalism), blending their respective principles into a coherent legal framework. This synthesis has practical and theoretical advantages, but it also introduces inherent tensions. One key contradiction arises from the limitation of natural law within the confines of official state power and law. A fully consistent natural law perspective, as envisioned by the Stoics with their idea of a universal cosmopolitan state where every person is a citizen, rejects the differentiation between human rights and citizen rights. Jus naturalism does not recognize the politically confined interpretation of natural human rights as merely private rights, nor does it accept the exclusion of individuals from the public-political dimension of law based on their citizenship status.

Theories like Marxism, civilizational approaches, and libertarian views provide frameworks for understanding how states emerge and evolve

This unresolved tension between jusnaturalism and legalism persists in the modern legal state. While their coexistence in a natural-positive framework allows for the recognition and protection of both individual and collective rights, it does so within the constraints of practical governance and the realities of state sovereignty. The result is a system that balances the universalism of natural law with the particularism of positive law, reflecting the complexities of contemporary legal and political order.

The typologies of state—ethnic, class, individual-political, and natural-positive—represent successive stages in the historical development of human freedom. From antiquity to the present, these forms have evolved to expand and refine the recognition and organization of freedom. The modern natural-positive state stands as the most advanced stage of this progression, embodying the ideals of universal rights and legal order while grappling with the inherent challenges of integrating diverse legal traditions and political realities.

4.5 Types and Forms of State

The type, or form of state refers to the method by which state power is constituted, organized, and exercised. It represents a comprehensive framework for understanding the legal mechanisms involved in the establishment, distribution, and operation of state authority. This concept encompasses three interconnected dimensions: **(1) the form of governance, (2) the form of state structure, and (3) the form of political regime**. Together, these aspects provide a holistic characterization of how state power is organized and functions within a legal and political system, reflecting the interplay between institutional arrangements, territorial organization, and the nature of the political environment.

The form of governance: it refers to the **method of organizing and establishing supreme state authority.** It addresses fundamental questions about how the sovereign authority of a state is structured, which institutions and officials are entrusted with this power, how they are constituted, and how power is distributed among them. Based on the form of governance, states are traditionally classified into two primary categories: **monarchies** and **republics.**

A monarchy, derived from the Greek term monarchia meaning "rule by one", is a **form of governance where supreme authority is vested in a single individual, typically based on the principle of inheritance**. Monarchies are further divided into two main types: absolute monarchies and representative monarchies. In an **absolute monarchy**, the monarch's authority is unrestricted by any representative, advisory, or legislative body. Historical examples include the rule of French kings prior to the French Revolution of 1789 and Russian emperors before the establishment of the State Duma in the early twentieth century. In contrast, a **representative monarchy** limits the monarch's power through the presence of representative institutions with advisory or legislative functions.

Representative monarchies historically took two forms: estate-representative monarchies and constitutional monarchies. **Estate-representative monarchies** featured assemblies composed of representatives from various social estates, such as the clergy, nobility, and the upper tiers of the emerging third estate (merchants, artisans, etc.). These assemblies, whose convocation and authority depended on the will of the monarch, were characteristic of the transition from feudal fragmentation to the centralization seen in absolute monarchies. **Constitutional monarchies**, which later replaced absolute monarchies, limit the monarch's power through constitutional frameworks or similar legal instruments. In these systems, the legislative authority is vested in a parliament, typically composed of a lower house elected by the populace and an upper house formed through inheritance, appointment by the monarch, or other methods.

Within constitutional monarchies, there are distinct developmental stages. In an early or dualistic constitutional monarchy, the monarch retains significant powers, including the formation of government, appointment of ministers, an absolute veto over legislation, and the ability to dissolve parliament at will. Parliament's role in such systems is often confined to legislative matters and budgetary approval. Dualistic monarchies were prominent in countries like Germany, Austria, and Italy during the late nineteenth and early twentieth centuries. In contrast, modern constitutional monarchies, as seen in nations like the United Kingdom, Belgium, Spain, the Netherlands, Norway, Sweden, and Japan, have largely ceremonial monarchs who act as heads of state. Here, legislative power is fully vested in parliament, and the government, typically formed by the majority party or coalition in parliament, is accountable to this body. Additionally, governments often exercise legislative initiative and issue normative legal acts under delegated authority.

This evolution of monarchy from absolute to constitutional forms reflects a broader historical trend toward limiting centralized authority and promoting representative governance. In modern constitutional monarchies, the system balances the symbolic continuity provided by the monarchy with the practical demands of democratic accountability and the rule of law, emphasizing the primacy of representative institutions in the governance of the state.

A republic, derived from the Latin term res publica meaning "public or national affair", is a **form of governance rooted in the principle of electing the highest state authorities for a specified term**. The concept embodies the idea that governance is a collective responsibility of the people, famously expressed by Cicero as *Respublica est res populi* ("The republic is the people's affair").[16] In modern governance, republics primarily adopt two main forms: **parliamentary republics** and **presidential republics**. These forms represent distinct approaches to implementing the principle of separation of powers within a state governed by the rule of law.

In a **parliamentary republic**, the parliament serves as the supreme representative and legislative authority. It is responsible for forming the highest executive body, the government, and holds the power to oversee its actions through parliamentary control. This structure ensures that the executive branch remains accountable to the legislative branch, reflecting the foundational principle of popular sovereignty. The close relationship between the parliament and the government defines the functioning of this form of government, emphasizing collective decision-making and the integration of executive and legislative functions under parliamentary oversight.

---

[16] Cicero 1928.

In a parliamentary republic, the head of state, typically the president, is elected by the parliament and holds a range of powers and responsibilities. These include the authority to dissolve parliament, participate in the appointment of the head of government, engage in legislative processes (such as signing laws and issuing decrees), and serve as the supreme commander-in-chief of the armed forces. The government is formed by representatives of the parties holding a parliamentary majority and is accountable to the parliament. This parliamentary majority has the power to dismiss the government, while the government, with the support of the president, can seek the dissolution of parliament and call for new elections. Examples of modern parliamentary republics include Greece, Italy, and Germany, where this form of governance emphasizes a balance of power between legislative and executive branches under parliamentary control.

States are characterized by governance structures (e.g., monarchy, republic), territorial organization (e.g., unitary, federal), and political regimes (e.g., liberal, authoritarian)

In a **presidential republic**, governance is characterized by the direct involvement of the population in electing both the parliament (the supreme legislative and representative body) and the president, who serves as both head of state and head of the executive branch. Presidential elections may occur through universal direct suffrage, as in Russia and France, or through indirect methods, as in the United States, where the electorate selects electors who, in turn, elect the president. This form of government has several variations, reflecting different balances and structures of power.

The United States exemplifies a classic model of a presidential republic, marked by a strict separation of powers. Legislative authority is vested in Congress, which consists of the House of Representatives and the Senate. Executive power is held by the president, who also functions as the head of government, in the absence of a prime ministerial role. Judicial authority is exercised by the Supreme Court. The president presides over the executive branch, including the Cabinet, which functions as an advisory body. Cabinet members, including ministers, are appointed by the president with the advice and consent of the Senate. This structure ensures the president wields significant authority in both domestic and foreign policy, acts as the supreme commander-in-chief of the armed forces, issues by-laws, and exercises a suspensive veto over legislation.

In the U.S. model, the president operates independently of Congress, and neither the president nor the Cabinet is directly accountable to the legislative body. The president's tenure is secure from parliamentary dismissal, with removal from office possible only through the process of impeachment. This framework provides the president with broad executive powers while maintaining a system of checks and balances to regulate interactions among the legislative, executive, and judicial branches.

These distinctions between parliamentary and presidential republics highlight variations in the organization and balance of power within republican forms of government. While parliamentary systems emphasize collaboration and accountability between the legislative and executive branches, presidential systems prioritize a clear separation of powers, granting the president substantial autonomy in governance. Both forms reflect different interpretations of democratic principles and the practicalities of maintaining effective state authority.

The French model of a presidential republic incorporates significant elements of a parliamentary system, blending features of both governance structures. Alongside the President, who holds extensive authority, there is a distinct government body known as the Council of Ministers, led by the Prime Minister. The President wields considerable influence over the executive branch, appointing the Prime Minister and, based on the Prime Minister's recommendations, other members of the government. Additionally, the President presides over meetings of the Council of Ministers and has the authority to accept the resignation of the Prime Minister and other ministers.

The President also possesses substantial legislative powers, including the right to dissolve the lower house of parliament, the National Assembly, after consulting with the Prime Minister and the presidents of both parliamentary chambers. Despite these expansive powers, the French system ensures checks and balances through the role of the bicameral parliament, comprising the Senate and the National Assembly. The parliament is vested with the authority to oversee and control the actions of the government.

The National Assembly, in particular, exercises significant influence by holding the government accountable. Through a majority vote, the National Assembly can adopt a resolution of censure, compelling the government to resign. This mechanism ensures that the government, while appointed and supported by the President, must also maintain the confidence of the legislative branch.

The French model thus represents a hybrid system that integrates the strong presidential authority characteristic of a presidential republic with the parliamentary oversight and accountability mechanisms found in parliamentary systems. This fusion allows for a unique balance of power, ensuring both executive strength and legislative scrutiny in the governance of the state.

The form of state structure: it encompasses the **method of territorial and national-territorial organization of state power and the distribution of authority among its subjects**. This dimension addresses the territorial structure of the state and the mechanisms for organizing state power across its regions. Based on the form of state structure in this context, states are classified as **unitary, federal, or confederations**, with each structure reflecting a distinct approach to the relationship between territorial entities and central authority.

A unitary state is a single, indivisible sovereign entity. In such a state, one constitution applies uniformly across the entire territory, and centralized authorities—representative, executive, and judicial—exercise state power. Legislation is unified, with no separate legal systems for different regions. Additionally, a unitary state maintains a single armed force and a unified tax and financial system. Modern examples of unitary states include Portugal, Finland, and France. The unitary form ensures a high degree of uniformity and centralized control, facilitating coherent policy implementation and governance throughout the state's territory.

A federal state is also a single sovereign entity, but it is organized as a union of semi-autonomous territorial or national-territorial entities, often referred to as states, provinces, or regions. These entities possess their own state and legal status, recognized within the framework of the federal constitution. Each entity has its own system of governance, including legislative, executive, and sometimes judicial bodies, and it operates under its own legislation. However, the sovereignty of the individual entities exists only within the bounds of the overarching sovereignty of the federal state. This structure allows for a balance between regional autonomy and national unity, accommodating diversity while maintaining central authority.

The confederation, in contrast, is a form of union between sovereign states. Unlike unitary and federal states, a confederation is not a single sovereign state but rather a cooperative arrangement among independent states. The member states retain their sovereignty and independence while coordinating on certain matters, often through agreements or common institutions, typically in areas like defense or trade. Confederations are generally looser in structure and may lack the cohesive strength of unitary or federal systems.

These forms of state structure reflect the diversity in how states organize their authority and manage relationships across their territories. While unitary states emphasize centralization and uniformity, federal states promote regional autonomy within a sovereign framework, and confederations prioritize the independence of member states within a cooperative structure. Each form addresses the complexities of governance and structuration in different historical, cultural, and geographic contexts.

The form of the political regime: this one reflects the character, nature, and quality of the legal framework through which state power is exercised. It addresses how state authority is implemented, focusing on the methods, procedures, and structures that define its operation. According to the libertarian-legal perspective,[17] the state, as a legal form of organizing and exercising public power, inherently operates within a legal order. In contrast, despotism—whether in the form of tyranny, dictatorship, totalitarianism, or other manifestations—represents an anti-legal regime, characterized by the absence of true legal structures. Despotic regimes, such as military-police, fascist, racial-Nazi, or party-class systems, fall outside the realm of legitimate statehood, as they lack the essential legal framework that defines the state. In essence, a genuine state regime is always state-legal (state of law),[18] distinguished by the presence of specific legal procedures, techniques, and methods for the implementation of power.

Political regimes can be classified according to their legal characteristics and the degree of legal development they exhibit. This classification divides regimes into two broad categories: **liberal** and **authoritarian**. These two types represent the extreme

[17] For this particular form, the libertarian explanations appear to be the most suitable and logical ones.

[18] See Chap. 5 for the description of the concept of state of law.

poles of the spectrum, from the most legally developed forms of governance to the least. Between these poles exist numerous intermediate forms, reflecting varying degrees of legal evolution in the implementation of state power. However, the fundamental distinction between liberal and authoritarian regimes lies in their contrasting approaches to the role of law, civil rights, and public accountability in governance.

A **liberal state and legal regime** is characterized by its foundation in modern constitutional democracy and civil society. It is marked by the official recognition and practical enforcement of fundamental, inalienable human rights and a wide range of civil liberties. Key features of this regime include the rule of law, the separation of powers (legislative, executive, and judicial), constitutionalism, parliamentarism, and ideological and political pluralism. A multi-party system, free elections, referenda, and mechanisms for public oversight of government actions are integral to its functioning. Independent institutions of civil society play a vital role in maintaining transparency and accountability in governance. The liberal regime embodies the core principles of democracy, particularly the sovereignty of the people, and is thus often referred to as a liberal democratic regime, underscoring its commitment to democracy in legal form.

In contrast, an **authoritarian state and legal regime** is prevalent in systems where the foundations of civil society and the rule of law remain underdeveloped. Such regimes lack the institutional safeguards necessary to protect human and civil rights, uphold the rule of law, and curb the arbitrary exercise of state power. They are marked by the absence of effective mechanisms for public oversight and accountability. Authoritarian regimes often emerge during the early stages of state development, where elements of civil society and legal legitimacy are nascent or absent. In such contexts, a blend of authoritarian and liberal elements may coexist, reflecting transitional phases in the evolution toward a modern legal state and civil society.

The distinction between liberal and authoritarian regimes highlights the fundamental importance of the legal framework in shaping state power. A liberal regime prioritizes the rule of law, human rights, and democratic principles, while an authoritarian regime reflects the lack of these features. The existence of intermediate forms between these extremes illustrates the dynamic and evolving nature of state regimes, as societies progress toward more developed legal and democratic systems. Ultimately, the form of a state regime serves as a critical indicator of its commitment to legality, legitimacy, and the protection of individual freedoms.

4.6 Functions of State

The functions of the state represent the primary forms of its activity, reflecting the essence of the state. The state's essence, as revealed through its functions, lies in its role as a legal, sovereign organization of public power for free individuals. From this perspective, the legitimacy of the state's activity depends on its alignment with its intrinsic nature and purpose. Only actions that arise from and correspond to the state's essence can be considered legitimate. Conversely, any actions by the state, its institutions, or officials that exceed the bounds of these inherent functions are unlawful and, by definition, cannot be regarded as genuinely state actions.

The core of all state functions is the organization, implementation, and protection of a state and legal order that governs the life of free individuals. This order is shaped by the socio-historical context within which the state operates. The functional activity of the state is unified in essence, as all its functions work collectively to create, sustain, and enforce this legal and societal framework. While the state's functions are interrelated and integrated, they can be distinguished into relatively independent aspects that focus on specific dimensions of state activity.

The primary functions of the state include the **law-making function**, which involves the creation of legal norms that establish the framework for governance and social order; the **law-implementing function**, which ensures the practical application of these legal norms in the administration and operation of the state; and the **law-protecting (human rights) function**, which safeguards the legal order and ensures compliance with established laws. Additionally, the **foreign-state (external) function** encompasses the state's activities in international relations, including the negotiation of treaties, the maintenance of diplomatic relations, and the defense of the state's sovereignty on the global stage.

These functions are not merely technical operations but reflect the state's broader purpose of enabling and protecting the freedom of its citizens within a structured legal framework. Each function contributes to the unified goal of establishing a just and sustainable legal order, ensuring that the state's authority is exercised within the confines of law and legitimacy. The legitimacy of the state is thus intrinsically tied to the fulfillment of these core functions in service of its foundational role as a legal and sovereign entity for free individuals.

The functions of the state can be broadly categorized into **internal** and **external** functions, each corresponding to the exercise of the state's sovereignty within its territory or in the realm of international relations. The first three functions—law-making, law-implementing, and human rights—are internal and reflect the state's role in exercising internal sovereignty. The fourth, the external function, represents the state's activity in implementing its external sovereignty. While distinct, these functions are deeply interconnected, complementing and reinforcing one another to ensure the effective operation and legitimacy of the state both domestically and internationally.

The **law-making function** encompasses the state's activities in establishing the sources and norms of current law. This includes enacting laws and other normative legal acts, recognizing and institutionalizing legal precedents, sanctioning customs, and formally affirming the priority of natural rights and freedoms. Through this function, the state creates the legal framework within which its authority operates and ensures that its legal system reflects fundamental human rights and principles of justice.

The **law-implementing function** involves the application and enforcement of the established legal framework. Its purpose is to ensure that the laws created by the state are consistently and effectively operational, maintaining their status as the current and binding legal standards. All state activities, including those of its bodies and officials, are fundamentally law-implementing in nature. This includes the issuance of normative legal acts as part of the legislative process and the execution of administrative and executive duties. Through this function, the state translates its legal framework into actionable and enforceable governance.

The **human rights function** focuses on the protection of individual rights and freedoms, the establishment of legality, and the maintenance of law and order across all spheres of public and political life. A critical element of this function is the state's responsibility to combat offenses and crime, including the implementation of preventive measures to uphold public safety and security. Protecting and promoting human rights is a fundamental obligation of the state, underscoring its legitimacy and commitment to serving its citizens.

The state performs law-making, law-implementing, human rights protection, and external (international) functions to maintain order and sovereignty

The **external function** reflects the state's activities as a sovereign actor in international relations. This includes ensuring national defense and protecting the population from external threats, fostering cooperation with other states in political, economic, cultural, scientific, and technical fields, and safeguarding the rights and interests of its citizens abroad. Additionally, the external function encompasses the state's role in promoting international solidarity, preventing conflict, and contributing to global peace and stability. Through this function, the state participates actively in the broader international community.

Together, these functions illustrate the multifaceted role of the state in organizing, implementing, and safeguarding the legal and social order. Internal functions ensure the state's legitimacy and effectiveness within its borders, while the external function reinforces its role and responsibilities in the global arena. This interconnected framework underscores the state's dual obligation to uphold justice and order domestically and to contribute constructively to the international community.

4.7 State Mechanism

The **mechanism (or apparatus) of the state** refers to the system of organs, institutions, and officials that, in accordance with legal procedures, are vested with state powers to carry out the functions of the state. It represents the organizational structure through which state power is implemented and serves as the institutional framework for the existence and operation of the state. Viewed from a human-centered and rational perspective, the state consists of free individuals—its citizens—and the state mechanism functions as institutionalized groups of citizens, organized within a legal framework, who are granted specific powers to exercise state authority.

In its institutional and functional dimension, a **state body, institution, or official position** constitutes a structural element of the state apparatus. Each of these elements is endowed with specific state powers, collectively referred to as competence. The creation, operation, and scope of these bodies and positions are determined by legal norms and are regulated by laws and other normative acts. The legal framework outlines the powers, procedures, and methods of operation for all components of the state mechanism, ensuring that their activities align with the established legal order.

The **hierarchical organization** of the state apparatus is based on the principle of subordination, where lower bodies are accountable to higher ones. This hierarchy ensures that the sovereign power of the state is expressed cohesively through the competencies of various state bodies, all of which are ultimately led by higher bodies vested with overarching sovereign authority. Within this structure, each body, institution, or official possesses a defined competence, tailored to its position in the hierarchy and aligned with the competencies of other bodies, ensuring coordinated and lawful functioning.

The **competence of a state body or official** encompasses its rights and obligations. These rights are not merely privileges but duties to act within the scope of authority granted by law, performing actions that fulfill the state's objectives. Similarly, the duties imposed on state bodies and officials inherently include the legal right to perform corresponding actions necessary for executing state power. The specific organization, powers, and functions of the state apparatus vary depending on the type and form of the state.

The state mechanism consists of institutions and officials organized hierarchically to execute state functions within a legal framework

In modern (legal) states, the state apparatus is built on the principle of **separation of powers** into three branches: legislative, executive, and judicial. Legislative power is exercised by a representative parliament (unicameral or bicameral), while executive power is vested in the head of state (such as a president or constitutional monarch), the government, ministries, and various central and local administrative bodies. Judicial power is carried out exclusively by courts, including general, constitutional, and arbitration courts. Judges operate independently, guided solely by the constitution and laws, with safeguards like irremovability and immunity to preserve judicial impartiality.

Despite its essential role, the state apparatus is often criticized for tendencies toward **bureaucracy, corporatism, and alienation from the public**. These shortcomings, such as prioritizing institutional interests over public welfare, abuse of power, and neglect of legal obligations, are particularly pronounced in the state apparatus of post-Soviet countries. Addressing these challenges requires continuous efforts to enhance accountability, transparency, and adherence to the rule of law, ensuring that the state mechanism serves its true purpose of advancing the common good and upholding justice.

The fight against both traditional and emerging shortcomings of the state apparatus requires a multifaceted and systematic approach. This author would recommend the following key strategies and directions for addressing these issues:

1. ***Strengthening legal foundations:*** Developing robust legal principles, frameworks, and procedures to guide the organization and functioning of all components of the state apparatus. This ensures that state activities are firmly grounded in legality and transparency.
2. ***Enhancing personnel training:*** Improving the processes for training and retraining qualified personnel for the state apparatus. This involves equipping civil servants with the knowledge and skills needed to meet the demands of their roles effectively and ethically.
3. ***Raising professional standards:*** Increasing the standards for the professional competence, moral integrity, and legal culture of civil servants. Emphasis on ethical behavior and adherence to the rule of law is crucial in fostering accountability and public trust.
4. ***Enforcing legal responsibility:*** Strengthening mechanisms for holding state employees accountable for misconduct. This includes enforcing measures of legal responsibility to deter and address offenses committed by officials within the state apparatus.
5. ***Empowering citizens and civil society:*** Encouraging greater legal awareness and activism among citizens and public associations. By actively participating in the defense of their rights and legitimate interests, citizens contribute to the accountability and responsiveness of the state apparatus.
6. ***Enhancing oversight:*** Continuously improving the forms and methods of public and state control over the activities of all state bodies, institutions, and officials. Effective oversight mechanisms ensure that state power is exercised responsibly and in alignment with the public good.

Questions for Students

1. *What are the key distinctions between legal and legitimate power, and why are both important in governance?*
2. *How does state sovereignty manifest internally and externally?*
3. *What is the integrative theory's view of the state as a political and legal organization?*
4. *How do different theories, like Marxism or the civilizational approach, explain the formation and evolution of states?*
5. *What distinguishes unitary, federal, and confederal state structures from one another?*
6. *How do the law-making, law-implementing, and human rights functions collectively define the role of the state?*

References

Aristotle (1995) Politics, Book III. Oxford University Press
Baitin A (1990) General Theory of State and Law (in Russian). Moscow
Burlatsky F, Keyzerov K (1989) Political Science: Theory and Methodology (in Russian). Moscow
Cicero (1928) On the Republic, Book I. Harvard University Press, Cambridge
Hegel GWF (2001) Lectures on the Philosophy of History. Oxford University Press, Oxford
Marx K, Engels F (1976) The German Ideology. Progress Publishers, Moscow
Plato (1937a) Republic, Book I (transl. Shorey P). Harvard University Press, Cambridge
Plato (1937b) Republic, Book VIII (transl. Shorey P). Harvard University Press, Cambridge
Spengler O (1926) The Decline of the West. Oxford University Press, Oxford
Toynbee A (1934) A Study of History. Oxford University Press, Oxford
Weber M (1978) Economy and Society: An Outline of Interpretive Sociology. University of California Press, Berkeley

Chapter 5
Rechtsstaat (State of Law) and Civil Society

Contents

Abstract This chapter provides a comprehensive examination of the concept of the Rechtsstaat, or State of Law, tracing its historical roots, theoretical evolution, core principles, and practical relevance especially in post-Soviet contexts. The chapter begins with a detailed historical account, highlighting the contributions of thinkers from Solon and Aristotle to Locke, Kant, Montesquieu, and beyond, who shaped the idea of law-bound statehood, grounded in justice, individual rights, and the limitation of power. It distinguishes *Rechtsstaat* from mere legalism, emphasizing that legality alone is not sufficient: laws must be just, fair, and serve human dignity. The chapter then presents key elements that define a *Rechtsstaat*: rule of law, supremacy of human rights and freedoms, mutual responsibility between state and citizen, separation of powers, high legal culture, and the essential role of civil society. It underscores that civil society is not only a component but a precondition for the realization of a true State of Law, providing both accountability and participation in public life. In conclusion, the chapter reflects on the challenges and prospects for post-Soviet states aspiring to build functioning *Rechtsstaaten*, arguing that this ideal demands more than constitutional declarations—it requires deep legal culture, just legal frameworks, vibrant civic engagement, and long-term commitment to democratic principles.

Keywords Rechtsstaat (State of Law) · Rule of law and legal justice · Human rights and freedoms · Civil society and governance · Separation of powers · Legal culture and awareness · Post-Soviet legal development

R. Atadjanov, *A Common Theory of Law*, https://doi.org/10.1007/978-94-6265-711-3_5

5.1 The History of the Idea of a *Rechtsstaat*

The idea of a modern State of Law, or, as it is more commonly known, a *Rechtsstaat*,[1] has a long instructive history as a special theoretical concept and corresponding practice. As the word itself suggests, the term '*Rechtsstaat*' (formed from the combination of two German words—*Rechts* meaning 'law', 'right', and *Staat* translated as 'State') originated and became established in the German legal literature during the first half of the nineteenth century, and it has become widespread ever since.[2] It is not generally used in the English-language legal literature; to a certain extent another term, 'rule of law', has been used as its equivalent.[3] When it comes to the content and ideas informing *Rechtsstaat*, in other words, the substance of the concept of a State of Law, those have first appeared already back in antiquity while the theoretically developed conceptions of a State of Law are first known from the sixteenth to seventeenth centuries.

Historically, this happened in the common course of origination and formation of progressive directions of legal and political thought, along with a crystallization of a new secular legal outlook, the development of the ideas of humanism, freedom and equality of all people as well as a search for various State and legal means, designs and forms directed against the usurpation of public political power and its impunity and irresponsibility before society.[4] Many prominent individuals have contributed to this process of conceptualization of 'legal statehood'—in the sense of State of Law as a lawful State, from Solon to Cicero, from Thomas Aquinas to Hegel. All its novelty (as it appeared novel for its time) notwithstanding, the theoretical concept of State of Law developed in their works has drawn upon the experiences of the past, the achievements of the preceding legal, social and political theory and practice and historically established universal values and humanistic traditions. What follows is

[1] Several alternative terms have been proposed or used to denominate this phenomenon: 'legal state', 'lawful state', 'state of justice', 'rule-of-law state', 'law-state', 'justice-based state', 'constitutional state', and so on. It appears more proper to employ a qualifying term such as 'State of Law', which may be interpreted as 'state based on law', which is in line with one of its most important characteristics—domination of *ius*, see Sect. 4.3, and which corresponds to the working definition of *Rechtsstaat* offered in Sect. 4.2. 'State of Law' also serves as an appropriate translation into English of the equivalent of *Rechtsstaat* in the Russian language—'pravovoe gosudarstvo' [правовое государство].

[2] Contrary to what is commonly believed, it was not Immanuel Kant (Kant 1996) who came up with the term "*Rechtsstaat*" itself although as it is described further on in the main text he was behind an elaborated philosophical justification of the liberal theory of the State of Law. The term first appeared in the works of Carl Theodor Welcker (Welcker 1813), a German law professor and politician, and Robert von Mohl (Von Mohl 1817), a German jurist.

[3] It appears more proper and logical to use the term *rule of law* in its more exact, or literal, connotation as a critical principle of law as well as one of the fundamental conditions/characteristics of *Rechtsstaat* rather than substitute it by the 'umbrella' concept of State of Law. See Sect. 4.3 for a brief description of the *rule of law* in that capacity.

[4] For the descriptions, definitions and subsequent discussion of such phenomena as society and public power, see, respectively, Chaps. 2 and 3.

a brief account of the contributions those personalities made to the evolution of the notion of the State of Law and its theoretical justification.

One of the famous so-called Seven Sages of Greece, Solon (ca 638–559 BC), the Athenian reformer, statesman and legislator, insisted on the fundamental significance of the rule, or domination, of the law (laws) in political affairs. According to Aristotle, Solon conducted his famous reforms with the help of 'the power of the law' combining force with law.[5] His idea of unity of force ('force' meaning the official power of the State) and law also allowed him to conclude that any transformations, or reforms in the State must always be done in a legal way, on the basis of official and universal law.[6] These ideas have been aimed at counteracting the notion that force creates right (i.e., law), or that the mighty and the strong are always right, or that the strong always have the powerless to blame, and so on. The subsequent development of ancient Greek political and legal thought has been accompanied by a further deepening of secular theoretical views on the relationship between law and State as well as better forms and mechanisms of legal mediation and/or regulation of political power relations.

Solon was not the only ancient thinker to develop the ideas of the rule of law in a Greek polis. In his famous dialogues, 'Republic' and 'Laws', Plato (ca 423–347 BC) wrote that 'where the law does not have force and remains under someone's power', the 'State's death is imminent' and that 'where the law is the lord over the rulers and the latter are slaves to the law I see the State's salvation'.[7] Certainly, it would be wrong to equate Plato's idea of a lawful State with *Rechtsstaat*. However, these two notions do have clear similarities: when Plato talks about the laws he implies not just any mandatory rule stemming from a power-wielding establishment but only the reasonable and fair binding rules. An essential feature of such a law as well as of the State itself, as estimated by Plato, is the expression and protection of a common interest. Without this feature there will be no law, nor State, nor fairness; instead, we would have only the abuse of these ideas in the context of violence, political divisions and domination of interests of a narrow group of individuals. It appears these same words could be repeated by contemporary proponents of *Rechtsstaat* and just law.

Another prominent philosopher of Ancient Greece, Aristotle (384–322 BC), also tried to justify the conception of the rule of rational laws from a natural legal perspective. In expressing his position towards state power, law (*ius*) and law as *lex*, Aristotle insisted that 'ruling against the law may not be a matter of proper lex, and desire to forcefully subjugate others contradicts the idea of law itself'. Law must dominate everything; where there is no 'rule of law (*lex*) there is no place for (any) form of State power.' In Aristotle's understanding, various forms of political and state structure must correspond to the principle of fairness and justice, and the idea of law; in other words, they carry a legal character. Only those forms of State system, according to Aristotle, that imply common benefit are correct and appropriate; they correspond to the principle of absolute justice. Those forms which serve only the private interests

---

[5] Solon, in Aristotle 1984.

[6] Aristotle 1996, at 41.

[7] Plato 1937, 1926, 715d.

of the rulers are wrong and are based on despotic ways of governance. The State is (should be) an interaction of free people. These conclusions allow us to see that there was a *Rechtsstaat* conception in Aristotelian teachings.

The legal approach to the State, i.e. its legal understanding and interpretation, was substantially developed, deepened and crystallized in the works of ancient Roman authors: statesmen, writers, lawyers, and historians. Their humanistic views echoed the ideas of progressive ancient Greek thinkers about law, freedom, human dignity and humanism. This is especially true with respect to the works of Marcus Tullius Cicero (106–43 BC), the famous Roman orator, politician, jurist, and intellectual whose big achievement (within the context of this section in Chap. 4) was a naturalist legal interpretation of the state as a coordinated and harmonized legal communion of people and common legal order. In his works 'On Laws', 'On Republic', 'On Duties', he asks: What is the State? To whom does it belong? Cicero himself provides an answer: The state is a property of the peoples, with 'peoples' understood as not just any kind of collectivity of people united in any way but as a conglomerate of many people tied together and with each other by a general agreement in the matters of law and commonality of interests.[8] For Cicero, State—from the perspective of its relationship to the law—is nothing else than common legal order. It flows out of this conception that the laws enacted by the state must necessarily correspond to the requirements and demands of natural law which posited that the human rights and freedoms are not bestowed or established by anyone or due to anyone's desire or will but belong to them by nature. Unjust laws, according to Cicero, 'would deserve the title of the law no more than the decisions adopted by brigands'.[9] It was Cicero who formulated the important state legal principle 'Everyone should be subject to the law,[10] which later served as one of the cornerstones of *Rechtsstaat*. Only in the State where law is applied equally towards all is a true legal equality of citizens and individuals possible. These humanistic motives and ideas of freedom and equality of all people, their occupation and status in the society notwithstanding, can be traced in the working and treatises of many other Roman philosophers, including for example, Seneca the Younger (ca 4 BC–AD 65).

Ideas and concepts of authors of Antiquity have found their further development and reinforcement in the work of intellectuals of the European Middle Ages, Early and Late Modern periods, and in contemporary history. Contrary to popular belief that not many deserving developments took place in terms of legal theoretical concepts during the Middle Ages, medieval jurisprudence, legal and political science, philosophy and theology played an important connecting role between the ideas of antiquity and modernity. This was true also for the evolution of the theoretical basis for the subsequent teaching on natural rights, separation of powers, representative system and other elements that make up the contemporary notion of *Rechtsstaat*.

In this sense, the political and legal views of Thomas Aquinas (1225–1274) and Marsilius of Padua (ca 1275–1342) deserve to be mentioned. The former developed a

---

[8] Marchenko 2019, at 197.

[9] Cicero 1998, II, at 13.

[10] Ibid., III, at 17.

number of political and legal ideas of ancient authors, especially Aristotle's ideas on the political nature of man and political forms of governance. According to Aquinas, natural law demands recognition of and respect towards the dignity of the human being as a reasonable creature. He posited that the State and human—positive—law must recognize and respect human dignity.[11] Within this understanding the state as a political form of expression of common good is called upon to provide decent living conditions, namely, conditions corresponding to people's dignity. In his turn, Marsilius of Padua maintained that the people is a source of any power—both secular and spiritual, a carrier of sovereignty and a supreme legislator.[12] He was one of the first individuals in the history of political thought to justify the conception of separation of legislative and executive powers based on the supremacy of the legislature. The principle of electivity of all positions in the state was another element of *Rechtsstaat* that Marsilius propounded.

During the Early and Late periods of Modern history, the ideas of State of Law developed in line with achievements of the preceding political and legal thought, including naturalistic legal understandings of freedom and human rights, priority of natural law before positive law, legal forms and limitations of carrying out state power, delineation of powers among different bodies, and more. A range of elements pertinent to the theory of State of Law was advanced by English philosopher John Locke (1632–1704), commonly referred to as the 'Father of Liberalism'. His vision of State of Law consisted of a state where the supremacy of civil law corresponding to the eternal and all-embracing universal law of nature is established. In this state the permanent constitutional laws are declared and adopted, inalienable natural individual rights and freedoms are recognized, state power is divided into legislative, executive (which also includes the judiciary) and federal—or external executive, powers. Locke contraposed such a state that provides for life, freedom and property of the people and where state power is limited by the common good, to a despotic state. Based on the ideas of the people's sovereignty and social contract that form legal grounds for and constitute the source of statehood, Lock offered a 'doctrine of legality of resistance to any unlawful exercises of power'.[13]

Another influential individual, this time a French lawyer and judge, Charles-Louis Montesquieu (1689–1755), offered a systematic elaboration of the concept of separation of powers that proved to be key to the State of Law. He first proposed the separation of state power into three main branches as we know them today: legislative, executive and judicial. Montesquieu argued that in order to prevent the abuse of power it would be necessary that each one of those three branches of power should mutually restrain each other. Separation and mutual restraint (something that modern constitutionalists refer to as a "system of checks and balances"), according to him, represent the main condition for ensuring political freedom in its relation to state organization. Montesquieu also considered political freedom with respect

[11] Nersesyants 2016, at 298.

[12] Ibid., at 299.

[13] Locke 1960, at 116.

to separate individuals wherein it would consist in the latter's' security.[14] Ideas of both Locke and Montesquieu about the supremacy of law in the state, natural rights as well as separation/restriction of powers, have considerably influenced the ensuing theoretical understandings of *Rechtsstaat*. The theory and practice of the so-called legal statehood ('State-of-Law-ness') has also been contributed to by some outstanding figures of the American Revolution, such as Thomas Jefferson (1743–1826),[15] Alexander Hamilton (1757–1804),[16] John Adams (1735–1826),[17] James Madison (1751–1836),[18] and others.

An account of the evolution of ideas of State of Law would not be comprehensive without noting the contribution made by Immanuel Kant (1724–1804). At the end of the eighteenth century the prominent German philosopher proposed a deep philosophical justification for the liberal theory of the State of Law. He noted that the state is a conglomerate of a multitude of people who are subject to just laws.[19] The benefit of having the state is in the highest degree of consistency of the state organization with legal principles. Reason demands from us that we aspire to achieve such a consistency through the categorical imperative. In law, this categorical imperative of reason presents itself in the form of a requirement of the universal law. It says, 'Act in such a way that the free expression of your arbitrary behavior is compatible with the freedom of each individual in accordance with the universal law'.[20] In the sphere of statehood, Kant's categorical imperative demands that the state be of necessity organized as a public state system based on separation of powers; justice in such a state is to be carried out by a jury elected by the people. According to Kant, the State of Law does not represent an empirical reality; rather, it is an ideal theoretical construct or model which we need to be guided by and which serves as a requirement of reason as well as the eventual purpose of our efforts in practically organizing the public and state legal life.[21] In other words, *Rechtsstaat* in Kantian understanding is a duty, an 'ought', and not an 'is'.

Not all descriptions or teachings on the State of Law were based on naturalistic legal views. A number of famous individual influencers subscribed to positivistic (legalistic) interpretations of the State of Law which became especially influential during the nineteenth and early twentieth centuries. Those individuals would include Rudolf von Jhering (1818–1892),[22] Carl Friedrich von Gerber (1823–1891),[23] Nikolai Korkunov (1853–1904),[24] and many others. The essence of their

---

[14] Montesquieu 1955, at 298.

[15] Jefferson 1975.

[16] Hamilton et al. 1987.

[17] Adams 1971.

[18] Hamilton et al. 1987.

[19] Kant 1996, at 233.

[20] Ibid., at 140.

[21] Nersesyants 2016, at 304.

[22] von Jhering 1915.

[23] von Gerber 1869.

[24] Korkunov 1909.

positivist conceptions of legal limitations upon the state consists in the effort to create various constructs for self-restraint of the state by a positive law established by that very state. The distinction between *ius* and *lex* was to be discarded while law had to be reduced to a set of written norms established, enforced and protected by the state. This type of understanding and interpretation of State of Law, or law and state (and their relationship) in general, goes back to and is based on the ideas and notions offered by Thomas Hobbes (1588–1679),[25] John Austin (1790–1859),[26] Hans Kelsen (1881–1973)[27] and Gabriel Shershenevich (1863–1912).[28]

It follows from the foregoing brief account that the ideas of natural law, human rights and freedoms, and the latter's inalienable character have had a significant impact on the whole process of the formation and development of understanding of what a State of Law is, what elements and characteristics it must include, and how its ideal needs to be achieved. The contemporary understanding of the meaning and significance of human rights as an essential component of the *Rechtsstaat* is based on the rich experience of mankind, first of all in the sphere of legal forms of organization of public and political life of the people as well as on the history of the evolution and crystallization of ideas and institutions dealing with human rights and freedoms.

5.2 What Is a State of Law?

A State of Law is one of the significant achievements of human civilization in terms of its influence upon the decision-making processes in the history of state formation. It is a multidimensional and developing phenomenon. In the course of social progress, it acquires new content and new features that correspond to the concrete conditions of societal existence and the level of societal development. And for any State of Law the enduring common element is its boundness by law.

There exist multiple definitions of the State of Law. Some of those definitions highlight the constitutional element: "A *Rechtsstaat* is a 'constitutional state' in which the exercise of governmental power is constrained by the law."[29] It is related to constitutionalism while often tied to the concept of *rule of law*; however, it also emphasizes what is just. Under such a definition, *Rechtsstaat* means that the power of the state is limited in order to protect citizens from the arbitrary exercise of authority. Close to this description are those where "the state in its realization of its governmental and judicial functions is restrained and limited by law; it stands under

[25] Hobbes 1996.

[26] Austin 1998.

[27] Kelsen 1967.

[28] Shershenevich 1995.

[29] Schmitt 2007, at 7.

law and not outside or above it" and where "*Rechtsstaat* is a state dominated by law".[30]

Another definition underlines the element of relationships between various actors and the state: "A State of Law is a special form of organization and activities of state power which is built on the relationships with individuals as well as with their various associations, and is based on [norms of] law".[31] Here, the relational/collaborational component may be understood as the main purpose of this form of organization (state) where such collaboration should stay within the limits of legal norms.

A Rechtsstaat ensures the rule of law, limits state power by law, and guarantees the protection of individual rights and freedoms

A more complicated description of the State of Law may be presented as follows. *Rechtsstaat* can be defined as a permanent unified organism of institutions which are being guided, supported and activated by a common will and which have as a task the promotion of the permitted goals of a certain people on a given territory.[32] This task encompasses and is addressed to both separate individuals and the whole society. This is probably a definition where the indication of what the State of Law must eventually be is most directly present.

Some simpler definitions of *Rechtsstaat* appear to stem from the well-known theory of social contract: "A law-state is a state giving [its] individuals law-state protection within its territory."[33] This description prioritizes only one function the State of Law performs which is to provide protection to persons on its territory. It does not include other important elements pertinent to the *Rechtsstaat* and considered in the next subsection, and seems to be rather simplistic or restrictive.

A general critique of the above attempts to define *Rechtsstaat*, as proposed by some authors could be that the notion of state in those definitions is given not within its historical context but in an idealized representation.[34] Instead of determining what a state *is* they try to define what it *should be*. In other words, such descriptions lay out an idealized version of what the state must be. While perhaps properly capturing an ought-to-be characteristic of *Rechtsstaat*, this critique is lacking in the realization that no single state in the world has truly become a State of Law. There are state actors that have come very close to being labeled as *Rechtsstaat*, but on the European continent it would be unrealistic to suggest that there exists a state that may claim a one-hundred percent denomination as State of Law. Hence, it appears the definition of *Rechtsstaat* will probably stay as an idealized form of political organization for the foreseeable future (see further the discussion in Sect. 5.5).

---

[30] For a popular description of *Rechtsstaat* based on a liberalist constitutionalist view, see von Hayek 2018, at 254–271.

[31] Khropanyuk 2019, at 80.

[32] von Mohl 1817; Shershenevich 1995, at 171.

[33] Frändberg 2014, at 57.

[34] Marchenko 2015, at 115.

Out of the multitude of *Rechtsstaat*'s definitions, one appears as perhaps the most comprehensive one in terms of its content, coverage, and elements as well as its teleological perspective.[35] According to this definition

> State of Law represents a form of organization of political power characterized by rule of law, legitimacy of power, and a high prestige and efficiency of the law, that ensure legal protection of the individuals and their unimpeded use of their democratic rights and freedoms in their legitimate (lawful) interests.[36]

This definition provides a list of some of the most important as well as relevant features of *Rechtsstaat*—which will be looked at in the next subsection—while indicating, or at least hinting at some of its main tasks and objectives such as guarantying protection by law and providing for human rights and the lawful interests of citizens. It (the definition) also contains a somewhat indirect reference to an ideal version of what a modern state should be or strive to become but that does not make it less deserving or less informational. For the purposes of this textbook, this definition of the term *Rechtsstaat* is used as a working one.

Based on this definition, the following main objective of the *Rechtsstaat* may be extracted. The purpose of the State of Law is the creation of conditions for the fullest provision of rights and freedoms of individuals as well as the consistent restriction of state power with the help of law in order to prevent abuse of power and its transformation into dictatorship or despotism. The achievement of this noble goal does not seem feasible without a proper application of two principles that are well known to lawyers but not always well understood and that directly relate to the matter of legal regulation.[37]

The first one states: 'Only what is prescribed by law is allowed'. This principle is concerned with a specific circle of legal subjects—state bodies and officials—and is sometimes referred to as the 'permissive binding' principle. It provides the subject of law with the amount of rights that is necessary for the performance of their duties. Here, the rights and obligations of the subject are quite accurately defined, and everything that lies outside of those rights and obligations is withdrawn from the scope of regulation. In this manner, the legal status of the state and state bodies, their subjects of jurisdiction and powers, are regulated.

The second principle, often labeled as a constitutional principle,[38] stipulates: 'Everything which is not directly forbidden by law is allowed'. It is an opposite of the first one and is applied towards the other subjects of law such as individuals (nationals/citizens and foreigners, i.e., natural persons) and legal persons. In this

[35] For a comparative perspective and more or less inclusive treatment of the concept from contemporary German authors, see *passim* Silkenat et al. 2014.

[36] Leonov 2005.

[37] The third classical principle of legal regulation that does not fall within the ambit of regulation in the *Rechtsstaat*, or the so-called 'permissive principle' will be described in the subsequent chapter of this textbook, Chap. 6, in Sect. 6.3.

[38] Indeed, it may be found although not in a directly referenced manner in the constitutional legal provisions of most of the post-soviet states' legal systems such as Kazakhstan, Uzbekistan, Russia and so on.

way, as a rule, the legal status of the individual as well as the implementation of civil and business turnover is regulated. The person bears responsibility before the state only in cases directly foreseen by law; individuals are obliged to fulfill only those requirements that are based on the law.

Having said this, it must be noted here that law will play a primary role in the State of Law only if it serves as a *measure of freedom* of all and everyone and if acting laws *really* serve the interests of the people and society while their realization and implementation represent an embodiment of justice and fairness. One needs to keep in mind that the fact that there exists a comprehensive and developed system of legislation with detailed laws and normative acts in a given state does not yet signal the actual '*Rechtsstaat*-ness'. There have been numerous examples of legal systems where normative legal sources have regularly been enacted, with their enforcement being rigorously and strictly ensured but such a form of legal regulation constituted anything but State of Law. The biggest examples here would be the totalitarian states of the past such as the Nazi German state and the former Soviet Union.

5.3 Main Characteristics and Principles

Based on the working definition of the State of Law provided in the preceding subsection, several fundamental key features of the *Rechtsstaat* which characterize it as such and which make it stand out from non-State of Law expressions of the state, may be discerned.[39] In order to constitute a true State of Law, it needs to include every one of the following elements, and none may be said to be more important or deserving than the other.

The first one is the principle of *rule of law*. Widely used not only in legal but also in political and academic parlance, this concept is a rather broad and elusive one. There have been a number of differing definitions offered to explain this critical concept, but all of those appear to agree on its one unifying aspect: it is viewed as a constraint on individual and, importantly, institutional (state) behavior. This means that the state and its organs are only allowed to perform particular tasks if they have been given the power to do so by law and to the extent that these tasks are allowed by law.[40] But the notion of rule of law is more holistic than simply a restraint on state action.

The Oxford English Dictionary defines the rule of law as "[t]he authority and influence of law in society, especially when viewed as a constraint on individual and institutional behavior; (hence) the principle whereby all members of a society (including those in government) are considered equally subject to publicly disclosed

[39] For the explanation of the state as a legal concept, see Chap. 3, Sect. 3.3.

[40] Frändberg 2014, at 185.

legal codes and processes".[41] This rather formalistic definition captures a significant aspect of the principle, namely, its applicability to all; in other words, the rule of law implies that *every person* is subject to the law, including legislators, law enforcement officials, judges and other state representatives. Without such inclusiveness the principle would lose its meaning and appeal.

A substantive description of the rule of law would imply primacy of law (*ius*) not only in terms of its formal aspects such as universality of the law, its generality, equality, publicity, certainty, consistency and prospective application, but also its content. This means the rule of law necessarily entails protection of individual human rights, either some or all of them. In that sense, primacy of *ius* suggests it goes in line with the theory and philosophy of human rights and human dignity as well as international human rights law. That is confirmed by the following substantive and very comprehensive definition of the rule of law: 'a principle of governance in which all persons, institutions and entities, public and private, including the State itself, are accountable to laws that are publicly promulgated, equally enforced and independently adjudicated, and which are *consistent with international human rights norms and standards* [emphasis added]. It requires, as well, measures to ensure adherence to the principles of supremacy of law, equality before the law, accountability to the law, fairness in the application of the law, separation of powers, participation in decision-making, legal certainty, avoidance of arbitrariness and procedural and legal transparency.'[42] Here, the consistency with international human rights norms and standards is a requirement for the law that rules and that connects it with another important element of *Rechtsstaat*—supremacy and ensuring of human rights and freedoms considered further below.

The rule of law means all members of society, including the government, are equally subject to publicly disclosed laws and accountable to them

The legal theory in the post-Soviet countries mostly adheres to a formalistic view whereby rule of law is defined as domination of law in all spheres of public life. At that, law in this connotation is understood as *lex*, i.e., the positive normative act of highest degree and force.[43] In accordance with this position, no state body, or state official, or a collectivity, or public organization, or any individual is free from the obligation to comply with the law. Some theorists even highlight that the rule of law is not to be confused with the rule of *ius*.[44] Laws regulate the most important spheres of life of a society. All legal acts issued by state power bodies must of necessity

[41] Oxford English Dictionary online (accessed 6 April 2025). Black's Law Dictionary provides several definitions; one of those is 'supremacy of regular as opposed to arbitrary power'. Black's Law Dictionary 2009, at 1448.

[42] United Nations Security Council 2004, at 4, para 6.

[43] On the dichotomy of *ius* and *lex*, see Chap. 6, Sect. 6.6.

[44] Marchenko 2019, at 213.

correspond to the laws and they may not contradict them.[45] Some positions offer certain specifications or compromises. For example, one author argues that it is not enough for the State of Law that all of its subjects obeyed the laws; it is necessary that those laws be in accord with *ius*.[46] In other words, the legislative acts must be just, they must conform to the requirements of law as a universal, necessary form and equal measure of the freedom of individuals. To reach that, the state must proceed based on the principles of law (*ius*) when formulating its legislative acts and enforcing their implementation.[47] But in general, the interpretation of the notion of the rule of law in the post-Soviet space remains largely formalistic, or positivistic.

The second feature of the *Rechtsstaat* is *supremacy of human rights and freedoms*. This one involves both the rights and interests of individuals and rights and freedoms of citizens. Here, the concept of freedom plays a critical role. In a true *Rechtsstaat*, freedom of the individual in social and political life constitutes their right. Such a State of Law fully recognizes this individual freedom and does not allow itself to intervene in it. The state power's duty not to intervene corresponds to the individual right to demand the fulfilment of this duty. In case this right is violated, it is to be fully redressed and ensured by proper judicial protection.[48] These conditions enable the above noted second principle of legal regulation (see the preceding section), namely, the general permissive principle ('everything which is not directly forbidden by law is allowed') to really work. It is imperative that supremacy of human rights and freedoms is not just expressed in a nominal recognition and establishment in the domestic legislation of the fundamental rights and freedoms of individuals; it must be actually guaranteed in reality, with a concrete possibility to enforce and fulfil those rights, interests and freedoms.[49] As for the specific human rights categories, those include all the major internationally recognized types of rights and freedoms: civil rights, political rights, social, economic and cultural rights, and so on. In this way, it would be possible to speak about the fullest and most efficient legal protection of the individuals that is possible to imagine in such a State.

The third characteristic would be the *principle of mutual responsibility of the state and the person*. It means that the relationship between the state as a carrier of political power on the one hand, and the individual as a full-fledged participant in the formation and fulfilment of that power, must be built upon the basis of equality, justice and fairness. Determining in its laws the measure of individual freedom, the state within the same boundaries limits itself in its own decisions and actions. It takes upon itself the obligation to ensure fairness in its relations with each individual. Obeying the law, state bodies cannot violate its rules and are responsible for violations or non-fulfillment of this obligation. The binding nature of the law for state power is

[45] Ibrayeva et al. 2017, at 60.

[46] Nersesyants 2016, at 309.

[47] Ibid.

[48] Khropanyuk 2019, at 83.

[49] Ibrayeva et al. 2017, at 59.

ensured by a system of guarantees that exclude and leave no room for administrative arbitrariness.[50]

The responsibility of the individual before the state is constructed on the same legal basis. The use of state coercion must always have a lawful character; it should not violate individual freedom, and it must correspond to the degree of gravity of violation of law committed by the individual. The legal nature of mutual responsibility of the state and the person is an important constituent part of the law that emerges objectively in society, and it is not—and it should not be—a product of the expression of the state's will. Compliance with requirements of the law is a legal duty of all, beginning with the state. This emphasizes the inalienability of natural human rights in a state governed by the rule of law.[51]

The fourth element of *Rechtsstaat* is the *principle of separation of powers* which can be said to serve as the basic underlying principle of organization and action of the State of Law. This implies the separation of the state (public) power into three relatively autonomous and independent branches: legislative, executive and judicial. This tripartite division operates on the so-called 'system of checks and balances' whereby the balance of interaction among all three branches is supported by special legal organizational measures/provisions that ensure not only their proper interaction but also, very importantly, their mutual limitation and restraint. Such a separation of the unified public power into three branches in this manner prevents potential abuses of power and a possible emergence of a totalitarian governance not bound by law. The following three paragraphs briefly describe each one of those branches.

The legislative power is generally perceived as the priority branch because it establishes the legal basis of the state and social life as well as the main directions of internal and external policy of the state. Therefore, it eventually determines the legal organization and the form of activity of the executive and the judiciary.[52] The dominant position of legislative bodies (mostly, parliaments are vested with the legislative power) in the mechanism of the *Rechtsstaat* conditions the highest juridical force of the laws they enact and lends a generally binding character to the legal norms formulated in those laws.

The executive power is engaged, via its bodies and structures, in the actual realization of legal norms adopted by the legislator. Its activities must be based on the law and it must be carried out within a legal framework. Executive bodies and state officials are not entitled or authorized to issue generally binding acts that establish rights or duties for citizens and organizations not foreseen in the law. The executive power may be called upon to exercise a legal (legitimate) character only when it represents an authority subordinated to the law and when it acts on the basis of legality. The containment of the executive may also be achieved by way of its subordination and responsibility to the representative bodies of state power. In a true State of Law, each

[50] Khropanyuk 2019, at 84.

[51] Ibid.

[52] Ibid., at 85.

citizen can protest or appeal against any unlawful actions of the executive bodies and state officials in a court of law.[53]

The judicial power aims at protecting law and legal foundations of public and societal life from violations no matter who commits them. Justice in the State of Law is carried out and delivered only by judicial bodies such as courts. No one may usurp or appropriate the functions of a court. In its law-enforcement/law-applying work the court is to be guided only by law; it should not depend on any subjective influences of the legislative or executive power. Independence and legality of justice constitute the most significant guarantee of rights and freedoms of individuals as well as serve as one of the pillars of a State of Law.

The fifth component that is ascribed to the *Rechtsstaat* is the *high legal culture and advanced level of legal awareness* (or alternatively, the so-called 'sense of justice') in the society. Legal culture may be understood as an achieved level of development in the legal organization of the life of the people in a given state at a given time. It represents an important part of general culture and includes all positive legal/law-related achievements; everything that has been accumulated by humankind in the field of law. Legal culture encompasses legal views and viewpoints, norms, institutions as well as behavioral relations based on law. Essentially, the high legal culture in the *Rechtsstaat* signifies a culture of recognition, protection and realization of human rights and freedoms as among the highest values of society.[54] If legal awareness is understood as a form of realization of the law as a specific phenomenon of social reality, then the advanced level of legal awareness would include a good/solid/fair knowledge of the law, respect for the law and understanding of its relevance and importance for the life of the people in the society.

The sixth, and arguably the last key element of the State of Law is civil society which is dealt with in the immediately following section.

5.4 Civil Society as a Key Component of *Rechtsstaat*

Civil society constitutes one of the main components of the State of Law. Without it no true *Rechtsstaat* could be imagined. A developed civil society is therefore not just an integral part of the State of Law; it may be viewed as the most important prerequisite for building such a State.[55]

The term itself was proposed by John Locke and Adam Smith to designate a certain stage or degree in the historical development of society, its transformation from a primitive or less developed level of evolution to a more advanced, civilized and progressive condition.[56] But the concept of civil society has been analyzed and

[53] Ibid., at 85–86.

[54] Nersesyants 2016, at 272–274.

[55] A free civil society has been determined to be necessary for democracy while the absence of it would be a mark of totalitarianism. See Hage et al. 2017, at 317.

[56] Locke 1988; Smith 1982.

developed by many outstanding minds, from Aristotle to Hegel to Marx all the way up to the contemporary intellectuals of the twenty-first century. The multiplicity of various explanations and descriptions of this phenomenon may be contributing to the difficulties in trying to propose a proper definition for it.[57]

Different approaches towards looking at and explicating civil society and its nature have been proposed. Some posit it as a contrast or juxtaposition to anarchy. Others distinguish civil society from church and clergy. A popular view is that civil society represents a set of public relations distinct from or even opposite to the state. Often these positions are accompanied by a proposition that civil society is a concrete phenomenon and product of western civilization.

Civil society consists of autonomous public, social, and economic institutions that interact with the state while promoting individual rights and freedoms

As noted above, civil society seen as a set of certain public relations reflects a rather popular view. In that sense, it is often defined as an aggregate of public, moral, social, economic, national, religious and family relations and institutions that help satisfy the individual as well as group needs in a given society. The main ideas here would be the primacy of the individual (person, man) in society, the notion of the individual's autonomy and independence, the capacity to develop and carry out activities independently based on ethical principles and respect for the law. At that, the state generally should not, and is not expected to, interfere with the life of civil society, doing so only in cases of violations of law.

If one were to offer an even more expanded definition of civil society, it would make sense to do so in the following manner: *civil society constitutes a free democratic legal society aimed at separate individuals, and is conducive to the environment of respect for legal norms and universal humanistic values and ideals. It promotes freedom of creative activities and business/entrepreneurship, and establishes possibilities for the achievement of well-being of citizens as well as a full-fledged realization of human rights.* It reaches these objectives also by creating mechanisms of control and restraint on state action. As one might see, the notion of civil society is detached from a classical notion of the state and is a 'non-state society' in that sense; however, it does not mean that it operates fully in isolation from the state. Its independence does not exclude interaction and cooperation with the state.

The following primary features of civil society may be listed: (1) the fullest possible 'insurance' of human rights and freedoms; (2) legitimacy and democratic nature of the public power; (3) freely formed public opinion and pluralism; (4) universal awareness and a real fulfilment of the right of individuals to information; (5) the dominating principle of coordination in the life of society as opposed to the principle of subordination typical to state mechanisms; (6) a diversified economy

[57] For a very succinct overview of some of those explanations or definitions, see Ibrayeva et al. 2017, at 64–65.

and protection of private property; (7) healthy competition among various structures, institutions and groups of individuals in the society; (8) a high level of civil culture and education; (9) domination by the middle class in the population, and (10) strong social policy providing for a decent level of life for members of the society. At the same time, these ten features of civil society can be called the pre-requisite conditions for its existence. While it does not seem necessary to describe each of those items here, in general this list provides a fair picture of what the ideal civil society must look like.

Some authors identify a number of systems in the structure of civil society. The first one would be a social system. It consists of, e.g., objectively formed communities of individuals; families; various social groups such as trade unions and so-called creative unions; people's associations, i.e., religious and public/social formations, political parties, as well as a complicated network of relationships among these various groups. They constitute the primary and fundamental foundation of civil society that determines or at least greatly influences the functioning of its other system components. It goes without saying that individuals in this system can move from one category in the civil society to another during their lifetimes. The interests of each one of those groups should be taken into account by the state, thereby creating a social balance or compromise between different, often competing group needs.[58]

The second system is an economic or material system. It represents a set or complex of economic ties/connections in which people in the society enter in the course of realization of property relations, production relations, processes of distribution and exchange of material goods and welfare, and so on.[59] Here, the civil society elements of a diversified economy, private property protection as well as support for businesses and entrepreneurship (see the working definition above) come into play.

The third system is a political one. The fact that the civil society as a public phenomenon is rather detached from the state apparatus does not mean that members of civil society have no say in the political life of the state and the country involved. At this level, individual and group members of civil society participate in the political life, engage in political activity and make individual choices based on political preferences, beliefs and values. This system implies a formation and maturity of an individual's concrete political positions, with individual and group preferences being realized with the help of political parties, movements, interest groups, 'pressure groups', and other political forms.

The fourth system is a cultural system which is constituted by a system of non-material, spiritual and cultural relations and institutions that implement these relations. These would be relations in the sphere of education, science, culture, arts, religion, and so on. The cultural component in the civil society is both relevant and important; several of the key elements of civil society cannot be imagined without a properly functioning set of cultural relations, including a high level of civil culture and general education as well as an advanced level of legal awareness and legal culture in the State of Law in the whole.

---

[58] Ibrayeva et al. 2017, at 66.

[59] Ibid.

The last system is a so-called informational system that is developed as a result of people's communication with one another, be it in a direct manner or by way of mass media and social networks. Its constituent elements would be those social and private organizations, institutions and even enterprises as well as individual citizens and their associations that are responsible for the production and release of media.[60] This system is relevant for the human rights component of civil society and *Rechtsstaat* as it directly involves the fulfilment of the right to freedom of information.

While such a structured description of civil society may appear somewhat artificial or non-comprehensive it still helps, in the opinion of this author, to illustrate how civil society organizes itself and what kind of system levels it operates upon. Further, it shows what structural 'units' or components it includes and how they may or should interact with each other.

The division of legislative, executive, and judicial powers ensures checks and balances, preventing abuse and safeguarding democracy

It is a commonly accepted view that civil society represents the highest and most progressive stage in the development of society and the most modern form of human community possible, even if it sounds idealistic. Some might even argue (but not this author) that progress is tied to the withering away of the state, with the latter being gradually taken over by civil society[61] slightly reminding one of the Kantian cosmopolitan society. This is probably too extreme a view. Be that as it may, one thing is clear: the building of a State of Law and civil society will necessarily imply narrowing the scope of state regulation of the life of members of society. This is closely related to the fact that in a true *Rechtsstaat* the individual and the state are considered equal partners; the two actors are not operating in a sovereign-subordinate paradigm.

When the post-Soviet states gained their independence in the early 1990s, they declared their intention of building up civil society and eventually achieving a real State of Law in their respective territories. A good and progressive example here would be Kazakhstan. Article 1, para 1 of the Constitution of the Republic of Kazakhstan stipulates that "The Republic of Kazakhstan *proclaims* [emphasis added] itself as a democratic, secular, State-of-Law, and social state whose highest values are the individual, his life, rights and freedoms." What this essential provision signifies is that Kazakhstan in its Supreme Law recognizes the State of Law as an eventual aim to which it should aspire but has not yet achieved, unlike some other states in the neighborhood such as, for example, the Russian Federation that stated they it has—in its respective Constitution. In other words, *it does not state* that Kazakhstan *is already* a State of Law; rather, it proclaims itself. This demonstrates a realistic perspective on the side of the legislators (or rather the drafters of the Constitution of 1995) and the state. Indeed, achieving the ideal of the *Rechtsstaat* appears to be

[60] Ibid., at 66.

[61] Ibid., at 67.

if not almost impossible then very difficult. The question is: is it achievable at all? That is the main topic of the next, last section of this chapter.

5.5 From Idea to Ideal

Consideration of issues dealing with formation and functioning or, even more so, the achievability of the *Rechtsstaat* is of a principal interest for any state in the world but it becomes especially relevant for the post-Soviet states who declared and put forward the task of building up 'States-of-law' in their respective territories. Most of them have included this element in their Supreme Law. When it comes to creating and maintaining a successful State of Law one needs to ask about certain real, objective and also subjective conditions[62] needed to reach that goal. What are those?

First of all, any state that truly aims at establishing a State of Law has to realize the necessity of achieving a *high level of political and, by extension, legal awareness and culture among its people.* Their active participation in political and public/social life is needed. At that, it becomes clear that the fifth element of the *Rechtsstaat* described briefly above in Sect. 5.3 is more than just a constituent part of it; it represents an essential factor without which the *Rechtsstaat* does not appear plausible. Indeed, without an actively concerned, well-informed and educated population it would be hard to hope that the principle of mutual responsibility between the state and the members of the society is fully implemented; that—and even more importantly—the key principle of rule of law could be realized: if people do not care for the law (*ius*) and are unwilling to comply with it, they are not informed or do not want to be informed about the law and legal norms, then no matter how hard the state may try to build other elements inherent in the State of Law, it will ultimately fail. Raising an advanced level of culture may be done in different ways (even if it is difficult and requires a lot of patience, resources and time) including systemic educational measures—in the sphere of legal education as well, development of science, support for arts and cultural life, and so on.

Another significant factor contributing to the success of efforts to build the State of Law is the *creation of a just, fair, unified, harmonious and realistic legislative framework.* Again, what is important here is not a high level of complexity of such a legal system. The quantity and level of detail in the regulative scope of laws does not appear here as relevant. Instead, the state significantly raises the chances of its people respecting and complying with its laws if it makes sure those laws correspond to the meaning of *ius*; in other words, they are just and they serve the interests of the individual and collective interests of the society as a priority and not interests of the state itself.[63] Also, laws need to be regularly updated, so that they will respond

[62] Marchenko 2019, at 217–220.

[63] Which does not suggest in any way that state interests are not to be protected by laws and normative regulations. They are, but the priority must be accorded to the members of that state's society.

to the societal needs and address the newly appearing problems in time. It goes without saying that laws have to be formulated in a sufficiently clear manner so that they are understood and made possible to be obeyed. The often unnecessarily difficult and sophisticated language of normative rules in legislative acts and statutes is notoriously well known. That hinders the very possibility of the legal frameworks being followed and complied with, hence making it more difficult to ensure the rule of law.[64]

Finally, it appears that some authors would also list the *existence of civil society* as a precondition for forming a successful State of Law. Thus, civil society would not only be considered as one of the constituent elements of the *Rechtsstaat* but in fact it would come as a necessary factor for the latter. The relationship between *Rechtsstaat* and civil society has been described above in Sect. 5.4. As noted before, civil society is frequently viewed as a system of relations, positions and actors contrasted or contraposed to the state. So, curiously enough it appears that the presence of the state-opposed independent set of relations comes as a required condition to have an 'ideal' state. In a way, civil society serves as a safeguard against the state and state structures violating the rules of law they had themselves enacted; it will be taking all the lawful measures to make sure the state bodies return to the path of law. Therefore, civil society is not just an element, it is in fact a condition necessary for the State of Law to exist and develop.

A true *Rechtsstaat* requires high legal culture, just laws aligned with societal needs, and an active civil society to maintain accountability and justice

To a certain extent, all the major characteristics of the State of Law considered in this chapter may be thought of at the same time as its preconditions. Indeed, without even one of them it is not feasible to picture a full-fledged law-state. Removing one of those elements from the picture will immediately endanger the whole construction: no rule of law—no supremacy of human rights and freedoms, or no separation of powers—no civil society. But perhaps, one last condition may allow us to summarize this conclusion: to ensure a true *Rechtsstaat*, *principles of real democracy* must be consistently followed, implemented and realized in the political, economic, social, scientific, cultural and educational spheres of life of the society.

When reflecting on the achievement of a State of Law one needs to take into account the main four bases constituting the *Rechtsstaat*. The *political* nature of the State of Law is probably most obviously expressed in its sovereignty. Thanks to sovereignty, various interests of state and non-state actors, organizations, entities and so on, are coordinated, their fair legal equilibrium and free development can be ensured. The State of Law is a sovereign state. The *social* basis of the *Rechtsstaat* is made of a self-regulated civil society that unites free individuals—'carriers of public

[64] For the description of how the written law (*lex*) is structured and how the system of law operates, see Chap. 10.

progress'. The individual and his/her needs and interests are the focus of attention of the state with a strong social element. The *economic* basis of the State of Law is composed of industrial relations built on a diversified economy, various forms of ownership—private, public, personal, collective, etc., that are equally protected from the legal point of view. Here, the property belongs to the producer and consumer; economic freedom is fervently protected. Finally, the *moral* foundation of the State of Law is formed of the universal principles of humanism and fairness, equality and freedom, honor and dignity of each person. The functioning regime of *Rechtsstaat* really affirms the highest ethical values of the person, provides for their determinative role in the life of society, and excludes arbitrariness and violence against the person.

All of these conditions, factors and bases need to be figured out and comprehensively 'taken care of'—in a positive sense if a state truly aims at achieving the status which comes closest to be labeled as *Rechtsstaat*. The tasks appear very difficult, and they are. This is also due to the fact that only focusing on one or two or three components of the State of Law while ignoring others will not bring any tangible results. The approach here needs to be holistic. There is no guarantee against failure—that goes without question. Certainly, as societies and states develop their ideals may not remain the same, they are subject to change, evolution and crystallization. The problem of achieving those ideals, though, will remain constant.

To many, civil society would appear as an ideal form of society while State of Law would represent an ideal modern state. There is nothing wrong with looking at these two notions in this way. By the same token, any suggestion that one be realistic in seeking to achieve these ideals does not imply the reverse, viz., that one must be skeptical about any such efforts. It constitutes nothing more than the acknowledgment that these ideals might not be fully reachable and that it takes constant, systematic, and regular effort over generations to establish the rule of law and a proper legal framework, raise the level of legal culture, assert the supremacy of human rights, consistently implement the separation of powers and independence of the judiciary, promote democratic principles and true constitutionalism. Patience, time and unswerving belief in the *Rechtsstaat*'s ideals are needed.

This is fully pertinent to the post-Soviet states. The formation of the State of Law and civil society in this region has only just begun. There are currently many problems at the local and regional levels that will have to be overcome if the states here are serious in the intentions proclaimed in their respective constitutions and other laws. The solution of those problems will eventually depend not only on the states themselves, but also on their societies and specifically on the individuals who comprise those societies. Simply put, building up a successful *Rechtsstaat* will have to be a collective effort. That is what the states in this region need to realize beyond mere proclamations and statements.

Questions for Students

1. *What are the main features of a Rechtsstaat, and how do they ensure justice and accountability?*
2. *How does the principle of rule of law apply to individuals and state authorities alike?*
3. *Why is civil society considered a key component of a Rechtsstaat, and how does it interact with the state?*
4. *What role does the separation of powers play in preventing state overreach and maintaining democratic governance?*
5. *What are the essential conditions for a state to transition into a true Rechtsstaat, especially in post-Soviet contexts?*

References

Adams J (1971) A Defence of the Constitutions of Government of the United States of America. Da Capo Press, New York
Aristotle (1984) The Athenian Constitution (Rhodes P (transl)). Oxford University Press, Oxford
Aristotle (1996) Constitution of the Athenians (in Russian). Moscow
Austin J (1998) The Province of Jurisprudence Determined (Campbell K (ed)). Hackett Publishing, Indianapolis
Black's Law Dictionary (2009) 9th edn. Thomson Reuters
Cicero (1998) On the Laws and On the Republic (Zetzel J (transl)). Cambridge University Press, Cambridge
Frändberg A (2014) From *Rechtsstaat* to Universal Law-State. An Essay in Philosophical Jurisprudence. Springer
Hage J et al. (eds) (2017) Introduction to Law, 2nd edn. Springer
Hamilton A, Madison J, Jay J (1987) The Federalist Papers (Isaac K (ed)). Penguin Books, London
Hobbes T (1996) Leviathan (ed. Tuck R). Oxford University Press, Oxford
Ibrayeva A et al. (2017) Theory of State and Law (in Russian), 3rd edn. Zhety Zhargy, Almaty
Jefferson T (1975) The Portable Thomas Jefferson. In: Peterson M (ed). Viking Press, New York
Kant I (1996) The Metaphysics of Morals (Gregor M (ed/transl)). Cambridge University Press, Cambridge
Kelsen H (1967) Pure Theory of Law (Knight M (transl)). University of California Press, Berkeley
Khropanyuk V (2019) Theory of State and Law (in Russian), 13th edn. Omega-L, Moscow
Korkunov N (1909) General Theory of Law (in Russian). St. Petersburg
Leonov I (2005) Social State of Law: Difficulties of Formation (in Russian). 2 Law and Governance: 21st Century 17
Locke J (1960) Selected Philosophical Works, Vol. II (in Russian). Moscow
Locke J (1988) Two Treatises of Government (Laslett P (ed)). Cambridge University Press, Cambridge
Marchenko M (2015) State of Law and Civil Society (in Russian). Prospect, Moscow
Marchenko M (2019) Theory of State and Law. An Elementary Course (in Russian), 3rd edn. Norma, Moscow
Montesquieu (1955) Selected Writings (in Russian). Moscow
Nersesyants V (2016) Common Theory of Law and State (in Russian). Norma INFRA-M, Moscow
Plato (1926) Laws (Bury R (transl)). Harvard University Press, Cambridge

Plato (1937) Republic (Shorey P (transl)). Harvard University Press, Cambridge
Schmitt C (2007) The Concept of the Political (Schwab G (transl), Strong T (ed)). University of Chicago Press, Chicago
Shershenevich G (1995) Common Theory of Law (in Russian), Vol. I. Moscow
Silkenat J et al. (2014) The Legal Doctrines of the Rule of Law and the Legal State (*Rechtsstaat*). Springer International Publishing AG
Smith A (1982) Lectures on Jurisprudence (Meek RL, Raphael DD, Stein P (eds)). Liberty Fund, Indianapolis
United Nations Security Council (2004) The Rule of Law and Transitional Justice in Conflict and Post-Conflict Societies. Report of the Secretary-General, S/2004/616, 23 August 2004
von Gerber CF (1869) Das Problem der Gesetzgebung [The Problem of Legislation]. Mohr, Tübingen
von Hayek FA (2018) The Constitution of Liberty (in Russian). New Publishing Moscow
von Jhering R (1915) The Struggle for Law (Lalor M (transl)). Callaghan & Company, Chicago
von Mohl R (1817) Encyclopedie der Staatswissenschaften. Berlin
Welcker CT (1813) Die letzten Gründe von Recht, Staat und Strafe: Philosophisch und nach den Gesetzen der merkwürdigsten Völker rechtshistorisch entwickelt. Heyer, Gießen

Chapter 6
The Notion of Law

Contents

Abstract This chapter addresses one of the most foundational and contested questions in legal theory: what is law? The chapter surveys the major approaches to understanding and defining law (normativist, naturalist, and sociological) highlighting their respective strengths and limitations. It argues that each perspective captures essential but partial truths, and makes the case for an integrative or synthetic approach as the most comprehensive and context-sensitive understanding. Law, in this view, is a system of normative standards rooted in justice and equality, protected by society, and designed to regulate the interactions of free wills in a pluralistic environment. The chapter explores the core characteristics of law: normativity, generality, systematicity, binding nature, and the balance between stability and dynamism. It presents law as a distinctive social regulator, contrasting it with morality, religion, and custom. Further sections analyze the legal significance of volition and interest, the concepts of legal object and subject, and the critical dichotomy of *ius* (law as justice) versus *lex* (law as state-enacted norm). The chapter concludes that a meaningful theory of law must reconcile moral principles with formal legal structures, especially in post-Soviet societies still influenced by rigid positivist legacies.

Keywords Definition of law · Integrative legal theory · Normativist vs. naturalist approaches · Sociological jurisprudence · Law as a social regulator · Volition and legal interest · Legal object and subject · *Ius* and *lex* dichotomy

R. Atadjanov, *A Common Theory of Law*, https://doi.org/10.1007/978-94-6265-711-3_6

6.1 The Definition of Law

One of the first main questions that any textbook on law should (purport to) answer deals with the exact definition and nature of law. While the need for the characterization of the nature of law and its proper definition is obvious, it is a need that is not easy to be satisfied. It appears that modern English-speaking authors tend to avoid proposing such definitions due to the difficulty and ambiguity of the exercise.[1] Within the post-Soviet (read: Russian-speaking) space, however, the legal science contains a big number of proposed individual definitions of what law is, and those definitions differ from one another either quite significantly or at least in certain separate nuances.[2] This multiplicity, or variety of definitions of the concept of "law" may be explained by the peculiarities of its cognition, which is associated with the separation of certain qualities and properties of law and the underestimation of other qualities, but also by the variety of manifestations of law, which can exist in the form of legal norms, or in the form of ideas and understandings about (perceptions of) law, or in the form of social relations that generate norms of law and are, in turn, affected by these norms.[3]

Depending on which of these peculiarities or forms one or another doctrinal researcher adheres to, several different approaches (or theories) to law, to its understanding, or rather, several types of law-understanding (and hence its definition/description) have so far emerged: normativist approach, naturalist approach, sociological approach, psychological approach, and integrative, or synthetic approach.[4] This author does not describe here all major existing theories of law for the purposes of this particular chapter; for example, theological or organic or economic theories are purposefully omitted from this overview.[5] Only those approaches have been chosen which either help elucidate the most convincing approach (or, alternatively, the one having the least number of shortcomings and gaps), provide a proper comparative perspective, and/or serve as illustrative examples of the most influential or impactful descriptions of law in the region. What follows is a brief description of each one of those approaches and their respective definitions of law culminating in this section's proposed definition based on the so-called synthetic approach.

---

[1] For example, Hage et al.'s textbook while trying to explain certain important aspects of legal rules and attempting to describe what nature of law means, does not define "law". See Hage et al. 2017. Almost the same could be said about another doctrinal source where the definitional attempt at law is limited only to the following: "...law is a construct of the human mind". See van Schilfgaarde 2019, p. 18.

[2] This is noted in Lazarev et al. 2022, pp. 142–143.

[3] Morozova 2021, p. 176.

[4] See ibid., p. 176; Lazarev et al. 2022, p. 114.

[5] The subsequent chapter, i.e., Chap. 7, deals with a more detailed discussion of the main theories of the origin and nature of law.

In the **normativist** approach (it is sometimes called statist or "etatist" from the French word "État" meaning "state") the law is defined as **a system of rules regulating human behavior, emanating from the state and protected by it**. This particular approach is based on what is known as positivist theory of law, which equates law and statute. State power is the source of law. A person has rights by virtue of their enshrining in acts of the state, and not by virtue of their nature. Consequently, only the norms of laws are true law.[6]

The advantages of this approach would be the following:

1. Fixation of the boundaries of permitted and prohibited behavior by means of legal norms;
2. Indication of a direct connection between law and the state, and its universal binding nature;
3. Emphasis on law having formal certainty, which is expressed in normative legal acts, in particular in laws;
4. Law is always a compulsory order established by the state;
5. Law is a volitional act of the state.[7]

But the normative approach to understanding law also has its own shortcomings which would be as follows:

1. Only that which comes from the state is recognized as law, and natural inalienable human rights are denied;
2. The role of the subjective factor in the formation of law is emphasized, i.e. an illusion is created that the adoption of a law is sufficient to solve any social problems;
3. It does not reveal the effect of law, its driving forces, regulatory properties, including its connection with social relations. In other words, it does not reveal law "in action";
4. Law is identified with the form of its expression and embodiment—legislation.[8]

Unlike legal normativists and positivists, natural law proponents view law as a **system of rules and principles that are inherent in human nature and can be discovered through human reason and reflection**. According to this perspective, law is not merely a set of arbitrary or socially constructed rules, but rather a reflection of universal moral principles that govern human conduct. According to Chloros, the traditional view of natural law is that it is a body of immutable rules superior to positive law. It is an ideal law since it consists of the highest principles of morality towards which humanity [mankind] is striving. It is also an absolute law since it is not the result of any convention, but is discoverable by the exercise of human reason.[9] In other words, from the point of view of natural law, law is a set of moral requirements

---

[6] Morozova 2021, p. 177.

[7] Ibid.

[8] Ibid.

[9] Chloros 1958, p. 609, cited in Atadjanov 2019, p. 51.

for the law and the state. **Naturalist approach** can also be said to constitute a moral, or philosophical, or even metaphysical approach to understanding and defining law.

The advantages of the naturalist approach would be as follows:

1. Law is interpreted as an unconditional value; law is recognized as the measure of freedom inherent in a given society, and measure of equality as an expression of general (abstract) principles and ideas of morality, fundamental human rights, justice, humanism, and other values. The legislator should be guided by this idea when adopting new legal norms: the priority is the natural rights of man;
2. Natural law exists independently of the state, society, and human consciousness, i.e., it is a social reality;
3. Natural law is constant and unchangeable, it is absolute good and is not subject to damage, spoilage and/or corruption;
4. It distinguishes between law and right; not every written (positive) law is legal.

The following can be recognized as shortcomings of the naturalist approach to understanding law:

1. It encompasses a vague idea of law, since high but abstract ideals, for all their significance, cannot in themselves replace the authoritative normative regulator of relations between people or serve as a criterion for lawful and unlawful behavior;
2. Unequal subjective understanding by participants of social relations of such values as justice, freedom, and equality;
3. A negative impact on attitudes toward the law, legality, and the possible emergence of legal nihilism;
4. The possibility of subjective and even arbitrary assessment of laws and other normative legal acts by citizens, officials, state and public bodies. Assessing a particular norm as contrary to the natural rights of man, a citizen or other subject may refuse to comply with it on this basis;
5. The impossibility of separating law from morality.

The **sociological approach** to understanding and defining law is aimed at understanding law as a social phenomenon that is relatively independent of the state. It gives preference to actions or legal relations. Moreover, legal relations are opposed to legal norms and constitute the central link in the legal system. Law is not what is conceived and written down, but what has actually happened in the practical activities of the addressees of legal norms.[10] In other words, the sociological theory of law defines law as **a social institution that is deeply interconnected with society's norms, values, and social structures**. Proponents of this theory view law not just as a set of rules or commands imposed by the state, but as a dynamic entity that evolves with society.

The sociological approach to understanding law (and this is its merit) attaches great importance to judicial and arbitration practice, freedom of judicial discretion, and the study of the effectiveness of legal norms and legal practice. However, the sociological school also has its own shortcomings. Firstly, there is a danger of blurring

---

[10] Morozova 2021, p. 179.

the concept of law: it becomes very vague and unclear. Secondly, there is a danger of arbitrariness on the part of judicial and administrative bodies, since any actions of the state apparatus and officials will be recognized as law. Thirdly, the fact that law is not the activity of subjects itself, but a regulator of their activity and social relations is ignored. Actions cannot be endowed with the properties of a regulator.[11]

As one can see, the naturalist and sociological approaches to law form the so-called *broad* understanding of law, while the normativist one forms the narrow understanding of it. Each of the named legal understandings has its own foundations, therefore it has its supporters. Thus, philosophical legal understanding is essential for legal education as well as for the development of current legislation. Without normative legal understanding, certainty and stability of social relations, legality in the activities of state bodies and officials are impossible. Through sociological legal understanding, law acquires concreteness and implementation in practice, without which law remains a simple declaration and abstract wishes. If laws are not embodied in a system of legal relations in which the diverse interests of members of society are expressed and agreed upon, i.e. ordered, then law does not work.[12]

Consequently, all types of legal understanding/definitions are as correct as they are disputable; they have their own advantages and disadvantages, and each concept serves as a counterweight to the other and does not allow extremes to prevail. Law in any of its parts can be a reflection of freedom, and an instrument of enslavement and tyranny, and be a compromise of public interests, and serve as a means of oppression and ensuring the rights and freedoms of the individual, and be legalized lawlessness, etc. It is not the abundance of concepts that causes concern, but the misconception that law is capable of solving any social problems and that it is enough to pass a law to solve them. Law is not omnipotent.[13]

Certain existing authoritative definitions of law seem to incorporate at least some of the elements described above and supported/propounded by either one or more approaches considered earlier. For example, two first major definitions of the term "law" contained in the Black's Law Dictionary are formulated as follows: "*(1) The regime that orders human activities and relations through systematic application of the force of politically organized society, or through social pressure, backed by force, in such a society; the legal system ...; (2) The aggregate of legislation, judicial precedents, and accepted legal principles; the body of authoritative grounds of judicial and administrative action; ...*"[14] Several elements in these two definitions include order, force (coercion, compulsory), society, system, principles—these are all figuring, in this or that form, in either normativist, or naturalist definitions; curiously enough, rules and norms are not mentioned as such—as is the state (replaced instead by a more flexible and comprehensive "politically organized society").

[11] Ibid., p. 180.

[12] Morozova 2021, p. 180.

[13] Ibid., p. 181.

[14] Garner 2004, p. 900.

Law is a set of normative standards rooted in equality and justice, protected by society, and regulating the interactions of free wills

There is one approach to law in legal theory that stands out aiming to combine the major features of all three explanations of law briefly described above. Recognition of the value of the provisions of different legal schools and different approaches to understanding law by theoretical legal science in the post-Soviet space made it possible to relatively recently propose the so-called **integrative approach** to understanding law. It is also sometimes called the **synthetic** approach. According to this approach, law is a **set of normative standards of equality and justice recognized in a given society and provided with official protection, regulating the struggle and coordination of free wills in their relationship with each other**.[15] Some scholars, alternatively, defined law as a system of normative settings (or guidelines) based on the ideas of human justice and freedom, expressed mostly in legislation and regulating social relations.[16]

The emergence of an integrative explanation of law can be attributed to the synthetic nature of legal phenomena; after all, the norms that reflect them cannot but be different. The integrative approach strives to unite different methodologies, covering both the existing and the due, and the ideal, and the realities of different theories, paying attention to economics, politics, as well as social unity.[17] The so-called integrative jurisprudence (a special separate direction in jurisprudence based on the integrative theory/understanding of law) seems to meet the modern demands of the time, caused by the processes of globalization. There are various legal families in the world with the most diverse legal systems included in them, which in turn cover various national legal systems.[18] But for some time now there has been a tendency towards the integration of law.[19]

The integrative approach to law has a number of rather positive aspects, namely:

1. It relieves tension in the confrontation of one theory with another, recognizing each of them as having its own relative truth;
2. It is based on the recognition of the pluralism of values, considering them also relative depending on place and time;
3. It allows us to construct a general definition of law that includes a full coverage of the legal values known to history and inherent in different civilizations;
4. It singles out among all values the essential ones, those without which law would not be law, recognizing among them equality in the free expression of personality.
5. It does not focus on either the creator of the law or its sources, recognizing here the diversity of both;

[15] Lazarev et al. 2022, p. 138, citing Lazarev 1992, p. 123.

[16] Morozova 2021, p. 181.

[17] Lazarev et al. 2022, p. 140.

[18] For more on that particular topic, see Chap. 12.

[19] Lazarev et al. 2022, p. 141.

6. For utilitarian and pragmatic purposes, the integrative approach allows for a conventional beginning in the recognition by law of a certain value for a certain place and time;
7. It allows one to look at law through the eyes of one who learns it, through the eyes of a practitioner and through the eye of a philosopher, without questioning its value and at the same time the difference in goals in each of these cases.[20]

This author finds this particular approach's definition of law the most convincing one so far, for the following elements it contains. First of all, it **eliminates** or at least **reduces** the role of the **state** as the only law-protecting, law-emanating and law-empowering phenomenon thus removing the strong statist characteristic of the normativist/positivist approach, and instead **accentuating the role of the society**.[21] Second, it does not deny the law its **normative nature**; it recognizes and confirms that law is a norm-based notion. Third, it highlights the **value-oriented** direction of the law (equality, justice, freedom). Fourth, the law's **regulatory** function is reinforced by "regulating the struggle and coordination".[22] Finally, the **volitional aspect** of law's teleology is prioritized (that aspect is considered below in Sect. 6.4).

6.2 The Nature of Law and Its Main Elements

The matter of exact nature of law has not been dealt with comprehensively or exhaustively in either Western or Eastern literature. In answering the question "What is law?" certain scholars tend to apply a non-dogmatic stand and to limit themselves to the simple and neutral idea that law is a construct of the human mind.[23] Others note that due to law's changing at such a high speed (because of current globalization processes) that it is impossible to give a short explanation of law from the outset but certain few characteristics of law may still be mentioned.[24]

It is true that there exists no single concept of the essence of law that is inherent to all times, peoples, and different societies, since the state of the economy, the national composition of the country's population, historical factors, the level of legal and political culture of society, etc. have a great influence on law and its essence/nature.[25] However, one thing can be said with more or less high degree of certitude: there are certain distinguishable characteristics of law that make it stand out and that allow us to speak about its inherent qualities and unique nature.

One of those qualities or features would be the **normativity** of the law which is one of its main characters. It cannot be denied that law consists of norms, i.e., binding

[20] Ibid., p. 142.

[21] For the analysis of the role of the state as a legal concept and political organization, see Chap. 4. For an overview of the society as a legal phenomenon, see Chap. 3.

[22] For a review and description of the functions of law, see Chap. 8.

[23] Such as, e.g., van Schilfgaarde 2019, p. 18.

[24] For example, Hage et al. 2017, p. 2.

[25] Morozova 2021, p. 183.

rules of general behavior that regulate social relations. The word "norma" can be translated from Latin as a "standard", a "rule", and/or a "pattern". The normative regulation of social relations represents an establishment of general or common rules for a particular group of specific situations (cases). Hence, it makes sense not to connect this quality of law only with such a source of law as, e.g., normative act.[26] A norm may be contained in other sources as well, such as, for example, a judicial decision or Ulpian's statements.[27]

Law consists of general, binding norms that govern social relations, ensuring consistency and predictability in behavior

Another determining quality of law related to the first one above would be its **general** nature. Indeed, law has a non-personified (unpersonalized), non-specific and general character; it does not have an individual "addressee", so to speak, because law regulates a number of similar situations. It spreads its effect upon all who find themselves in certain situations and in certain capacities. It is further characterized by repetition and duration (continuity) of its action.

But law constitutes not simply a sporadic set of norms, it is their defined system. Legal norms may demonstrate and exercise their regulatory properties only in a system and in their ordered interaction. The closer the consistency of legal provisions, the more effective the law will be. Hence, the law can be said to have a **systemic** character. This system can accommodate all kinds of legal sources. And law represents a system of **formally determined** norms, meaning such norms whose content has been expressed precisely, unambiguously and not vaguely.[28]

Law's **binding** nature belongs to the set of its inherent characteristics. Its compliance is mandatory for individuals, organizations and states/state bodies to whom it is addressed. The law's binding nature (its "bindingness", so to speak) and its realization is to be guaranteed by the state. While most of legal norms are followed, complied with and executed voluntarily by their addressees (subjects of law),[29] there is a possibility of state coercion behind every legal norm for compliance and enforcing responsibility for its violation. For many individuals it may be a factor that ensures lawful conduct.[30] One must be careful and precise here, though: while law as social regulator ensures order in social relations, regulates the behavior of a person and communities of people, expressing the ideas of justice, freedom and equality of people, and serves the good of society and its interests, it should not mean that law has no coercive force, but coercion does not mean violence, although it does not exclude legal responsibility. Thus, it is all about the extent and means of coercion,

---

[26] For an overview of various types of sources of law, see Chap. 9.

[27] Lazarev et al. 2022, p. 143.

[28] Ibid., p. 144.

[29] On subjects of law see further below in this chapter.

[30] See Chaps. 5 and 12 for more discussion on legal awareness, legal culture, and factors influencing lawful/unlawful behavior.

and not its presence or absence. Therefore, law does not exclude coercion, but it excludes coercion in the form of violence and suppression.

Finally, law possesses such important qualities as **stability** and **dynamism**. Along with societal development law does not stay static and unchanging; new legal norms are constantly created, old ones are regularly abolished, many legal requirements and regulations are periodically reformulated, or stated and expressed, or grouped differently (e.g., they may merge into larger normative acts or statutes). But lawyers tend to be supporters of stability in social relations. For example, they may condemn or decry certain practices such as amendments into normative instruments which have not yet entered into legal force.[31]

6.3 Law as a Social Regulator

It also makes sense to look at law from the perspective of it being a social normative regulatory system. Without this, the description of its nature would not be comprehensive. The law, as a social regulator, serves to organize, control, and guide human behavior in a society by establishing norms and rules that individuals (i.e., its subjects) are expected to follow. As a public or social regulator, the law is central to creating a stable, predictable, and just society where individual rights are balanced with the community's needs. What follows is a closer look at why law is a critical normative regulator and how it distinguishes itself from other social norms.

As follows from Chap. 7, the primary function of law (typified in that chapter as regulatory and protective) is to maintain social order and protect the rights of individuals by clearly delineating acceptable behaviors and establishing penalties for misconduct. Laws cover broad areas of public and private life, from criminal justice and contract enforcement to family and property law, reflecting society's evolving values and standards. From the point of view of public interest, laws (legal norms) are designed to serve the greater public interest, focusing on safety, health, and welfare. They promote collective values that foster cooperation and social harmony.

But why call law a "public or social regulator"? There are several considerations in favor of that. One of those is about **public accountability**. Unlike private norms or cultural customs, laws are enforced by public institutions, such as the police (law enforcement) and the judiciary, ensuring transparency and accountability. Another consideration involves **universal applicability**: laws are created to apply universally within a given jurisdiction, establishing consistent standards that all citizens are expected to follow, regardless of individual beliefs or backgrounds. Furthermore, **institutional enforcement** comes into play, too: the enforcement of law is carried out by designated bodies, including the courts and law enforcement agencies, which operate with a mandate to uphold public order and safety. Finally, there is a built **adaptability** in law, that is, laws can be amended or repealed through democratic

[31] Lazarev et al. 2022, p. 144.

processes to reflect changes in public opinion, values, and societal needs, which makes them dynamic and adaptable as regulatory mechanisms.

As a normative regulator in society, law prescribes rules for acceptable and unacceptable behavior, which are derived from moral, social, and ethical considerations. It shapes what society deems to be "right" and "wrong". By setting normative standards and imposing sanctions for violations, the law influences behavior and decisions, creating a culture of responsibility and accountability. One should also not forget about conflict resolution: law provides a formal structure for resolving conflicts, with codified rules that ensure fair and impartial adjudication, which prevents disputes from escalating into chaos or vigilante justice.

Law organizes and controls behavior through rules that balance individual rights with societal needs, ensuring justice and stability

When it comes to law's uniqueness compared to other social normative systems (such as morality, customs, traditions, religion, and social etiquette), its following attributes need to be mentioned. ***(1) Enforceability***, namely, unlike customs or moral codes, which rely on social approval or disapproval, law is enforceable through formal sanctions, including fines, imprisonment, and other penalties; ***(2) institutional authority:*** it means that laws are backed by governmental authority, making their enforcement mandatory rather than voluntary. This differs from other social norms that are often maintained through social pressure rather than formal mechanisms; ***(3) objective framework*** meaning that laws provide an objective framework that is less susceptible to individual interpretation or personal beliefs. This helps in maintaining a consistent standard across society, unlike moral or religious norms, which can vary widely between groups and communities; and, importantly, ***(4) rights and duties:*** The law not only restricts behavior but also establishes and protects individual rights and freedoms, which is not typically the role of other normative systems like tradition or religious doctrine.

In essence, the law is a distinctive regulatory system because of its enforceability, public mandate, and role in balancing individual and collective interests. As a formal, adaptable system with explicit mechanisms for enforcement, law stands out among social regulators as a robust, resilient means of maintaining order and promoting social welfare.

6.4 Volition, Interest and Their Legal Significance

In legal theory, **volition and interest** are pivotal concepts that ground the structure and application of law, shaping its very purpose and its influence over human behavior. The law is more than a static set of rules;[32] it is a system designed to channel and direct the behavior of individuals and groups, reflecting the interplay between normative requirements and the volitional (or will-based) engagement of legal subjects.[33] Volition, or the will, thus serves as the underlying force that enlivens the legal system. This volitional aspect transforms the law from mere instruction into a dynamic framework that prescribes, motivates, and sometimes coerces specific forms of behavior among its participants. Legal norms are binding—as rules flowing out of a normative system, but they gain efficacy through their capacity to align with or influence the volitional actions of those they govern, bridging psychological intent and legally prescribed action.

Volition (will) drives compliance with legal norms, while interest reflects the societal and individual values law aims to protect

The role of volition in law can be thought of as a **complex psychological phenomenon that encompasses individual, collective, and societal will**. At the individual level, volition manifests as personal intentions and decisions that drive compliance or challenge legal norms, reflecting a person's conscious engagement with the law. However, volition in the legal context extends beyond the individual to encompass collective intentions, such as those of communities, organizations, or societies as a whole. In these collective contexts, volition embodies shared **ideals**, social **values**, and common **interests** that the law seeks to uphold or protect. The legal system, therefore, does not merely impose rules but actively engages with these layers of volition, seeking to integrate individual and collective will into a structured regulatory framework that promotes social order and justice. The psychological dimension of will thus become instrumental, influencing not only compliance but also the legitimacy and adaptability of legal norms in various social contexts.

Interest, in legal terms, represents the values, needs, and objectives that law is intended to protect or fulfill for individuals or groups. It is a vital component of the legal system as it defines the aims of legal norms and grounds them in social relevance.[34] Unlike volition, which is concerned with the active intent or disposition toward compliance, **interest refers to the stake or benefit individuals or groups derive from legal norms**. For example, laws protecting property rights reflect an underlying interest in security and economic stability, while labor laws embody the

[32] See further in Chap. 10 on legal norms.

[33] The next section, Sect. 6.5, deals with the question of legal subjects and objects.

[34] The scope of interests and values protected by law/legal norms, may be called the protective scope of law.

interest in fair treatment and safe working conditions. These interests are not merely subjective preferences; they are recognized and protected by law because they are deemed essential for maintaining a functional, equitable society. Thus, the concept of interest in law serves as the rationale for creating legal norms and is a touchstone for interpreting and applying these norms in various cases.

The interplay of volition and interest in law reveals why these concepts matter so profoundly to the legal system. Together, they shape the content and purpose of legal norms, anchoring them in the lived realities of social actors (which is quite important as law is a social regulator as explained in the preceding section).

Volition matters because it determines the degree to which individuals and groups internalize and follow legal norms, while interest provides the justification for these norms, explaining why they ought to exist and why society values their enforcement.

Without volition, the law would lose its connection to the human behaviors it seeks to influence, becoming an abstract set of commands disconnected from real-world application. Without interest, the law would lack a substantive basis for its rules, rendering it arbitrary and potentially oppressive rather than serving the public good.

Ultimately, the role of volition and interest in law highlights that the law is not just a rigid set of instructions and rules but a responsive, interactive social institution or phenomenon. It is designed to respect and incorporate the wills of individuals and groups while addressing and securing their interests within a structured legal framework. By doing so, the law reflects the values and priorities of society, balancing between guiding behavior and respecting the autonomy of those it governs. In this sense, volition and interest are not peripheral or passive aspects of legal phenomena; they are fundamental forces that define, justify, and animate the legal system in pursuit of a balanced, orderly, and just society.

6.5 Legal Object and Subject

The question of the object and subject of a legal relationship is legal (juridical) in the sense that only the law determines who can be a subject of law and under what circumstances, and that only in the law, understood in the broadest sense, is it determined which social relations are subject to mediation by means of legal norms and act as legal, and which are not regulated by means of legal norms and remain non-legal.

In modern legal theory, the "object of law" (or "object of a legal relationship") refers to the specific entity or interest that legal subjects—such as individuals, corporations, or states—are concerned with or act upon within a legal framework. This object could be a tangible item, such as property or money, or an intangible interest, such as intellectual property or a legal obligation. The object of law exists **within the scope of a legal relationship** and is defined by the rights, duties, and responsibilities imposed on the subjects involved. For example, in a contractual agreement, the object of law could be the services provided or the goods exchanged, which serve as the focus of the legal relationship between the contracting parties. The concept is foundational in distinguishing between the components of legal relationships, as it highlights what is at stake or regulated in these interactions.

Understanding the object of law involves recognizing its function as separate from the "subject of law" (see further below). While subjects of law are the individuals or entities that hold rights and bear duties, the object of law is what these rights and duties pertain to or impact. This distinction clarifies roles within legal structures: subjects operate within the law, interacting with one another, while objects are the focus of these interactions. For instance, in property law, a person (subject of law) may have ownership rights over a piece of land (object of law). Similarly, in criminal law, the object could be the legally protected interest, like public safety or individual bodily integrity, which the law seeks to safeguard. This separation of subjects and objects is essential, as it enables a structured application of rights and responsibilities.

For the sake of clarity, the terms "object of law" and "legally protected interest" are related but not identical. A **legally protected interest refers to an aspect or value that the law aims to preserve or safeguard**, often abstractly, like personal security, privacy, humanity,[35] human dignity, or freedom of expression. In contrast, the **object of law is the specific entity or thing** around which legal rights and obligations revolve. While legally protected interests can sometimes align with objects of law—such as when laws protect intellectual property rights to foster innovation—the two concepts are not always interchangeable. Legally protected interests are broader principles that justify legal protections, while objects of law are the tangible or specific items those laws regulate. Therefore, legally protected interests are a subset of the broader framework, guiding which objects become regulated within legal relationships.

According to the concept established in the scientific literature, a subject of law is understood as a person or organization (entity) that is recognized as having the ability to be bearers of subjective rights and legal obligations. In modern legal literature, the concept of "subject of law" is most often used as a synonym for the terms "subject" or "participant in legal relations". In legal sources of the late nineteenth–early twentieth centuries, the concept of "subject of law" was used only to denote a "bearer of subjective rights".[36]

More specifically, the "subject of law" refers to **individuals, entities, or organizations that have legal capacity**, meaning they can possess rights and obligations within a legal system. In modern legal theory, subjects of law are divided into two main categories: natural persons (humans) and legal persons (entities such as corporations, governments, or non-profits created by law to perform certain functions). As subjects of law, these persons can enter into legal relationships, own property, be held accountable for actions, and seek protection of their rights. For example, a corporation, as a legal person, can enter contracts, sue or be sued, and be held liable for its actions. The status of a "subject of law" thus **grants an entity legal personality**, enabling it to participate fully within the scope of legal rights and duties

---

[35] See, for example, Atadjanov 2019.

[36] For example Marchenko 2015, p. 607.

established by a jurisdiction. This concept is fundamental to the functioning of legal systems, as it delineates who can actively participate in and be governed by law.

The object of law refers to what is regulated (e.g., property), while the subject of law refers to those with rights and duties (e.g., individuals, corporations)

It is important to note that states can be subjects of law, particularly in the realm of public international law. As sovereign entities, states possess legal personality, enabling them to enter into legal relationships with other states, international organizations, and even individuals under certain circumstances. This legal subjectivity allows states to sign treaties, make international agreements, and be held accountable before and by international courts like the International Court of Justice (ICJ). Despite their sovereignty, states are bound by certain international obligations and can assert rights—such as territorial integrity, non-interference, and diplomatic immunity—that are recognized by the international community.[37]

In addition to their roles in international law, states can also act as subjects of law within their own national jurisdictions, typically through government entities or officials that represent the state in domestic and administrative law matters. Thus, states are unique subjects of law as they operate on both national and international levels, governed by a complex mix of domestic laws and international norms.

Legal capacity is the ability and legal opportunity of a person to acquire rights and obligations, exercise and fulfill them by their actions, as provided by legal norms. Types of legal capacity are transaction capacity, i.e., the ability (possibility) to personally, with their actions, conclude civil-law transactions, and tort capacity—the ability to bear legal responsibility for a committed offense, as provided by legal norms.

6.6 Dichotomy of *Ius* and *Lex*

The dichotomy of *ius* and *lex* reflects two foundational, yet often competing, concepts in legal theory. *Ius* represents a notion of law rooted in justice, fairness, and universal principles that transcend specific legal systems. Originating from Roman law, *ius* embodies values of natural law, encompassing moral and ethical dimensions aimed at preserving human dignity and individual rights. In Roman times, *ius* was considered the source of natural justice, and the Romans distinguished between *ius civile* (civil law) and *ius gentium* (law of nations). The latter, *ius gentium*, was crucial for establishing principles of international law, as it was based on what the Romans viewed as common laws universally applicable across different societies. Over time,

[37] See more on that in Shaw 2017, pp. 155–204.

ius developed as a set of guiding values—fairness, justice, freedom, and the protection of individual rights—that would influence ethical principles across various legal fields, particularly in human rights and international law.[38]

In contrast, *lex* refers to specific statutes, regulations, or codes enacted by a legislative authority. *Lex* embodies positive law, meaning laws that are explicitly created by legislative bodies within a given jurisdiction. Legal positivism, a school of thought that emerged prominently in the nineteenth and twentieth centuries, supports this view by asserting that law is derived from specific, verifiable sources and should not necessarily depend on moral or ethical considerations. Notable legal positivists, like Hans Kelsen, with his "Pure Theory of Law", argued that law is a hierarchy of norms, where each law derives its validity from a higher norm until reaching the so-called "Grundnorm", or fundamental norm.[39] H.L.A. Hart also contributed significantly to this theory, emphasizing that law is a system of rules enforced by social institutions, separable from moral content.[40] However, the limitations of *lex* become apparent when laws enacted solely for national interests result in injustices that conflict with the universal standards embodied in *ius*. This division suggests that while norms based on *ius* inherently aim for justice, not every *lex* aligns with this ideal, leading to instances where positive law may uphold narrow state interests rather than, or to the detriment of, justice.

The divide between *ius* and *lex* highlights an inherent tension in law: *ius* norms are always just and aim to protect universal principles, while *lex*, as positive law, may diverge from these ideals if enacted for particularistic purposes. Throughout history, states have often implemented *lex* to serve their national interests, resulting in unjust outcomes that contradict the principles of *ius*. For instance, laws that discriminate against certain groups, suppress individual freedoms, or endorse authoritarian practices may be legally valid as *lex* but unjust by the standards of *ius*.[41] This conflict has led to critical discussions on the legitimacy of positive laws and whether legal systems should strive to align all laws with the values represented by *ius*. The criticism of unjust *lex* has fueled legal reforms, pressing for laws that are not only procedurally valid but also morally sound.

***Ius* represents universal justice and moral principles, while *lex* refers to codified, state-enacted positive laws, highlighting their interplay and potential conflict**

It must be said that the historical interaction between proponents of *ius* and supporters of positive law has played a beneficial role in the evolution of legal systems worldwide. This "competition", or rivalry, has fueled progress, pushing societies to

[38] For a brief historical and definitional analysis of the concepts of natural law and *ius gentium*, see Atadjanov 2019, pp. 50–53.

[39] Kelsen 1967.

[40] Hart 1961.

[41] The Nazi laws in Hitler's Germany in 1933–1945 can serve as an outright example.

develop laws that not only adhere to codified statutes but also align with ethical and universal standards of justice. The tension between *ius* and *lex* has prompted legal scholars, legislators, and judges to refine legal systems to address not only state interests but also the universal demands for fairness and justice. In the field of public international law, for example, this interplay has led to the establishment of treaties and conventions that protect human rights, environmental standards, and promote peace. International bodies such as the United Nations have emerged as platforms that try to balance state sovereignty (*lex*) with universal justice (*ius*), fostering a more cooperative and ethically conscious approach to global governance.[42]

This competition has also significantly influenced modern law by shaping fields such as human rights law, environmental law, and international criminal law (ICL). The rivalry between *ius* and positive law has, in the firm belief of the author, encouraged the international community to develop legal norms that transcend national interests, setting universal standards for human dignity and environmental stewardship. For instance, international human rights frameworks, such as the Universal Declaration of Human Rights and relevant treaty law, reflect an attempt to integrate *ius* principles with positive law, ensuring that all legal norms enacted by states align with global standards of justice. Thus, the ongoing dialogue between *ius* and *lex* has led to more sophisticated, principled legal systems that strive to harmonize state law with universal ideals, marking significant progress toward a more just world.

Questions for Students

1. *How does the integrative approach to defining law reconcile various perspectives like normativist, naturalist, and sociological?*
2. *What are the key characteristics that define the normative nature of law?*
3. *In what ways does law function as a social regulator, and how does it differ from other social norms?*
4. *Why are volition and interest important concepts in understanding the purpose and application of law?*
5. *What is the distinction between the object and subject of law in legal relationships?*
6. *How does the dichotomy of ius and lex reflect the tension between justice and state-enacted laws?*

References

[42] Neff 2014.

Atadjanov R (2019) Humanness as a Protected Legal Interest of Crimes against Humanity - Conceptual and Normative Aspects. International Criminal Justice Series, vol 22. TMC Asser Press, The Hague
Chloros A (1958) What is Natural Law? The Modern Law Review 6:609–622
Garner BA (ed) (2004) Black's Law Dictionary. Thomson West
Hage J et al. (eds) (2017) Introduction to Law, 2nd edn. Springer
Hart HLA (1961) The Concept of Law, 3rd edn. Oxford University Press
Kelsen H (1967) Pure Theory of Law (transl. from the 2nd German edn.). University of California Press
Lazarev VV (1992) Theory of State and Law (in Russian). Moscow
Lazarev VV, Lipen SV, Saidov AKh (2022) Problems of the Common Theory of jus (in Russian). Norma, Moscow
Marchenko M (2015) Problemy obshhej teorii gosudarstva i prava [Problems of Common Theory of State and Law], Vol. 2, 2nd edn. Prospect
Morozova LA (2021) Theory of State and Law (in Russian), 6th edn. Norma, Moscow
Neff S (2014) Justice among Nations. A History of International Law. Harvard University Press, Cambridge/London
Shaw M (2017) International Law, 8th edn. Cambridge University Press
van Schilfgaarde P (2019) Law and Life. Why Law? Springer

Chapter 7
The Main Theories of the Origin and Nature of Law

Contents

Abstract This chapter offers a comprehensive and structured overview of the key theories explaining the origin and nature of law, tracing their development from mythological and religious conceptions to modern libertarian legal thought. Beginning with ancient beliefs in divine or supernatural sources of law, the chapter explores how early civilizations justified authority and legal norms through the will of gods. It then moves to patriarchal and paternalistic conceptions, examining how historical legal systems reinforced gender hierarchies and limited personal autonomy under the guise of care and protection. The organic theory likens society and the state to living organisms, with legal institutions functioning like interdependent organs. Classical natural law and social contract theories are discussed as foundational rationalist frameworks, highlighting law's moral underpinnings and its legitimacy through collective agreement. Legalist (positivist) and Marxist theories present contrasting views, portraying law either as a product of state authority or as an instrument of class domination. The psychological theory, developed by Petrażycki, redefines law as a psychological experience shaped by internal impulses and emotions. Finally, the libertarian theory emphasizes law as the institutionalization of formal equality, presenting it as the normative framework through which individual freedom is realized. The chapter equips readers with a nuanced understanding of how legal thought has evolved across time and ideologies, emphasizing the continued relevance of these theories in shaping modern legal systems, especially in post-Soviet contexts.

R. Atadjanov, *A Common Theory of Law*, https://doi.org/10.1007/978-94-6265-711-3_7

Keywords Origin of law · Legal theory typologies · Natural law and social contract · Legal positivism and normativism · Marxist theory of law · Psychological theory of law (Petrażycki) · Libertarian legal theory · Patriarchal and paternalistic legal conceptions · Organic theory of state and society

This chapter presents a holistic overview of the main influential theories of origin and nature of law, starting from mythological and religious conceptions through to the libertarian theory of law. Providing such an overview adds considerable value by offering a comprehensive, but also chronological framework that aids the reader's understanding of how legal thought has evolved over time. Such an approach illuminates the cultural, philosophical, and ideological shifts that have influenced contemporary legal systems,[1] helping us appreciate the historical context of modern legal principles. This exploration serves an informative purpose, equipping readers with a basic foundation to analyze the evolution of legal theories and their varying interpretations of justice, authority, and freedom, ultimately fostering a hopefully well-rounded understanding of legal theory and philosophy.[2]

7.1 Mythological and Religious Conceptions

The mythological (mystical) and religion-informed concepts are based on the idea of a supra-human and supernatural (or heavenly, or divine) source and origin of both man himself and the proper order in the common life of people, including the corresponding generally binding rules of conduct and common authority. Such ideas, which appeared during the formation of primitive human communities, in one form or another retained their cognitive and explanatory significance even after the emergence of law and the state. Moreover, in these, as in many subsequent concepts of the origin of law and the state—for example, in patriarchal, psychological and organic teachings, or in the social contract theories up until the nineteenth century, there is no distinction between society and the state, so that essentially uniform ideas about generally binding rules of conduct and common power are extended (in them) both to the pre-state and to the "static" state of people's common life.

The dominance of mythological and original religious ideas is clearly manifested in the fact that all ancient peoples such as Egyptians, Babylonians, Hindus, Chinese, Assyrians, Jews, Persians, Greeks, and others, trace their orders—including the laws and powers established and operating in their societies (and states), to superhuman, heavenly forces and beings, to gods. They attribute their laws, forms of government, and institutions of power directly to the gods or their chosen ones and protégés (such

[1] For an overview of the contemporary legal systems, see Chap. 13.

[2] The main ideas and descriptions in this chapter are mostly based on the conclusions and explanations from *passim* Nersesyants 2016.

as mythical demigods and heroes—founders of city-states, legislators like the Indian Manu, the Spartan Lycurgus, the Athenian Theseus, the Jewish Moses, etc.).

The Greek historian Herodotus (fifth century BC) tells us about the corresponding views of the **Egyptians** that during his visit to Egypt, the priests told him that there had been 341 pharaohs in Egypt, all of whom were people. "It is true," Herodotus reports from the priests, "that before these people, gods reigned in Egypt, who lived together with people, and one of them was always the most powerful. The last of these kings was Or, the son of Osiris, whom the Greeks call Apollo. Having overthrown Typhon, he became the true king-god in Egypt."[3] Plato (fifth–fourth centuries BC), who also refers to information from the Egyptian priests, gives a slightly different version of the myth about the initial rule and legislation of the gods, their establishment of states and teaching people the basics of joint state life, gives a slightly different version of the myth about the initial rule and legislation of the gods, their establishment of states and teaching people the basics of joint state life. According to this version of the myth, the state appeared in the era of Zeus and the Olympian gods, and before that, under Kronos, there was no state, and people were directly governed by the gods and lived happily. "Under the rule of the god," writes Plato about the time of Kronos, "there were no states; there were also no women and children in property."[4]

According to ancient **Indian** mythology, the ritu—the general cosmic and earthly order, its law and custom—was established by the god named Indra. He also maintains this order and law. In the Rig Veda, which contains the sacred hymns of the Aryans (2nd millennium BC), it is said: "By establishing ritu, Indra also maintains it; the power of ritu grows quickly and brings wealth. The expanses of the earth and heaven belong to ritu." According to ancient **Chinese** mythology, the order in the Celestial Empire (i.e. in China), including the organization of power, rules of conduct, etc., is generated and conditioned by the will of the divine Heaven. The Emperor (the supreme ruler of the Celestial Empire) is characterized as the "son of Heaven". The divine origin of their power and their laws was also persistently emphasized by the **Sumerian** and **Babylonian** rulers. Thus, establishing his laws, Hammurabi (eighteenth century BC) proclaims: "By the command of Shamash, the great judge of heaven and earth, let my justice shine in the land, by the word of Marduk, my lord, let no one be found who would cancel my plans".

Law originates from divine or supernatural sources, with rules and authority granted by gods or higher powers

The ancient **Jews**, according to Old Testament traditions, were in special contractual relations with God. Thus, God gave the Jewish forefathers Abraham, and then Isaac, a promise (a vow, an oath) to multiply their family and make their descendants the chosen people, if they; for their part, strictly fulfill the covenant of God and

[3] Herodotus 2003.

[4] Plato 1925.

properly honor him. In this spirit, the Bible also covers the exodus of the Jews led by Moses from the Egyptian Dlen to Canaan by the will and with the help of Yahweh. On Mount Sinai, this God gave Moses the "tablets of the covenant", which contained the commandments of the laws by which the Jews must live (Ex. 20–23).

The idea of the divine origin of all authority is also inherent in **Christian** theology. Thus, the Apostle Paul already stated: "Let every soul be subject to the higher authorities. For there is no authority except from God: the authorities that exist have been ordained by God. Therefore whoever resists the authority resists the ordinance of God… For the ruler is God's servant for your good… Therefore you must obey, not only for fear of punishment, but also for conscience' sake" (Rom. 13:1–5).[5] The same approach was held by the greatest authority in Christian theology, **Thomas Aquinas** (1225–1274), albeit with a reservation: any authority is precisely by its essence divine and from God; but by the way it is acquired and used, authority can be contrary to God and tyrannical.[6] Similar ideas about the divine source of state power were developed in the twentieth century by the neo-Thomist J. Maritain.[7] Many other modern adherents of theological natural law teachings (A. Auer, E. Wolf, H. Dombois, F. Hurst, etc.) ultimately see the original foundation and source of law and state in God (his mind, will, creation, etc.).[8]

Theological interpretations of the origin of law and state have also become widespread in **Islam**. Thus, Shiite theologians (from members of the secret Islamic organization "Brothers of Purity" in the tenth century to modern Islamic fundamentalists) interpret Sharia (Muslim law) and Imamate (state) as a manifestation of the will, goodness, and wisdom of Allah, which are expressed in the Koran and in the prophetic words and deeds of Muhammad. The state (imamate) is considered as the support of Islam, a form of its protection and implementation in earthly life.

7.2 Patriarchal and Paternalistic Conceptions

Patriarchal conceptions of law are rooted in the idea that laws, historically, have often mirrored and reinforced male-dominated structures within society. A **patriarchal** legal framework typically aligns with a societal hierarchy where male authority presides over social, political, and familial life. This is evident in ancient legal codes, such as the **Code of Hammurabi**, which assigned distinct legal rights and obligations based on gender, often prioritizing male authority in familial and societal roles. The patriarchal view posits that legal norms and institutions serve to maintain male dominance, consciously or unconsciously embedding gender biases that influence everything from property rights to family law. In this conception, law functions not only as a governing structure but as a medium that reflects and reinforces societal norms that

[5] The Holy Bible 1989.

[6] Aquinas 1947.

[7] Maritain 1951.

[8] Auer 1971; Wolf 1961; Dombois 1971; Hurst 1959.

favor male authority. Scholars argue that this setup has systematically marginalized women's rights and agency, creating a legal culture where male-centered norms are normalized.

Legal **paternalism**, by contrast, is the idea that the law acts in a "protective" manner, exercising authority over individuals or groups for their supposed benefit, often at the expense of personal autonomy. Unlike patriarchal frameworks, which focus on hierarchical male authority, paternalistic legal conceptions are about authority over individuals in need of protection, regardless of gender, but frequently applied in ways that affect marginalized or vulnerable groups. For example, laws restricting certain professions or behaviors, historically justified to "protect" women and children, reflect a paternalistic belief that certain groups lack full capacity to make choices for themselves. This paternalistic notion has been critiqued for infantilizing adult individuals and curtailing personal freedom, while framing such restrictions as benevolent. Critics argue that paternalism in law can obscure issues of power and control, reinforcing inequalities under the guise of care or social welfare.

Laws historically reflect male-dominated structures and protective authority, often limiting individual autonomy under the guise of care

Although patriarchal and paternalistic conceptions of law have distinct theoretical bases, they often intersect and reinforce each other within legal systems. This intersection is particularly evident in laws regulating family, sexual, and reproductive rights, where legal frameworks have historically controlled women's autonomy, supposedly for their protection or in the interest of family unity. For instance, coverture laws in early modern England, which subsumed a woman's legal identity under her husband's, are a clear example where patriarchal authority combined with paternalistic justifications, framing a husband's control over his wife as a form of "protection". This intersection illustrates how patriarchal systems exploit paternalistic reasoning to sustain broader social control, embedding systemic biases within the law that limit the agency and rights of certain groups under the pretense of protection or moral order. These patterns reveal how legal systems, under patriarchal influence, often conflate protection with control, particularly impacting women, children, and marginalized communities.

Modern legal theorists and activists have criticized patriarchal and paternalistic conceptions of law as restrictive and ethically problematic. Feminist legal theory, in particular, has exposed how patriarchal assumptions in law perpetuate gender inequality, and paternalistic legal norms limit personal agency. Scholars such as Catharine MacKinnon argue that patriarchal laws institutionalize gender-based biases, perpetuating discrimination under the guise of neutrality.[9] Meanwhile, critiques of paternalism, including those from libertarian and human rights perspectives, challenge the notion that law should override individual autonomy

[9] See, for example, *passim* MacKinnon 1989.

for supposed well-being. They argue that paternalistic laws undermine self-determination, assuming that certain groups need state intervention to make "better" choices. This critique calls for reforms that dismantle gender biases in law and uphold individual autonomy, encouraging laws that recognize and empower the personal agency of all individuals rather than imposing a top-down control.[10]

In contemporary legal systems, patriarchal and paternalistic conceptions of law continue to have implications, though they are often more subtly embedded. Issues such as reproductive rights, domestic violence laws, and workplace equality are frequently areas where patriarchal and paternalistic assumptions intersect. Today, legal reforms aim to dismantle these lingering biases, promoting gender equality and protecting individual rights without undermining personal autonomy. For example, shifts towards recognizing marital rape, equal pay, and parental leave aim to address the structural inequities within patriarchal legal legacies. Similarly, reducing paternalistic laws that restrict individual autonomy, like drug laws or restrictions on certain consensual behaviors, reflects a growing recognition of personal freedom and the rights of individuals to make autonomous choices. As legal systems evolve, there is an increasing emphasis on developing laws that are inclusive and responsive to diverse experiences, moving away from the restrictive frameworks of the past toward principles rooted in equality and respect for individual agency.

7.3 Organic Conceptions

The idea of society and the state as a living organism and their organic origin goes back to ancient times. According to such organic ideas, society and the state are also organisms, a set of interconnected organs. The place, significance and power of each class and institution in the hierarchical system of organization of social and state life are determined by the function and role of the corresponding organ in a living organism. In this sense, a more important organ corresponds to a higher status and more significant power in the organic system of society and the state, which is of a hierarchical-rank nature. Analogies between the state and the organism were widely used by thinkers of antiquity such as Plato and Cicero, and philosophers of modern times—Hobbes, Rousseau, and Hegel. Organic ideas about society, the state and law were thoroughly developed in the works of the founders of positivistic sociology such as Comte and Spencer and their followers. The ideas of social Darwinism had a certain influence on their views. Representatives of the organic school in sociology—Schaeffle in Germany, Worms in France, Lilienfeld in Russia, went significantly further than their predecessors in the so-called "biologization" of social and political phenomena.[11] Thus, according to Lilienfeld, the government carries out the functions of the brain, and trade—the functions of blood circulation, etc.[12]

[10] Feinberg 1986.

[11] Schäffle 1875–1878; Worms 1896; von Lilienfeld 1873.

[12] Nersesyants 2016, at 213.

Society and the state are seen as living organisms where institutions function like organs, each fulfilling specific roles

7.4 Natural Law and Social Contract Theories

The traditional view of natural law is that it is a **set of universal and immutable principles that stands above the positive law created by human authorities.**[13] This view posits that natural law represents the highest moral standards towards which humanity aspires, serving as an ideal form of law rooted in reason and independent of human conventions.[14] Hugo Grotius, an influential thinker in natural law theory, argued that natural law dictates what is morally necessary or forbidden based on rational principles inherent in human nature. Grotius famously proposed that natural law's principles are so immutable that even divine intervention cannot alter fundamental truths, such as mathematical certainties.[15] This rationalist aspect of natural law underscores its secular potential, illustrating that it is accessible through reason alone, without needing divine endorsement. This principle has persisted since the classical era, as Greek philosophers like Plato and Aristotle, and later Roman legal thought, all recognized the existence of a higher moral law, which later became foundational for Christian theological teachings and international law.

Social contract theory offers a contrasting perspective on the origin and nature of law by arguing that legal systems arise from human agreements rather than immutable moral dictates. In social contract theory, the **establishment of government and laws is understood as an outcome of a collective decision to create a structured society for mutual benefit**, often as a remedy to the perceived hardships of a pre-political state of nature. Thinkers such as John Locke, Jean-Jacques Rousseau, and Montesquieu each developed unique social contract theories, with varying views on human nature and the conditions justifying authority. Although natural law and social contract theory may initially appear divergent, these traditions intersect through a shared emphasis on rational principles as the foundation of legitimate governance. Both theories seek to ground authority in reason, albeit through different pathways, making them complementary frameworks for understanding the moral basis of law.

John Locke's social contract theory emphasizes the protection of natural rights as the primary justification for establishing a government. According to Locke, individuals possess inalienable rights in a state of nature, such as life, liberty, and property, which any legitimate government must respect.[16] For Locke, the social contract is

[13] On the dualism of *ius* and *lex*, see Chap. 6.

[14] Chloros 1958, pp. 609–622.

[15] Grotius 2005.

[16] Locke 1988.

an **agreement among individuals to create a government that protects these rights, with the understanding that failure to do so would render the government invalid.**[17] Locke's contract theory thus incorporates natural law by suggesting that certain moral principles (those governing natural rights) precede any formal agreement. Locke's approach demonstrates an integration of natural law's moral absolutism with the pragmatic need for a structured authority, creating a harmonious blend of immutable moral values with social contract principles.

Jean-Jacques Rousseau, while also grounded in social contract theory, diverged significantly from Locke in his vision of human nature and governance. Rousseau viewed the state of nature as a peaceful and egalitarian condition, corrupted by the emergence of private property and social inequalities. In his concept of the social contract, Rousseau argued that l**egitimate authority could only be based on the "general will", i.e., the collective will of the people directed toward the common good.**[18] For Rousseau, the social contract reestablishes equality and communal values, aligning with natural law's moral aspirations by advocating for a society based on reason and the pursuit of collective moral goals.[19] Rousseau's approach suggests that law, though emerging from human agreement, should aspire to fulfill moral principles similar to those posited by natural law theory, particularly regarding equality and justice.

Montesquieu's perspective further enriches the connection between natural law and social contract by emphasizing the need for balanced government to prevent abuses of power. In "The Spirit of the Laws", Montesquieu argued that the structure of government should reflect the social and environmental factors of a given society while also ensuring a separation of powers to protect individual freedoms.[20] Although Montesquieu did not focus explicitly on a social contract *per se*, he supported the view that a **government's legitimacy depends on its adherence to universal principles of justice**, similar to natural law. Montesquieu's emphasis on rationally designed institutions echoes natural law's ideals by ensuring that governmental structures aim to uphold justice, stability, and the preservation of rights, thereby embedding natural law principles within a practical governance framework.

Natural law derives from universal moral principles, while social contract theory views law as an agreement among individuals for mutual benefit

The intersection of natural law and social contract theory is particularly relevant for post-Soviet states, where questions of legitimacy and authority remain central to the legal discourse. Natural law's emphasis on universal moral standards can provide a foundational ethical framework, suggesting that laws and institutions

[17] Ibid.

[18] Rousseau 2004.

[19] Ibid.

[20] Montesquieu 1989.

should align with rational, universally applicable values. Simultaneously, social contract theory offers a pathway for these states to legitimize authority through public consent and structured agreements, particularly in societies transitioning from authoritarian regimes to more participatory governance models. This combination of moral idealism and pragmatic legitimacy provides a compelling basis for developing legal systems that respect individual rights while maintaining social cohesion.

In sum, natural law and social contract theories offer complementary yet distinct perspectives on the nature and purpose of law. Natural law provides a vision of law grounded in immutable moral principles accessible through reason, while social contract theory underscores the role of human consent and collective agreement in establishing legal authority. When considered together, these theories suggest that law can be both a rational expression of universal moral values and a practical framework for maintaining social order. For post-Soviet states, integrating elements of both theories could foster legal systems that not only command respect through adherence to moral principles but also gain legitimacy through democratic engagement and consensus.

As I view it, both theories advocate for law's grounding in rationality—natural law through universal principles and social contract theory through agreed-upon rules—which positions them as enduring resources for states striving to build just and stable legal systems. As post-Soviet states continue to define their legal identities, these theories offer a means to harmonize ideals of justice with the realities of governance, reflecting a nuanced approach to the origins and purposes of law in modern society.

7.5 Legalist (Positivist/Normativist) Theories

The legalistic type of legal understanding is characterized by the identification of law as a certain objective entity, independent of the will and arbitrariness of official power and the law as a compulsory and obligatory establishment of power. According to legalism, **law is an arbitrary product of the state, its order** (compulsory establishment, rule, act, or norm). For legalism and, in general, "legal positivism", disregard for the rights of man and citizen, an apology for power, and the hypertrophy of its norm-making capabilities are very characteristic. In this sense, legalism is a normative expression of authoritarianism. The pathos and aspirations of legalism are the subordination of all to the rules and regulations of power. Here, the view of man as a subordinate object of power, and not a free being, dominates everywhere.

In modern times, the legalistic approach was substantiated by Thomas Hobbes, an apologist for the absolutist Leviathan state. "The legal force of the law," he emphasized, "consists only in the fact that it is the command of the sovereign."[21] By "law" here is meant all current (positive) law. Later, such an understanding of the law was adopted by representatives of various schools of the so-called "legal positivism"

[21] Hobbes 1996.

(and neopositivism), which is essentially not legal, but legalistic positivism (and neopositivism).

The main ideas and provisions of "legal positivism" include the interpretation of law as a creation of power, the coercive power as ultimately the only distinctive feature of law, formal-logical and legal-dogmatic methods of analyzing law, "purification" of the doctrine of law from various kinds of "metaphysical" provisions on the essence, nature, causes, values of law, etc.

Law is a system of rules established by the state, focusing on formal authority and state-enforced compliance

Similar ideas in the nineteenth century were developed by Austin, S. Amos and others in England, by Windscheid, Gerber, Bergbohm, Laband, Zitelman and others in Germany, by Cabantou and others in France, and by Vas'kovsky, Golmsten, Grimm, Pakhman, Shershenevich and others in Russia.[22] In the twentieth century, this approach is represented by such directions of "legal" neopositivism as "jurisprudence reformed by general linguistics" of Katkov, the "pure doctrine of law" of Kelsen, the "concept of law" of Hart, etc.[23]

One of the prominent representatives of English analytical jurisprudence, Austin, in his work on the "philosophy of positive law" characterized law as "an aggregate of rules established by a political leader or sovereign" and emphasized: "Every law is a command, an order." Amos also claimed that "law is an order of the supreme political power of the state with the purpose of controlling the actions of individuals in a given community." Shershenevich held similar views. "Every rule of law," he wrote, "is an order." Law, according to his assessment, is "a product of the state", and state power is characterized by him as "that initial fact from which legal norms proceed, clinging to each other."

By its order, state power generates law—such is the credo of this type of legal understanding. From this point of view, everything that the power orders is law. The distinction between law and arbitrariness is thus, in principle, deprived of objective and substantive meaning and has for adherents of this approach only a subjective and formal character: obvious arbitrariness, sanctioned by a certain subject (government body) in a certain form (in the form of one or another act—a law, decree, rescript, regulation, circular, etc.), is recognized as law.

The definition of the concept of law as **a system of norms established or sanctioned by the state and secured by its coercive force** has been widely used in legalistic literature. It is true that the provisions (norms) of officially valid (positive) law are established by the state and secured by state coercion, but this is not enough for a proper concept of law, for the interpretation of such official-authoritative

---

[22] Austin 1998; Amos 1874; Windscheid 1906; von Gerber 1869; Bergbohm 1892; Laband 1876; Zitelmann 1880; Cabantou 1900; Vas'kovsky 1907; Golmsten 1901; Grimm 1900; Pakhman 1908; Shershenevich 1995.

[23] Katkov 1985; Kelsen 1967; Hart 1961.

establishments (norms) as legal phenomena (phenomena of legal essence), as law in general, since in such a legalistic definition there is no criterion for distinguishing law from arbitrariness, a legal norm from an arbitrary establishment of power, a legal law from an anti-legal law.

7.6 The Economic (Marxist) Theory of Law and State

The doctrine of socio-economic formations, developed by Karl Marx and Friedrich Engels from a materialistic, proletarian-class, communist position, underlies the Marxist typology of law and state. According to Marxism, **the determining role in socio-historical development is played by economic (production) relations**, which constitute the basis of society, which determines the corresponding superstructure, including the state and law.[24] According to this approach, the entire history of mankind is divided into five socio-economic formations: the primitive communal system, the slave system, the feudal system, the capitalist system, and the communist system.

Three class-antagonistic formations (i.e., slave, feudal, and capitalist), based on private property and class division, correspond to three types of law and state: the slave law and state, the feudal state and law, and the bourgeois (capitalist) law and state. Under the primitive system (primitive communism) there is no law and state yet, under communism the law and state as class phenomena will wither away. In relation to statehood and law in the first phase of communism (i.e. under socialism), Marx spoke of the dictatorship of the proletariat and the bourgeois "equal law" for regulating the measure of labor and consumption.

Later, in Soviet Marxist literature—in obvious divergence from the prognostic positions of the founders of Marxism themselves—they also began to distinguish a socialist type of law and state, which in fact demonstrated the absence and inconsistency of the predicted transition from socialism to full communism without a law and a state. Economic and class relations, along with other factors (spiritual, cultural, etc.), are undoubtedly of great importance in the process of the emergence, change, and development of the state and law. However, the hypertrophy of their role, characteristic of all Marxism, including the Marxist typology of the state and law, leads to significant vices. Among such vices is also the fundamentally negative approach of Marxism to the law (and state), their interpretation as instruments of class violence and oppression, as a machine of domination and suppression.

Law reflects and enforces class-based economic relations, serving as an instrument of oppression in class-divided societies

[24] Marx and Engels 1976.

The Marxist approach thus ignores the fundamental circumstance and the obvious fact of world history that human freedom in this world appears and develops precisely in state-legal forms. The real historical development and change of types of state and law (from early states to the modern legal state) testify—contrary to Marxist ideas and assessments—to the progress of human freedom (the expansion of the sphere and measure of freedom, the increase in the number of free people, etc.), and not at all to the progress of violence, suppression and domination of some classes over others, etc.

The Marxist doctrine of the law and state, including the corresponding typology of law and state, essentially rejects any positive attitude to law and state as a certain value, as an achievement in the development of human culture, freedom, etc. It is anti-legal in nature and, in principle, does not fit in with jurisprudence and the legal interpretation of law (and the state).

7.7 The Psychological Theory of Law (PTL)

The psychological theory of law, most famously developed by Leon Petrażycki, offers a distinctive perspective that conceptualizes law as an empirical phenomenon rooted in human psychology. Unlike traditional legal theories that rely heavily on external structures, such as statutes or judicial decisions, Petrażycki's approach, i.e., PTL, centers on the inner experiences of individuals. He posited that law manifests through specific psychological states—namely, emotions and impulsions—which form the basis of legal experiences.[25] These legal experiences imply a unique two-sided relationship: the recognition of a right on one side and a corresponding duty on the other. This dual relationship, according to Petrażycki, is the foundation of the legal phenomenon.

Central to Petrażycki's psychological theory is the **distinction between positive law and intuitive law, which hinges on whether the legal experience is tied to normative facts**. Positive law refers to legal experiences that are connected to external normative systems, such as statutes, court rulings, contracts, or social customs. These external systems provide objective reference points that validate the legal experiences as part of an organized societal framework. For example, the recognition of a contractual obligation as legally binding involves a legal experience that aligns with established rules or commands. Positive law, therefore, integrates the subjective legal experiences of individuals into the broader, objective legal order.

Law arises from psychological experiences, such as emotions and impulsions, and includes both positive (external) and intuitive (internal) law

[25] Petrażycki 1955.

On the other hand, intuitive law represents legal experiences that arise independently of external normative systems. Such legal experiences are spontaneous and intrinsic, often reflecting deeply personal or moral impulses rather than codified rules. For instance, an individual may feel an inherent duty to assist a neighbor in distress, even in the absence of any legal mandate. In this sense, intuitive law is more fluid and subjective, operating outside the structured boundaries of positive legal systems. Petrażycki viewed intuitive law as a vital component of human behavior, often guiding actions in areas where formal legal norms are absent or insufficient.

Petrażycki's psychological theory emphasizes introspection as the primary method for studying law. **By examining their own legal experiences, individuals can identify the emotional and impulsive states that constitute legal phenomena**. This approach challenges the traditional reliance on objective, external analyses of legal systems, suggesting instead that the essence of law lies within the subjective experiences of individuals. In the post-Soviet context, where legal systems are often marked by a tension between formal institutions and cultural norms, Petrażycki's theory offers a powerful lens for understanding the interplay between individual psychology and societal legal frameworks.

In conclusion, PTL provides a groundbreaking framework that reconceptualizes law as an inherently psychological phenomenon. By distinguishing between positive and intuitive law and highlighting the significance of introspection, this theory bridges the gap between subjective human experiences and objective legal structures. For post-Soviet states, where legal systems are in flux and often characterized by pluralistic norms, Petrażycki's ideas remain especially relevant. They underscore the need to consider the psychological dimensions of law in addressing the challenges of legal development and reform.

7.8 The Libertarian Theory of Law

The libertarian type of legal understanding is based on the **principle of formal equality**. The libertarian understanding of law includes not only the understanding of law as such (both the essence of law and the legal phenomenon in the form of a lawful *lex*), but also the legal understanding of the state as an institutional and authoritative form of expression and action of the principle of formal equality, as a legal form of organization of universal public authority.

The foundation for legally treating different individuals as equals lies in the recognition of individual freedom within social relations, expressed through their legal capacity and personality. Formal equality, as the essence and principle of law, consists of three interrelated and mutually reinforcing components: (1) a universal equal standard or norm, (2) the formal freedom of all individuals subject to this equal standard, and (3) the universal justice that ensures this form of regulation is equally fair for everyone. These components work together to uphold the principle of formal equality in law.

The libertarian-legal theory offers a balanced approach to understanding law by addressing the limitations of both *jus naturalism* and legalist theory. It establishes that the relationship between the essence of law (formal equality) and its manifestation (legal phenomenon) is both necessary and natural. In this view, the essence of law—formal equality—forms the foundation of a legal phenomenon, such as a generally binding law created by the state, which reflects and enforces this principle of equality. Conversely, a legal phenomenon, like a law, serves as the external expression of the underlying essence, formal equality. This reciprocal relationship ensures that the essence (formal equality) and its phenomenon (the law) are inherently connected and mutually reflective.

The libertarian theory states that only on the basis of and taking into account such a necessary connection between the legal essence and the legal phenomenon is it possible to achieve their desired unity in the form of a lawful *lex*, i.e. established by the state and officially operating generally binding positive law, expressing in a normatively concretized form the properties and requirements of the principle of formal equality. From the standpoint of legalism and *jus naturalism* (or natural law), such a unity of legal essence and legal phenomenon in the form of a legal law is unattainable.

We call this type of legal understanding and the corresponding concept of jurisprudence legal-libertarian (or libertarian), since, according to our interpretation, law is a universal and necessary form of freedom of people, and freedom (its existence and realization) in social life is possible and valid only as law, only in the form of law. The law implied by the libertarian legal understanding is only the necessary legal minimum, that is, without which there is no and cannot be law in general, including the rule of law.

Law is the formal equality of individuals, ensuring freedom and fairness through universally binding principles

Legal equality is the equality of the free and equality in freedom, the general scale and equal measure of freedom of individuals. Law speaks and acts in the language and means of such equality and, thanks to this, acts as a universal and necessary form of being, expression and implementation of freedom in the life of people together. In this sense, we can say that law is the mathematics of freedom.

In the social sphere, equality is always legal equality, formal legal equality. After all, legal equality, like any equality, is abstracted (by its own basis and criterion) from actual differences and therefore necessarily and by definition has a formal character.

The history of law is the history of the progressive evolution of the content, volume, scale and measure of formal (legal) equality while preserving this principle itself as the principle of any legal system, law in general. Different stages of the historical development of freedom and law in human relations have their own scale and measure of freedom, their own circle of subjects and relations of freedom and law, in a word, their own content of the principle of formal (legal) equality. So the principle of formal equality is a principle constantly inherent in law with historically changing content.

In general, the historical evolution of the content, scope, and sphere of application of the principle of formal equality (and its implementation in the current law and state) does not refute, but, on the contrary, reinforces the significance of this principle (and the system of norms that concretizes it) as a distinctive feature of law in its relationship and divergence from other types of social regulation (moral, religious, etc.). Taking this into account, it can be said that law is a normative form of expression of freedom through the principle of formal equality of people in social relations.

Legal equality and legal inequality are interconnected legal concepts that complement and presuppose each other, standing in contrast to actual differences. The principle of legal equality recognizes that while individuals are treated equally under the law, the rights and obligations they acquire may differ. Law transforms the disorder of real-world differences into a structured legal framework of equalities and inequalities, all organized around a common standard and unified principles.

Questions for Students

1. *How do mythological and religious conceptions explain the origin and authority of law?*
2. *In what ways do patriarchal and paternalistic conceptions of law influence legal systems, particularly regarding individual autonomy?*
3. *What is the key analogy in organic conceptions of law, and how does it apply to society and the state?*
4. *How do natural law and social contract theories differ in their explanation of the origins and purposes of law?*
5. *What are the defining characteristics of legalist (positivist) theories, and how do they relate to state authority?*
6. *How does the Marxist theory of law critique the role of law in class-based societies?*
7. *What is the distinction between positive and intuitive law in the psychological theory, and how do these concepts interact?*

References

Amos S (1874) The Science of Law. John Murray, London

Aquinas T (1947) Summa Theologica (Fathers of the English Dominican Province (transl)). Benziger Bros., New York

Auer A (1971) Autonome Moral und christlicher Glaube [Autonomous Morality and Christian Faith]. Matthias-Grünewald-Verlag, Mainz

Austin J (1998) The Province of Jurisprudence Determined (Campbell R (ed)). Hackett Publishing, Indianapolis
Bergbohm H (1892) Jurispudenz und Rechtsphilosophie [Jurisprudence and Legal Philosophy]. Duncker & Humblot, Leipzig
Cabantou A (1900) Le pouvoir d'État: étude de droit public et de philosophie politique [State Power: A Study in Public Law and Political Philosophy]. Sirey, Paris
Chloros AG (1958) What Is Natural Law? The Modern Law Review, Vol. 21, No. 6 (Nov. 1958)
Dombois H (1971) Das Recht der Kirche im pluralistischen Staat [The Law of the Church in the Pluralistic State]. Vandenhoeck & Ruprecht, Göttingen
Feinberg J (1986) The Moral Limits of the Criminal Law: Harm to Self. Oxford University Press, New York
Golmsten VV (1901) Lectures on the Encyclopedia of Law (in Russian), 2nd edn. St. Petersburg
Grimm DN (1900) Introduction to the Science of Law (in Russian). St. Petersburg
Grotius H (2005) On the Law of War and Peace (De Jure Belli ac Pacis), 2nd edn (Tuck R (transl/ed)). Oxford University Press, Oxford
Hart HLA (1961) The Concept of Law. Oxford University Press, Oxford
Herodotus (2003) The Histories, Book II (Waterfield R (transl), Dewald C (ed)). Penguin Books, London
Hobbes T (1996) Leviathan (Tuck R (ed)). Oxford University Press, Oxford
Hurst F (1959) Naturrecht und christlicher Glaube [Natural Law and Christian Faith]. Evangelische Verlagsanstalt, Berlin
Katkov AB (1985) Language and Jurisprudence (in Russian). Moscow
Kelsen H (1967) Pure Theory of Law (Knight M (transl)). University of California Press, Berkeley
Laband P (1876) Das Staatsrecht des Deutschen Reiches [Constitutional Law of the German Reich]. Mohr, Tübingen
Locke J (1988) Two Treatises of Government (Laslett P (ed)). Cambridge University Press, Cambridge
MacKinnon CA (1989) Toward a Feminist Theory of the State. Harvard University Press, Cambridge, MA
Maritain J (1951) Man and the State. University of Chicago Press, Chicago
Marx K, Engels F (1976) The German Ideology. Progress Publishers, Moscow
Montesquieu (1989) The Spirit of the Laws (Cohler AM, Miller BC, Stone HS (transls/eds)). Cambridge University Press, Cambridge
Nersesyants V (2016) Common Theory of Law and State (in Russian). Norma INFRA-M, Moscow
Pakhman SV (1908) Lectures on the General Part of Civil Law (in Russian). Moscow
Petrażycki L (1955) Law and Morality (Solomon HJ (transl)). Harvard University Press, Cambridge
Plato (1925) Statesman (Fowler HN (transl)). Harvard University Press, Cambridge
Rousseau JJ (2004) The Social Contract (Cranston M (transl)). Penguin Books, London
Schäffle A (1875–1878) Bau und Leben des sozialen Körpers [Structure and Life of the Social Body], Vols. 1–4. J.G. Cotta, Stuttgart
Shershenevich G (1995) Common Theory of Law (in Russian), Vol. I. Moscow
The Holy Bible (1989) New Revised Standard Version. National Council of the Churches of Christ, New York
Vas'kovsky EA (1907) Public Law: General Part (in Russian). St. Petersburg
von Gerber CF (1869) Das Problem der Gesetzgebung [The Problem of Legislation]. Mohr, Tübingen
von Lilienfeld P (1873) Gedanken über die Socialwissenschaft der Zukunft [Thoughts on the Social Science of the Future]. Duncker & Humblot, Leipzig
Windscheid B (1906) Lehrbuch des Pandektenrechts [Textbook on the Pandects], 9th edn. De Gruyter, Berlin
Wolf E (1961) Gesetz und Gesetzlichkeit in der Theologie und im Recht [Law and Legality in Theology and Law]. Mohr Siebeck, Tübingen
Worms R (1896) Organisme et société [Organism and Society]. Félix Alcan, Paris

Zitelmann E (1880) Die juristische Konstruktion [The Legal Construction]. Duncker & Humblot, Leipzig

Chapter 8
The Principles and Functions of Law

Contents

Abstract This chapter explores the foundational principles and core functions of law, explaining how they shape the nature, structure, and purpose of legal systems. It begins by defining principles of law as overarching ideas that guide the formation, interpretation, and application of legal norms, emphasizing their role in ensuring freedom, justice, and order in society. General principles such as social freedom, justice, democracy, humanism, equality, legality, and responsibility, are presented as universal standards embedded in both national and international law. The chapter also introduces cross-branch (interdisciplinary) and branch-specific principles, illustrating how legal coherence is maintained across diverse areas like criminal, civil, and procedural law. A key discussion focuses on the controversial yet increasingly accepted role of legal principles as sources of law, especially in filling gaps where written norms are absent. Drawing comparisons between domestic and international legal systems, the chapter highlights the growing recognition of principles in legal practice. Finally, it outlines law's two primary social functions: regulatory (structuring social relations) and protective (guarding society against harmful acts). Together, these principles and functions underscore law's dynamic role in promoting societal progress, legal certainty, and individual dignity particularly relevant for legal reform in post-Soviet states.

Keywords Principles of law · General and branch-specific principles · Cross-branch legal norms · Sources of law · Regulatory and protective functions · Legal system structure · National vs. international law · Legal reform and coherence

R. Atadjanov, *A Common Theory of Law*, https://doi.org/10.1007/978-94-6265-711-3_8

8.1 The Definition of Principles of Law

Law is built upon certain major principles that express its nature and social purpose.[1] They reflect the main features and particularities of law, which lend it the quality of social regulator as a measure of freedom and fairness in public relations. Principles of law are the main ideas, or main premises that lead the process of law's formation, evolution and functioning. They consolidate, in legal sense, the objective patterns of social life. Principles of law permeate the legal life of the society as well as the legal system of any given country while being reflected, first of all, in legal norms. The principles characterize not only the essence but also the content of law; they reflect its inner structure, its statics, and also the process of its application and its dynamics. Principles of law have a huge impact on the process of normative acts' formation and on their promulgation; they may be said to establish, so to speak, guarantees or assurances of compliance with legal requirements.[2]

The principles of law act as a kind of supporting structure on which not only its norms, institutions or branches, but also its entire system rest and are implemented. They serve as the main guideline for all law-making, law enforcement and law enforcement activities of government bodies. The level of coherence, stability and efficiency of the legal system depends on the degree of their compliance with principles of law. Having a generally binding nature, the principles of law help strengthen the internal unity and interaction of its various branches and institutions, legal norms and legal relations, subjective and objective law.[3]

Principles of law are foundational ideas guiding the formation, evolution, and application of law to ensure fairness, freedom, and justice in society

The principles of law are not arbitrary in nature as one might think. They are determined by the economic, social, and political system of society that exists in a particular country, the social nature of the law and state, the nature of the prevailing political and governmental regime in the country, the basic principles of the construction and functioning of the political system of a particular society.[4]

In accordance with the most widespread criteria of classification of principles of law found in academic legal literature, the principles of law that apply to the entire system of law and determine its nature, content, and its most important features and characteristics are called general principles. Among them are usually the principles of social freedom, social justice, democracy, humanism, equality before the law, unity of legal rights and obligations, responsibility for a guilty commission of offence, and

[1] For a systematic overview and advanced analysis of legal principles, see *passim* Stoilov 2022; Ávila 2007.

[2] Khropanyuk 2019, at 206.

[3] Ibid.

[4] Generally, ibid., p. 207.

legality. What follows is a brief description and explanation of each one of these principles.

8.2 General Principles

These include social freedom, justice, democracy, humanism, equality, legality, and responsibility, serving as core values for legal systems

The principle of social freedom: The main principle of legal regulation in a civilized state is to provide its subjects with: maximum freedom in choosing forms of labor activity and profession; living place; opportunities to use various social services of the state and private individuals; freely dispose of their income; participate in the distribution of common social benefits; and be protected from unemployment and other social conflicts. This principle ensures social security of the individual and provides real guarantees for a free and prosperous life.[5]

The principle of social justice: This principle has both moral and legal content. It ensures correspondence between the practical role of individuals in the life of society and their social status, between their rights and responsibilities, between work and reward, crime and punishment, a person's merits and their social recognition. Through law, the most optimal proportionality is achieved between possible and proper behavior and the assessment of its results. Justice is also one of the leading principles in the practice of legal regulation, when resolving specific legal cases (for example, when assigning a pension, allocating housing, determining criminal penalties, etc.).[6]

The principle of democracy: In a law-state, this principle permeates the entire legal system. It finds direct expression in legal norms regulating the order of organization and activities of government bodies, determining the legal status of the individual, and the nature of their relationship with the state.[7]

The principle of humanism: The foundations of humanism are characteristic of all civilized legal systems. They reveal one of the most important value characteristics of law. The law consolidates and actually guarantees the natural and inalienable rights and freedoms of every person: the right to life, health; personal freedom and security; the right to protect one's honor and reputation; protection from any arbitrary interference in the sphere of personal life, etc. The humanism of legal provisions is also expressed in the fact that legal provisions guarantee the inviolability of the person: no one can be arrested or illegally detained except on the basis of a court decision; Every person has the right to defense and to a fair and public hearing by

[5] Ibid., at 207.

[6] Ibid., pp. 207–208.

[7] Ibid., p. 208.

a competent, independent and impartial court; all persons deprived of their liberty have the right to be treated humanely and with respect for their dignity; and no one should be subjected to torture or cruel, inhuman or degrading punishment.[8]

The principle of equality (i.e., equality of all before the law): This key principle is enshrined in the Universal Declaration of Human Rights, the UN international covenants on human rights of 1966, and in the constitutional legislation of most countries of the world. These regulatory legal acts proclaim the equality of all citizens before the law, their equal right to the protection of the law, regardless of national or social origin, language, gender, political and other beliefs, religion, place of residence, property status or other circumstances.[9]

The principle of unity of legal rights and obligations: The essence of this principle is expressed in the organic connection and interdependence of the legal rights and obligations of participants in social relations: the state as a whole, its bodies, officials, citizens and various associations. With such an organization of social relations, the right to enjoy a certain social benefit corresponds to the obligation to perform socially useful actions in the interests of others. It is possible to talk about the reality of any right only if there is a corresponding legal obligation. In particular, a citizen's right to judicial protection is realized through the obligation of the courts to provide such protection. A citizen's right to social security in old age, in case of illness or loss of ability to work is ensured by the state through its special bodies, which are obliged to pay her/him pensions or benefits. At the same time, the law establishes that the exercise of rights by a citizen should not contradict the rights of other people.[10]

The principle of responsibility for a guilty commission of offence: In accordance with this principle, legal liability (responsibility) can be imposed on a person only if she/he is guilty of violating the requirements of a legal norm. Guilt is the leading principle that determines the basis of legal responsibility. If there is no guilt in a person's act, legal liability measures cannot be applied to her/him.[11]

The principle of legality: One of the cornerstone principles in law, this principle is of the most general and comprehensive nature. Its content is expressed in the demand for strict and complete implementation of the requirements of legal norms by all subjects of law. By ensuring the realization of the rules of law, this principle simultaneously promotes the implementation in the practice of legal regulation of other general legal principles mentioned above: justice, social freedom, and humanism.[12]

It should be noted that all general principles of law briefly described above are closely interrelated. If the principle of social justice operates, then humane relations between people are established. Conversely, the implementation of the principle of humanism means at the same time the establishment of fair relations in public life.

[8] Ibid.

[9] Ibid., pp. 208–209.

[10] Khropanyuk 2019, at 209.

[11] Ibid.

[12] Ibid., pp. 209–210.

As it is known, Aristotle noted that justice is closely related to the concepts of legality and equality of people, since justice acts as legal and equal, and injustice as illegal and unequal treatment of these people.[13]

8.3 Cross-Branch Principles

The so-called cross-branch, or inter-branch legal principles are guidelines that express the features of several related branches of law (for example, criminal procedure and civil procedure). The common principles of these branches of law are, for example, collegiality in the consideration of criminal and civil cases, publicity of judicial proceedings. At the same time, general legal principles fully apply to related (allied) branches of law. They appear separately in each industry and are integrated into cross-industry principles.[14]

Cross-branch principles, like equality of arms and judicial impartiality, apply across multiple legal fields, ensuring consistency and fairness

As an example, the following non-exhaustive list of principles of procedural law (in the continental legal system) which apply to both criminal law and administrative law, may be illustrative of cross-branch principles of law: equality of arms, adversarial process, establishment of truth, publicity of the court hearing, immediacy of the trial (as in "no intermediaries"), independence of the judiciary, judicial impartiality, right to defense in court, legal assistance to citizens in need, consideration and resolution of the case within a reasonable time, and some others.

8.4 Branch Principles

Branch legal principles characterize the most essential features of a particular branch of law (for example, administrative or civil). For example, the principles of civil law are equality of parties in property relations, ensuring contractual discipline, etc. The content of branch principles is usually discussed in more detail when studying the relevant sectoral legal disciplines.[15]

[13] Ibid., p. 210, citing Aristotle 1908, p. 3.

[14] Ibid.

[15] Khropanyuk 2019, at 210.

Specific principles within legal branches, such as legality and non-retroactivity in criminal law, define the essence of those legal areas

The following principles of criminal law may serve as good illustration of branch principles: principle of legality, or *nullum crimen/nulla poena sine lege*; *non bis in idem* (prohibition of double jeopardy); no application of the law by analogy, or *nulla poena sine lege stricta*; non-retroactivity of the law; equality before the law; inevitability of criminal responsibility; personal culpability; principle of fairness; and principle of humanism.

8.5 Principles as Sources of Law

One of the contentious issues when it comes to principles of law would be their character of being or serving as sources of law. It is important for both national and international law. Even if the exploration and understanding of principles of law within the common theory of law is mostly related to national law, a proper understanding of legal principles as sources of law may be helped by looking into how (general) principles are treated and perceived at international law, all the more so that the interaction between national/domestic and international law nowadays is becoming increasingly strong and active due to, *inter alia*, undeniable processes of globalization in the world.

If one compares the principles of national and international law, it becomes clear that there is no qualitative difference between them. This applies both to the definition of "principle of law" and to the purposes and functions of legal principles that they carry out in the legal regulation at their corresponding national and international levels. The difference between national and international law as concerns principles of law consists in how they are categorized and legally formalized, i.e., in what way they have been "sourced", that is, legally expressed.

The principles that underlie public international law (that is, form the basis of it) and apply to this law as a whole are called its general principles. They are frequently relied upon in the practice of international law; representing a non-treaty and non-customary source of international law, they differ from the special principles relating to particular or specific branches of international law. The general principles of international law reflect its nature and they reveal the peculiarities of this branch of law. A typical formulation of this source appears in Article 38(1)(c) of the Statute of the International Court of Justice, where, in the third place after treaties and international custom, the Court is instructed to apply "the general principles of law recognized by civilized nations" in deciding "in accordance with international law such disputes as are submitted to it".[16] The core list of these principles is established

[16] Janis 2003, pp. 55–56.

in the Charter of the United Nations,[17] UN General Assembly's Declaration on Principles of International Law[18] as well as in the Helsinki Final Act.[19] According to Janis, although at one time the term "civilized nations" was meant to restrict the scope of the provision to European states or states recognized as actors in the European system of international politics, such as the United States and, somewhat later, Japan, nowadays it is recognized that a search for general principles of law should include all corners of the globe.[20]

When comparing the principles and norms in the area of international law, the researchers of international law basically try not to starkly differentiate between the two. General principles of international law include the principles of sovereign equality of states, fulfillment of international obligations in good faith, prohibition of the threat or use of force, non-intervention in the domestic affairs of a state, settlement of disputes by peaceful means, and others. Due to the fact that both general principles of law (see Sect. 8.2) AND general principles of international law have commonly shared value roots, they may be said to characterize law as one single unified phenomenon which has two dimensions—national, or domestic, and international.

In both national and international law their general principles are legally expressed via sources of law. The difference is in the exact types of those sources; it is determined by the particularities of the nature of these two branches, or dimensions—as stated above, of law. In national/domestic law, the legal principles are either legislatively recognized, or they are referred to in judicial decisions and acts. In public international law, the general principles of law are formed by way of inclusion in treaties; this is because of the consensual nature of international law: an agreed, or consented will of states is necessary, and treaties are the result of that will (volition). Because of this, once can say that principles of public international law have a contractual, or rather, conventional origin.

Principles serve as sources of law, providing a foundation for legal rules and bridging gaps when explicit legal norms are absent

In international law, general principles determine the line of conduct of states and other subjects of international law. Together with international norms, they serve as legal basis for the qualification of conduct either as lawful or unlawful. In national law, the general principles, be they legislatively established or figure as references in the court acts, serve—or are supposed to serve, as legally valid lawful basis for

[17] Charter of the United Nations, opened for signature 26 June 1945, 1 U.N.T. S. XVI (entered into force 24 October 1945), Articles 1, 2.

[18] Declaration on Principles of International Law Concerning Friendly Relations and Co-Operation among States in Accordance with the Charter of the United Nations (GAR 2625), Adopted by the UN General Assembly Resolution 2625 (XXV) of 24 October 1970.

[19] Organization for Security and Co-operation in Europe 1975.

[20] Janis 2003, p. 56, citing Gong 1984.

directing the behavior of the subjects of law and resolving their disputes. In the post-Soviet space, in the Central Asian region in particular, there seems to be a problem in accepting or recognizing the validity or applicability of general principles on the side of local lawyers and judges—specifically where those principles have not been codified in written law (for examples, principles of criminal law not formulated in a criminal code). This may be attributed to the prevailing positivistic approaches to the law in the legal systems of this region; more on those systems see in Chap. 12. Indeed, when the judges realize that the principles that do not figure in a codified legislation as written law—even if they are convincingly argued on the side of the prosecutor or the defense attorney, they will most likely not apply those principles ("show it to me in the black and white on the paper").

Regarding the practical aspects of the application of general principles of law, as maintained by Janis and demonstrated by practice, the most usual approach to general principles of law as a source of international law relies upon techniques of comparative law.[21] The basic notion is that a general principle of law is some proposition of law so fundamental that it will be found in virtually every legal system. When treaties and customary international law fail to offer a needed international rule, a search may be launched in comparative law to discover if national legal systems use a common principle. If such a common principle is found, then it is presumed that a comparable principle should be attributed to fill the gap in international law.[22] In other words, the general principles of law play a gap-filling role from the practical perspective.

As for the national practice, search for general principles of law as an exercise in comparative law is a method familiar to lawyers in the common law tradition where courts often survey judicial decisions from other states. Although such foreign cases are not binding as precedent, the rulings from other jurisdictions do have some persuasive value.[23] In a similar sense, lawyers and judges in the civil law tradition are familiar with the problem of lacunae, gaps in the law, a concept based on the premise that only formal legislative institutions are empowered to make legal rules. When there is no statute available to settle a disputed matter, then there may need to be an explicit authorization permitting courts to fill the legislative vacuum. In this fashion, Article 38(1)(c) of the International Court's Statute can be read as expressly authorizing the Court to draw upon general principles of law to fill gaps left by conventional and customary law.[24] In any case, general principles of law, as gap fillers, are more a feature of court cases than of other kinds of international legal process.[25] And, comparatively speaking, there has been little problem in accepting general principles of law as a source of international law, relative to their perception and treatment and at the domestic level in the post-Soviet space.

---

[21] Janis 2003, p. 56, citing Friedmann 1962.

[22] Ibid.

[23] Ibid.

[24] Ibid., p. 57.

[25] Ibid., p. 58.

8.6 Functions: Regulatory and Protective

The active role of law in the life of society is expressed in its functions. If law affects various spheres of social life—economics, politics, culture, etc., then the concept of functions shows how it affects them and by what means it does so.[26]

The functions of law are the main directions of its influence on social relations and people's behavior and they can be considered in different planes. In many ways, but not in all, they coincide with the functions of state power (see Chap. 3). All main directions of state activity are carried out in legal forms, on the basis of legislative acts that determine the nature and content of this activity. On the one hand, we can distinguish economic, social, environmental and other functions of law, which correspond to identical functions of the state. On the other hand, according to the subjects of state power, one can distinguish between legislative, executive and judicial functions of law.[27]

The functions of law can be divided into types and depending on what specific main tasks they solve. This classification identifies such areas of legal influence that express/reflect the specificity of law as a regulator of social relations, its legal significance for these relations.[28]

Law performs regulatory functions to organize social relations and protective functions to safeguard society from harmful behaviors

The most important task of the legal system of any contemporary civilized country is to streamline social relations, introducing them into the framework of social freedom and justice. The law solves this problem through the *regulatory* function. Another important task of law is the protection of regulated social relations from various types of attacks by offenders. This problem is solved with the help of the *protective* function of law.[29] Let us briefly consider the content of both the regulatory and protective functions of law.

The regulatory function is a direction of legal influence that is designed to ensure a clear organization of social relations, their functioning and development in accordance with the needs of social progress. The regulatory impact of law is associated with positive phenomena of social life that arise in the sphere of property, financial, family and other types of relations.[30] The regulatory function of law affects social relations in the following way.

Firstly, they do so by consolidating these relations in regulatory legal acts. Legal norms give binding legal form to those relationships that form the basis for the

[26] Khropanyuk 2019, at 210.

[27] Ibid., p. 211.

[28] Khropanyuk 2019, at 211.

[29] Ibid.

[30] Ibid.

normal functioning of the society. In particular, the following are enshrined in the rules of law: the order of formation and competence of state bodies, as well as rights, freedoms and responsibilities of citizens.[31]

Secondly, law ensures a high degree of freedom and organization of social relations, their constant improvement and development. This impact of law is manifested in the direct regulation of the organization of social relations in economic, social and other spheres. As a result of legal regulation, the most optimal order of social relations is established, meeting the interests of the entire population of the country. Law contains the possibility of changing and improving existing relations, as well as the ability to bring to life new social relations, the need for which arises at each specific stage of social development (for example, enshrining in legislative acts the various forms of property during the transition from a totalitarian state to a democratic state of law, or a *Rechtsstaat*).[32]

The protective function is a direction of legal influence that is aimed at protecting positive and crowding out relationships that are harmful to society. The protective function is aimed at suppressing and preventing illegal behavior. The protective effect of law is expressed in the following: (a) establishment of prohibitions on commission of illegal acts; (b) establishment of legal sanctions for committing those acts, and (c) direct application of legal sanctions to persons who have committed offenses. These are the main directions of influence of law on social relations. They express the service role of law and its social purpose and goal setting.[33]

Questions for Students

1. *What are the main roles of the principles of law in shaping legal systems and ensuring justice?*
2. *How do general principles of law like justice, democracy, and equality influence legal regulation and enforcement?*
3. *What is the distinction between cross-branch principles and branch principles in law?*
4. *How does the regulatory function of law organize and facilitate societal progress?*
5. *In what ways does the protective function of law address illegal behavior and ensure societal safety?*
6. *How do principles of law act as sources in both national and international legal systems?*

[31] Ibid., pp. 211–212.

[32] Ibid., p. 212.

[33] Ibid.

References

Aristotle (1908) Aristotle's Ethics (in Russian). Saint-Petersburg
Ávila H (2007) Theory of Legal Principles. Springer
Friedmann W (1962) The Uses of "General Principles" in the Development of International Law. 106 Hague Recueil 1, 54 (1962)
Gong GW (1984) The Standard of "Civilization". International Society
Janis MW (2003) An Introduction to International Law", 4th edn. Aspen Publishers
Khropanyuk V (2019) Theory of State and Law (in Russian), 13th edn. Omega-L, Moscow
Organization for Security and Co-operation in Europe (1975) Final Act of the Conference on Security and Co-Operation in Europe. Organization for Security and Co-operation in Europe
Stoilov Y (2022) Principles of Law: Concept and Application. Prospekt, Moscow

Chapter 9
Sources of Law

Contents

Abstract This chapter provides a comprehensive examination of the diverse sources from which law derives its authority, structure, and guiding principles, especially within the complex legal cultures of post-Soviet states. It begins with a broad, pluralistic definition of "source of law" that includes not only formal state-issued instruments but also societal customs, judicial precedents, scholarly doctrine, and general moral principles. The chapter explores how legal custom, emerging from longstanding social practices, becomes a binding legal norm once recognized by the state. Judicial precedent is addressed as a means of ensuring consistency and adaptability, particularly in common law systems, with an emphasis on how precedent could be cautiously integrated into civil law traditions. Juridical doctrine is presented as an influential interpretive tool, often bridging the gap between codified norms and evolving legal needs. Normative legal acts including constitutions, statutes, and by-laws, are acknowledged as the dominant legal source in Romano-Germanic and post-Soviet systems, but with caution against overreliance and positivist rigidity. The chapter also emphasizes the crucial but often underused role of general legal principles such as justice, equality, and fairness, as both sources of law and interpretive tools, especially important where written law is silent or inadequate. Finally, religious texts are recognized as valid sources of law within faith-based legal traditions, while remaining formally excluded in secular legal systems like those of post-Soviet countries. The chapter argues for a more balanced and inclusive legal culture that acknowledges the complementary roles of all these sources in building responsive and legitimate legal systems.

R. Atadjanov, *A Common Theory of Law*, https://doi.org/10.1007/978-94-6265-711-3_9

Keywords Sources of law · Legal custom and tradition · Judicial precedent and case law · Juridical doctrine · Normative legal acts · General principles of law · Religious texts as legal authority · Post-Soviet legal systems · Legal pluralism and positivism

9.1 What Is a Source of Law?

A source of law refers to the origin from which laws derive their authority, legitimacy, and guiding principles. It encompasses the foundational elements that create, shape, and inform legal systems, going beyond mere positivistic notions of written statutes or governmental decrees. In the context of the post-Soviet states, where legal traditions often intermingle with social, cultural, and political dynamics, the concept of a source of law must be understood as pluralistic and adaptive. This inclusive understanding accommodates diverse influences such as historical practices, evolving judicial interpretations, scholarly insights, moral principles, and even religious values that collectively underpin the legal framework. In line with this understanding, the following definition is offered by this author: a source of law is **any origin or foundation, whether formal or informal, from which legal norms derive their authority, legitimacy, and guiding principles, encompassing both official legal instruments and broader societal, cultural, and moral influences.**[1]

Among the key sources of law is **legal custom**, which reflects the practices and traditions of a society that gain binding authority through consistent application over time. Customs are deeply embedded in societal norms and values, making them indispensable in contexts where written laws may be sparse or disconnected from lived realities. **Judicial precedent**, or case law, serves as another significant source, where decisions made by courts establish authoritative examples for resolving similar future disputes. This dynamic source of law highlights the judiciary's role in interpreting and shaping legal norms to address new challenges, thereby promoting flexibility and adaptability in the legal system.

A source of law is the origin or foundation from which legal norms derive authority, legitimacy, and principles, encompassing formal instruments and societal influences

Another vital source is **juridical doctrine**, encompassing the scholarly works of legal theorists and academics that influence the interpretation and development of law. These contributions often bridge gaps between formal legal norms and broader societal needs, offering innovative solutions and critical perspectives. **Normative legal acts**, including constitutions, statutes, and regulations, remain foundational as

[1] The main ideas and descriptions in this chapter are mostly based on the reworked conclusions and useful explanations from *passim* Nersesyants 2016.

explicit expressions of state authority. However, they must interact harmoniously with **general principles of law**, such as justice, fairness, and equality, which transcend specific legal systems and provide universal benchmarks for assessing the legitimacy of all other legal sources.

International law exemplifies this pluralistic approach by recognizing a variety of authoritative sources: **international treaties**, which formalize agreements between states; **customary international legal rules**, derived from consistent and widespread state practices; and **general principles of law**, which ensure coherence and universality across diverse jurisdictions. Additionally, in certain legal systems, religious texts may serve as a source of law, particularly in contexts where faith traditions are deeply interwoven with societal values and governance structures. This multifaceted understanding of the sources of law underscores the need for legal systems in post-Soviet states to embrace a progressive, inclusive framework that reflects the complexity of modern legal and cultural realities.

9.2 Legal Custom

Legal custom, or customary law, refers to **rules that evolve over a long period to regulate human behavior and social relations**, which are eventually recognized by the state as generally binding legal norms. These rules, arising organically from societal practices and traditions, gain legal significance when officially sanctioned by the state. This process of recognition transforms customs into a formal source of positive law, integrating them into the broader legal system while retaining their connection to societal practices.

The sanctioning of customs by the state can occur in various ways. One common approach is implicit or tacit sanctioning, where customs are consistently applied by state bodies such as courts, administrative agencies, or legislative representatives over time, without formal codification. Through repeated application in judicial or administrative decisions, these customs acquire legal authority and are treated as binding norms. Alternatively, customs may be explicitly recognized in written form through normative legal acts, where the state formally acknowledges their significance and incorporates them into the legal framework as positive law.

Another important dynamic between law and custom occurs when established customs are directly incorporated into formal legislation. In such cases, the content of the custom is explicitly reproduced within the text of a normative legal act. However, this does not constitute the recognition of the custom as an independent source of law; instead, the normative legal act itself becomes the source of law, with the custom serving as the inspiration or foundation for the written provision. This illustrates how custom and formal law interact in shaping legal norms, often blending their boundaries.

Customary law evolves from long-standing societal practices recognized by the state as binding norms

A similar relationship is observed in legal systems that rely on judicial precedent. In such contexts, courts may base their rulings on customary practices, effectively giving those customs the status of binding precedent. Here, custom becomes integrated into case law as the foundation for judicial decisions, gaining official legal significance through its transformation into precedent. This highlights the flexible role of custom in different legal systems, whether as an independent source of law or as an element woven into statutes or case law. Through these mechanisms, legal custom serves as a bridge between traditional societal norms and formal legal structures, ensuring the law remains connected to the lived experiences of the community.

9.3 Judicial Precedent

Judicial precedent, often referred to as "case law", or *stare decisis*, is a source of law rooted in the principle that **decisions made by higher courts serve as authoritative guidelines for lower courts when deciding similar cases**. This doctrine ensures consistency, predictability, and stability within legal systems by binding future rulings to established judicial interpretations. Judicial precedent is not merely a reflection of judicial decisions but also a dynamic process wherein courts interpret and apply legal principles to real-world disputes, thereby shaping the development of the law over time. In systems that recognize it as an official source of law, particularly in common law jurisdictions, precedent forms a critical part of the legal framework.

In legal systems where judicial precedent is embraced, such as in the United States, the United Kingdom, and other common law jurisdictions, its role extends beyond mere repetition of past decisions. It enables courts to adapt legal principles to novel circumstances while preserving the foundational values of the system. Precedent offers a bridge between legal tradition and societal change, as courts refine, distinguish, or even overturn previous rulings when necessary. By doing so, judicial precedent ensures that the law remains relevant and responsive to evolving norms, while maintaining continuity and coherence.

Judicial precedent, or case law, involves decisions by higher courts guiding future cases, ensuring consistency and adaptability

The positive aspects of judicial precedent lie in its ability to ensure uniformity and fairness, as similar cases are treated alike, fostering public trust in the legal system. It also allows for adaptability and gradual reform, as courts incrementally modify and refine legal principles to suit contemporary needs. However, its drawbacks include potential rigidity, as lower courts are bound by higher court decisions, even when those decisions may no longer align with societal values. Additionally, the complexity of managing extensive case law can lead to inconsistency, with conflicting precedents causing confusion. Moreover, judicial precedent relies heavily on the interpretive skills and perspectives of judges, which may introduce subjective biases into the legal system.

Although judicial precedent is a defining characteristic of common law systems, its integration into civil law traditions, such as those in continental Europe and post-Soviet states, is not impossible. Civil law systems typically prioritize codified statutes as the primary source of law, but many jurisdictions have begun to recognize the persuasive value of higher court decisions. For instance, constitutional and supreme courts in civil law systems often develop interpretive frameworks that influence lower courts. While full adoption of judicial precedent as a binding source of law may challenge traditional notions of legal hierarchy and codification, a hybrid approach that incorporates precedents as persuasive (but not binding) authority could enrich civil law systems. This approach could enhance consistency, foster judicial creativity, and provide practical solutions to gaps in codified laws, offering a valuable complement to legislative frameworks.

9.4 Juridical Doctrine

Legal, or juridical, doctrine refers to the **body of ideas, principles, constructions, and judgments about law developed by legal scholars**. In certain legal systems, these scholarly contributions hold binding legal authority and are recognized as a formal source of law. Often described as the "law of lawyers", doctrinal provisions carry particular weight in shaping the interpretation and application of legal norms. While legal doctrine is more commonly influential than formally binding in modern legal systems, its importance varies significantly across jurisdictions, reflecting its diverse historical and cultural roles.

Historically, legal doctrine was the primary source of law in Continental European legal systems, particularly during the era of Roman law, when scholarly interpretations dominated legal practice. This dominance persisted until the nineteenth century when state rule-making and codified laws replaced doctrine as the principal source of law. However, even after this shift, doctrine has retained significant influence in the Romano-Germanic legal tradition. Legal doctrine serves as a foundation for interpreting and filling gaps in codified law, guiding courts and legislators in adapting to complex or novel legal issues. It continues to shape the evolution of law, ensuring its coherence with broader theoretical principles.

Legal doctrine comprises scholarly interpretations that influence the development and understanding of legal norms

Legal doctrine also plays a central role in other legal traditions. In Islamic law, for example, scholarly interpretations of religious texts form a crucial part of the legal framework, highlighting the enduring authority of legal doctrine in shaping jurisprudence. In common law systems, while doctrine is not recognized as a formal source of law, it contributes to legal development by influencing judicial reasoning and guiding statutory interpretation. Despite these contributions, legal doctrine faces significant challenges as a source of law. In many jurisdictions, its authority may be questioned because it lacks the formal backing of state endorsement or widespread societal recognition, making its influence more indirect and subject to debate.

One of the primary difficulties with legal doctrine lies in its perception. As it originates from academic or scholarly work rather than state institutions, its authority can be seen as less democratic or representative of societal values. This skepticism can be especially pronounced in systems where state legislation or judicial precedent dominate. Moreover, the diversity of scholarly opinions may create inconsistencies, with competing doctrinal interpretations leading to uncertainty rather than clarity. Despite these challenges, legal doctrine remains a valuable source of law, particularly for addressing theoretical gaps, shaping the development of legal principles, and ensuring a deeper intellectual foundation for legal systems worldwide.

9.5 A Normative Legal Act

A normative legal act is a **written document issued by the state that establishes new legal norms within the current legal system**. It is distinct from other legal acts, such as those applying or interpreting existing legal norms, as well as from non-legal official acts, such as state declarations or statements or concepts. The defining feature of a normative legal act is its "legal-establishing" (or "law-establishing") nature, which introduces new rules to govern social relations. Within the Romano-Germanic legal family, normative legal acts are the principal source of law, forming the backbone of legal regulation in countries adhering to this tradition, including the post-Soviet states.

Normative legal acts exist in various forms, creating a structured hierarchy of legal authority within a national legal system. At the apex of this hierarchy is the Constitution, the supreme legal document that provides the foundational framework for the state's legal and political order. The Constitution is typically adopted through special procedures, such as referenda, constituent assemblies, or parliamentary processes, reflecting its fundamental importance. Below the Constitution are other laws, enacted by the legislature or sometimes through referenda, which address critical societal and legal issues. Subordinate to these primary laws are by-laws, or rather, the sol-called sub-normative legal acts, which include decrees, orders, regulations, instructions, and other administrative acts that provide more detailed rules based on the broader principles established by higher-ranking laws.

A normative legal act is a written document issued by the state to establish new legal norms, forming the backbone of many legal systems

In countries of the Romano-Germanic legal family, such as those in the post-Soviet space, normative legal acts play a dominant role in regulating social relations. They are often considered the most authoritative and comprehensive legal source for addressing the critical aspects of societal organization. Legislative acts, particularly the Constitution and primary laws, are seen as the ultimate legal regulators, governing issues fundamental to the nation's life and legal order. However, this reliance on written norms reflects a broader trend in these legal systems: the dominance of positivistic legal theory, which prioritizes codified laws over other sources of law, such as general principles, judicial precedents, or customary norms.

This overreliance on normative legal acts is particularly evident in the post-Soviet states, where judges, lawmakers, and state officials often limit their interpretations and decisions to codified laws. This tendency marginalizes other sources of law, such as uncodified principles, jurisprudential doctrines, and customary rules, which could provide greater flexibility and adaptability in governance. As a result, legal systems in the region tend to favor strict textual interpretations of the law, sometimes at the expense of fairness, justice, and broader societal considerations. This positivist approach, while offering clarity and predictability, risks neglecting the dynamic and evolving nature of law, limiting its ability to respond effectively to contemporary social and legal challenges.

9.6 General Principles of Law[2]

General principles of law are foundational ideas that express the essence, purpose, and structure of the legal system. These principles reflect the broader social, moral, and political values that law seeks to uphold, such as justice, fairness, and freedom. They serve as a measure of legal coherence and guide the formation, evolution, and application of legal norms. Unlike specific legal rules, general principles of law operate as overarching concepts, shaping the interpretation and implementation of all branches of the legal system. Their influence extends beyond codified laws, providing a framework for evaluating the validity and legitimacy of legal norms and practices.

In Romano-Germanic legal systems, and particularly in the post-Soviet states that are part of this tradition, general principles of law occupy a critical position as a source

[2] For the definition of principles of law as well as for a more detailed listing of general principles, see Chap. 8.

of law. These principles underpin the legislative process, ensuring that laws align with societal values and constitutional ideals. They are intended to guide not only the drafting of normative legal acts but also their application by courts and administrative bodies. However, the role of general principles in these post-Soviet systems, i.e., in contexts where legal positivism dominates, is frequently undermined. In practice, they are often neglected, misapplied, or entirely overlooked. This overemphasis on codified norms means that unless a general principle is explicitly codified, its practical application by lawyers, judges, and public officials remains limited.

These are foundational ideas, such as justice and equality, guiding legal systems and ensuring coherence across branches of law

One of the main challenges in the application of general principles in post-Soviet legal systems is the tendency to treat codification as a prerequisite for legitimacy. Principles like justice, equality, and legality are only consistently applied when explicitly mentioned in constitutions or normative acts (but it is not guaranteed even in case of codification as compared with some other sources such as normative legal acts). This approach reflects a deep-rooted positivist legal culture, where the focus is on formal, written sources of law rather than broader, uncodified ideas. As a result, general principles are often reduced to abstract declarations rather than being integrated meaningfully into everyday legal practice. This not only weakens their influence but also undermines their potential to address complex legal and social challenges that codified laws alone cannot resolve.

Despite these challenges, general principles of law remain indispensable for ensuring the cohesion, adaptability, and fairness of legal systems. Their application fosters unity across legal branches and serves as a corrective mechanism when written laws fall short or conflict with fundamental values. In post-Soviet states, greater emphasis on these principles could help balance the rigidity of positivism with the need for more equitable and dynamic legal solutions. To achieve this, legal education and judicial practice must shift toward a more integrated approach, recognizing that the legitimacy of law derives not only from its formal enactment but also from its alignment with the enduring values that general principles represent.

9.7 Religious Texts

Religious texts, often referred to as sacred books, serve as a significant source of law within systems of religious law. These texts, regarded as divinely inspired or spiritually authoritative, provide binding legal norms for the religious communities that adhere to them. For example, in Muslim law, the Qur'an and the Sunnah (sayings and practices of the Prophet Muhammad) are foundational texts that govern not only spiritual matters but also social and legal behavior within the Islamic community. Similarly, religious texts such as the Bible, Torah, and Vedas hold comparable authority in Christian canon law, Jewish law, and Hindu law, respectively. These sacred writings often include moral guidelines, rituals, and legal prescriptions, shaping the everyday lives of believers and ensuring cohesion within religious communities.

It is important to note that religious law functions primarily within the context of the corresponding religious community and is distinct from national-state legal systems. Religious legal systems, such as Muslim law or Hindu law, govern the behavior of adherents as members of a faith group rather than as citizens of a nation-state. For instance, Muslim law does not equate to the legal systems of predominantly Muslim countries, and Hindu law is not synonymous with the legal framework of India. Instead, these religious laws operate alongside, or sometimes in tension with, secular legal systems, often focusing on matters like personal status, marriage, inheritance, and religious obligations. The separation of religious law from national legal systems underscores the spiritual and community-oriented nature of these sources of law.

Religious texts, like the Qur'an or Bible, serve as legal sources in religious communities, governing moral and legal behaviors

Despite their spiritual foundation, the role of religious texts as sources of law poses challenges, especially in contexts where secular state systems dominate. Integrating religious norms into state law can be contentious, raising issues of inclusivity, equality, and human rights in pluralistic societies. Moreover, within religious communities themselves, the interpretation of sacred texts can vary, leading to disputes over their application and relevance in modern contexts. Nevertheless, religious texts remain a vital source of legal and moral guidance for millions of people worldwide, providing not only spiritual meaning but also a framework for organizing social relations in accordance with deeply held beliefs. In the post-Soviet space, where legal systems are of secular nature, religious texts do not serve as officially recognized sources of law.

Questions for Students

1. *What constitutes a source of law, and why is it essential for the legitimacy of legal systems?*
2. *How does legal custom transition from societal practice to a recognized source of law?*
3. *What role does judicial precedent play in ensuring legal consistency and flexibility?*

4. *How do juridical doctrines contribute to the interpretation and evolution of legal systems?*
5. *Why are normative legal acts considered the primary source of law in many jurisdictions?*
6. *What is the significance of general principles of law in bridging gaps where written statutes fall short?*
7. *How do religious texts function as sources of law within their respective communities, and what challenges arise when integrating them into secular systems?*

Reference

Nersesyants V (2016) Common Theory of Law and State (in Russian). Norma INFRA-M, Moscow

Chapter 10
System and Structure of Law

Contents

Abstract This chapter examines the internal system and structure of law, presenting it as an organized hierarchy of norms, institutions, and branches that regulate social relations. At its core is the legal norm, defined by a three-part structure: hypothesis, disposition, and sanction. These norms are classified by function (prohibitive, obligatory, empowering, and incentive) and by their role in either substantive or procedural law. Legal institutions are collections of norms regulating specific social relations, while branches and sub-branches organize these institutions into broader legal domains. The chapter distinguishes between public and private law, showing how each addresses different societal and individual needs. It also clarifies the difference between the legal system, i.e., the substance of law, and the legislative system, i.e., its formal expression. International law is explored as a unique, decentralized framework based on sovereign equality and mutual consent. The chapter concludes with a breakdown of how law operates in practice through four forms of implementation: compliance, execution, use, and application, demonstrating how legal norms are translated into real-world behavior.

Keywords Legal system and structure · Legal norms (hypothesis, disposition, sanction)) · Legal institutions and branches · Public law vs. private law · Legislative system vs. legal system · Forms of law implementation · Substantive and procedural law · International law and sovereignty · Post-Soviet legal framework

R. Atadjanov, *A Common Theory of Law*, https://doi.org/10.1007/978-94-6265-711-3_10

10.1 Introduction

The legal system is a doctrinally defined category and structure encompassing legal norms, as well as the legal institutions and branches of law that organize and integrate these norms. From a doctrinal perspective, the characterization of law as a system of norms implies that the legal norm serves as the fundamental systemic and systemic/ structural element of law. Within this framework, the legal system comprises a wide array of norms designed to regulate diverse social relations. However, there is a natural correspondence between the nature of the social relations being regulated and the characteristics of their normative legal regulation. Homogeneous social relations are governed by norms of a similar order, reflecting a cohesive approach to their regulation. Consequently, legal norms within the legal system are systematically grouped into legal institutions and further into broader branches of law, ensuring an organized and structured regulatory framework.[1]

10.2 Legal Norms

As previously noted in Chap. 2, legal norms constitute the most significant category within the broader framework of social norms. They form a fundamental component of law, representing its foundational element and serving as the primary concept underpinning the legal system. All legal structures, legislative processes, and the mechanisms for the formation and implementation of law are intrinsically linked to the concept of a legal norm.

A legal norm is a **general rule for regulating social relations**, according to which its addressees must, under certain conditions (hypothesis), act as subjects of certain rights and obligations (disposition), otherwise certain unfavorable consequences for them will follow (sanction).[2] Alternatively, it may also be formulated as follows: a legal norm (or legal rule) in its most simplified form can be defined as an **abstract, non-personalized, generally binding, formally defined rule of conduct established or sanctioned by society, acting as a regulator of social relations, provided with a certain compulsion and designed for repeated application**.

Legal norms emerge as the product of deliberate human activity, shaped by the collective interests of individuals, societal groups, and broader social strata. Consequently, the creation of legal norms is a multifaceted process influenced by a range of factors and conditions within society, including its international context.

Legal norms are designed to **regulate not all social relations but those deemed most essential to the functioning and well-being of society or specific segments**

[1] The main ideas and descriptions in this chapter are mostly based on the reworked conclusions and useful progressive explanations from *passim* Nersesyants 2016, as well as from *passim* Morozova 2021.

[2] See further down below in this same section for the description of all three elements of the legal norm.

of the population. This regulation is conducted through mechanisms that operate at the socio-political level, with legal norms often articulated through formalized state structures. The societal origins and functions of legal norms are central to their character.

Typically, legal norms encapsulate and formalize existing, recurring patterns of social relations. However, they also have a dynamic role in shaping societal evolution by programming the development of certain relationships and directing their progression in accordance with desired objectives. A legal norm functions as a model for regulated social relations that align with the ideals and priorities of society. These norms articulate relationships that are considered desirable and beneficial from a societal perspective.

Legal norms possess a distinct essence, form, and content. Their essence reflects the interests they serve and the collective will they express on behalf of society. While the essence of law may not be explicitly discernible in an isolated legal norm, it becomes apparent when norms are examined collectively—whether within specific legal institutions, branches of law, or the legal system as a whole.

A legal norm is a general, binding rule established to regulate behavior, featuring components like hypothesis, disposition, and sanction

A legal norm is characterized by several defining features that distinguish it from other forms of social regulation. These features ensure its role in governing social relations systematically and effectively:

General and abstract nature: A legal norm is designed to regulate general categories of relationships rather than specific, isolated situations. It addresses patterns of interaction that manifest across a multitude of individual instances, providing a universal framework for diverse factual circumstances.

Impersonality: Legal norms apply universally to an indefinite number of subjects. When a legal act refers to a specific individual or entity, it does not constitute a legal norm but rather an individual legal prescription tailored to that particular case.

Social/volitional nature: A legal norm appeals to the free will of participants in social relations, presupposing that the addressees have the autonomy to choose among behavior options. This feature ensures that legal norms are meaningful only in the context of voluntary human action. Additionally, legal norms embody the collective societal will, reflecting an intent to regulate specific types of relationships.

Close connection with society and its formal institutions: Legal norms are established or formally sanctioned by competent authorities within society's institutional framework. This connection underscores the organized and systematic nature of legal regulation.

Protection by organized enforcement mechanisms: The prescribed behavior within a legal norm is enforced through structured measures, including mechanisms of societal coercion. These measures aim to restore violated rights and impose penalties for noncompliance with obligations or prohibitions.

Formal certainty: Legal norms are characterized by precise definitions of the conditions under which they apply, the legal consequences they entail, and the qualifications required of participants in legal relations. This certainty ensures that norms are consistently interpreted and applied within recognized sources of law by those responsible for their enforcement.

Representative nature: Legal norms govern behavior through reciprocal relationships involving rights and obligations. Typically, a legal norm includes a right vested in one party and a corresponding obligation for another. However, not all legal norms adhere strictly to this structure; for instance, prohibitive, recommendatory, and specialized norms—such as conflict-of-law or operational norms—may deviate from this model.

General bindingness: Legal norms impose binding obligations on all entities or specific categories of persons as outlined within the norm. Their violation entails consequences enforced by societal mechanisms, ensuring compliance and accountability.

Systematic integration: A legal norm operates as part of a cohesive legal system. It interacts with other norms through various relationships—aligning, subordinating, or elucidating their content—thus contributing to the overall coherence of the legal framework.

Multiple application: A legal norm is intended for repeated application, addressing an unlimited number of instances of conduct (or non-conduct) that fall within its scope.

Presence of structure: A legal norm exhibits an inherent structure, typically comprising elements such as a hypothesis, disposition, and sanction. This structure facilitates its operational clarity and practical enforcement.

The **disposition** of a legal norm refers to the mutual rights and obligations of the participants involved in the relationship governed by the norm. Within this framework, each party possesses both rights and obligations. Furthermore, the right of one party inherently corresponds to the obligation of the other, and vice versa. This reciprocal relationship between rights and obligations underpins the bilateral nature of legal norms and, by extension, the law as a whole. Legal norms embody a dual granting-obligating (attributive-imperative) character, whereby the assignment of a right is inseparably linked to a corresponding obligation. The regulatory function of granting a right is rendered ineffective without the imposition of a corresponding obligation. For the proper regulation of social relations, the rights and obligations of the participants must be harmonized. This requires that the rights of one party precisely correspond to the obligations of the other and that this alignment is reciprocal. Such mutual correspondence is a fundamental principle of the legal regulation of social interactions, ensuring fairness and balance in the relationships it governs. Derived from the Latin term "dispositio" (meaning "arrangement"), the disposition of a legal norm signifies the deliberate and mutually agreed arrangement of the rights and obligations of the involved parties. This precise alignment ensures that the rights and obligations of one participant are directly correlated with those of the other, reflecting the essential structure and purpose of legal norms in regulating social relations.

The **hypothesis** of a legal norm defines the specific conditions under which the rights and obligations articulated in the norm's disposition come into effect. It outlines the circumstances or prerequisites that must be present for the legal norm to operate and regulate behavior effectively. A hypothesis serves to link an abstract, general model of behavior to specific circumstances, such as a particular case, time, or place. It often establishes criteria or conditions for applicability, such as the individual's citizenship within a given society, the attainment of a specified age, or the time frame during which the legal norm comes into force. By doing so, the hypothesis provides the necessary contextual framework for the operation of the legal norm.

The **sanction** of a legal norm refers to the adverse consequences imposed on a party that violates the requirements set forth in the norm's disposition and hypothesis. These consequences, unfavorable to the violating party, arise from the breach of rights and obligations established in the disposition, as well as the conditions governing their applicability as defined by the hypothesis. Understanding the interrelation between these structural elements—hypothesis, disposition, and sanction—is crucial for comprehending the logical and functional coherence of legal norms. Additionally, it is essential to distinguish between the form and content of a legal norm, as this distinction significantly impacts its interpretation and application within the framework of contemporary law. The form relates to how the norm is expressed or structured, while the content pertains to the substantive provisions it seeks to regulate.

Legal norms fulfill a variety of regulatory functions, which differ in nature, content, objectives, and goals. This diversity underpins the existence of various types of legal norms, distinguished by specific criteria used for their classification and grouping.

According to the *sectoral* criterion, legal norms are categorized based on their affiliation with specific branches of law, such as constitutional, civil, criminal, family, and labor law. Additionally, the division of law into substantive and procedural branches gives rise to two distinct types of legal norms.

Substantive legal norms constitute the foundation of primary legal regulation, governing the core aspects of social relations. These norms define rights, obligations, and legal statuses directly related to societal interactions. **Procedural** legal norms establish the framework and processes for the practical implementation and enforcement of substantive legal norms. They regulate how legal rights and obligations are applied and upheld within formal systems of justice. While procedural norms are sometimes viewed as secondary, this does not imply lesser importance; instead, they serve a complementary role, ensuring the effective operation of the legal system itself. As legal systems develop, the number and complexity of procedural norms tend to increase, resulting in the emergence of distinct procedural branches of law, such as criminal procedural law and civil procedural law. The critical role of procedural norms lies in their establishment of an orderly framework for the operation of the law, thereby ensuring its consistent application and enforcement.

Legal norms can also be categorized based on the forms of their regulatory impact or the modality of their regulatory force. This classification yields several distinct types of norms.

Prohibitive norms impose bans on specific actions deemed unlawful. These norms are particularly prevalent in branches such as criminal and administrative law, where they define prohibited behaviors (e.g., crimes or administrative offenses). However, prohibitive norms also exist in other branches of law. For instance, certain provisions in civil codes may prohibit acquiring rights or obligations under the name of another person, thereby ensuring the integrity of civil transactions. **Obligatory** norms prescribe actions that must be performed by legal subjects. These norms create binding duties that are essential for the functioning of specific social or legal relationships. **Empowering** norms grant rights or permissions, enabling legal subjects to engage in particular actions or relationships. These norms are instrumental in fostering autonomy and enabling participation in legal systems. **Incentive** norms encourage certain behaviors by offering benefits or rewards. These norms are often used to promote socially desirable actions and align individual interests with broader societal goals.

10.3 Legal Institutions

A legal institution refers to **a set of interconnected legal norms that collectively regulate a specific category of social relations**. These norms are uniform in nature and address particular aspects of societal interaction within a given branch of law. For instance, in civil law, the legal institution of property encompasses a cohesive group of norms governing property relations. Similarly, other institutions within civil law, such as those regulating persons, representation, or limitation periods, are defined by their focus on specific types of relations or legal concepts. The same principle applies across other branches of law. In criminal law, legal institutions include areas such as crime, punishment, the criminal liability of minors, and crimes against individuals. In family law, examples of legal institutions would include marriage and its dissolution, the rights and obligations of spouses, and the alimony responsibilities of family members. These institutions serve as integral components of the broader legal system, ensuring structured regulation of distinct areas of societal and legal interaction.

Based on the above, one can say that a legal institution is a **cohesive group of legal norms interconnected by subject-functional links that regulate a specific category of social relations**, thereby achieving relative stability and operational independence. Within a legal institution, sub-institutions may exist, differing in the scope of regulation and the range of norms they encompass. For instance, the sub-institution of legislative initiative operates within the institution of lawmaking in constitutional law, while the sub-institution of referendum belongs to the institution of democracy. Similarly, in civil law, sub-institutions such as property insurance, personal insurance, and entrepreneurial risk insurance function within the broader institution of insurance.

A legal institution is a group of related legal norms addressing a specific category of social relations, such as property or family law

Legal institutions can be classified as sectoral or inter-sectoral. **Sectoral** institutions consolidate groups of norms within a single branch of law. Examples include the institution of donation and the institution of inheritance in civil law, as well as the institutions of the presidency, electoral law, and local self-government in constitutional law. **Inter-sectoral** institutions, on the other hand, regulate social relations that intersect multiple branches of law. For example, the institution of human rights spans both international and constitutional law; the institution of contract applies to labor, civil, international, state, and administrative law; and the institution of legal responsibility extends across nearly all branches of law. This division reflects the multifaceted nature of legal institutions and their role in addressing complex and interconnected social relationships.

10.4 Legal Branches and Sub-Branches

A branch of law comprises a **cohesive set of legal norms regulating a specific category of social relations**. Within a given branch, legal institutions represent distinct groupings of relatively independent norms that address particular aspects of these relations, forming a unified and homogeneous legal framework. Branches of law are commonly divided into **substantive** and **procedural** categories, reflecting the nature of the norms they encompass.

Branches of **substantive law**, such as, for example, civil law, labor law, and criminal law, establish the foundational rights and obligations of legal entities within particular areas of social regulation. **Procedural law**, which includes branches such as civil procedural law and criminal procedural law, prescribes the methods and processes for implementing substantive norms, ensuring their practical realization. Procedural norms provide legal certainty to relationships among legal entities at all stages of law-making, law enforcement, and judicial activities. By offering structured legal forms and processes, procedural law serves as a vital safeguard for individual rights and freedoms, facilitating the effective functioning of the legal system as a whole. The degree of proceduralization within a legal system is a key indicator of the system's overall development and sophistication.

Branches of law, like civil or criminal law, represent coherent sets of norms regulating broad areas of societal interaction, divided into substantive and procedural categories

Sub-branches of law emerge within larger branches to address more specialized areas of legal regulation. For example, within substantive law, constitutional and administrative law often give rise to corresponding procedural sub-branches, such as constitutional procedural law and administrative procedural law. Similarly, sub-branches of substantive law may develop within a given branch, as seen in the evolution of social law (or social security law) within the broader framework of labor law. Sub-branches typically originate from one or more legal institutions, uniting a group of homogeneous norms to address specific regulatory needs. Over time, and under certain conditions—such as the emergence of new spheres of social relations or significant changes in the principles of legal regulation—a sub-branch may evolve into a distinct and independent branch of law. This process reflects the dynamic nature of the legal system, which adapts (or is supposed to adapt) to meet the growing complexity and diversity of societal relations.

10.5 Public Law and Private Law

The division of law into public law and private law is a well-established concept in legal literature, reflected in the categorization of branches into those associated with public and private domains. This division is typical for the family of continental civil legal systems (to which post-Soviet states' legal systems belong) and as a rule is not adopted in the common law systems. Branches of public law include constitutional law, administrative law, criminal law, civil procedural law, and criminal procedural law, among others. Private law, by contrast, is typified by branches such as civil law. Similarly, international law is divided into international public law and international private law, reflecting parallel distinctions at the global level. The recognition of public law, and its distinction and interaction with private law, fundamentally places the state—its organization, activities, and the powers of its bodies—under the authority of law. This signifies that the state and its institutions are not endowed with any special or exclusive rights but are instead subject to the same legal framework as other subjects of law, including private individuals. The state, its bodies, and officials must comply with the general rules of law, acting within the bounds of its universal principles.

Public law focuses on collective societal interests, while private law emphasizes individual rights and equality in legal relationships

However, the division of law into public and private domains should not be understood as a strict segregation of societal and individual interests into separate norms or branches. It is not the purpose of public law branches, such as constitutional or criminal law, to exclusively articulate what is socially beneficial (e.g., public goods, interests, or welfare), nor is it the purpose of private law branches, such as civil, family, or business law, to solely reflect private interests or benefits. Instead, the true significance of this division lies in the capacity of all legal norms and branches to balance and integrate both public and private interests. Legal norms, irrespective of their classification, are tasked with recognizing and expressing the interconnected and mutually reinforcing nature of public and private goods, ensuring their unity in the broader legal framework.

The features characteristic of public law include:

1. The *imperative* nature of norms, requiring strict compliance with prescribed rules;
2. A focus on satisfying *public and social interests*, emphasizing collective welfare;
3. *Hierarchical relationships* among the subjects of public relations, where authority and subordination are central;
4. The *unilateral expression of will* by subjects, particularly state entities, in the exercise of their powers;
5. A *broad sphere of discretion* granted to state bodies and officials, allowing them significant leeway in decision-making;
6. Sanctions of a *predominantly punitive nature*, designed to deter violations and enforce compliance;
7. A high degree of *centralized regulation*, ensuring uniformity in the application and enforcement of rules.

In contrast, private law is characterized by the following features:

1. The *equality of subjects* in legal relations, where parties engage on an equal footing;
2. An *optional content of legal regulation*, allowing for flexibility and adaptability in agreements;
3. The *free expression of will* by subjects in exercising their rights and entering into legal relationships;
4. A focus on *satisfying personal or corporate interests*, prioritizing individual or organizational needs;
5. *Self-responsibility for obligations and actions*, ensuring accountability is borne by the parties involved;
6. Sanctions that are primarily *restorative in nature*, aimed at rectifying harm rather than punishing wrongdoing;
7. *Decentralization*, where subjects can determine the terms of their behavior by mutual agreement, as seen in examples like a marriage contract in family law, a contract for work in civil law, or the terms of a copyright agreement.

The distinction between public and private law remains a contentious issue in legal science. According to this author, that is due to the mutual penetration and interplay of public and private principles across various branches of law. The boundaries between the two are inherently flexible, reflecting the interconnected nature of societal and individual interests. However, this fluidity does not alter the fundamental public or private law affiliation of a particular branch of law, which remains grounded in its primary focus and regulatory framework.

10.6 System of Law and System of Legislation

The system of legislation refers to the collection of normative legal acts that reflect the substantive and structural characteristics of law. In essence, legislation serves as the external form through which law is expressed. This definition aligns with a broad understanding of legislation, though a narrower interpretation limits it to a set of laws alone.

The legal system consists of norms, institutions, and branches that organize and integrate legal rules to regulate social relations cohesively

Regardless of whether legislation is understood broadly or narrowly, the legal system and the legislative system are deeply interconnected. Both are shaped by social factors such as economic, political, spiritual, and cultural influences. However, they differ in key respects:

- The legal system develops objectively in response to the social relations present in a given society, whereas the legislative system is largely subjective, shaped by the deliberate will and purposeful actions of the legislator.
- The legal system represents the internal structure of law, focusing on its substantive content. In contrast, the legislative system represents the external structure, emphasizing the formal organization of law.
- The legal norm is the foundational element of the legal system, while the normative legal act constitutes the primary unit of the legislative system.
- The legal system acts as the guiding framework for the legislative system. Rooted in the objectively existing patterns of social development, the legal system serves as the primary foundation upon which the legislative system is built. The legislative system should align closely with the legal system, reflecting processes such as integration, differentiation, or changes in the scope of legal regulation. The legal system thus provides essential direction to legislators in adopting, amending, or repealing laws.
- The legislative system encompasses a broader range of materials compared to the legal system. Beyond differentiating materials by their subject and method of regulation, the legislative system includes regulations and other provisions that address a wide variety of social relations, often employing multiple regulatory methods or their combinations. Consequently, the legal system is more strictly organized than the legislative system.
- While the legal system is primarily structured through horizontal connections based on sectoral distinctions, the legislative system incorporates both sectoral

and hierarchical relationships. These include variations in the legal force of normative legal acts and, where applicable, federal divisions within the legislative framework.

The legislative system is the formal expression of law, comprising normative legal acts like constitutions and statutes that mirror the substantive framework of the legal system

The legislative system also includes complex formations organized by functional purpose or by specific spheres of public administration. Examples of such formations include economic, customs, and agricultural legislation, among others. These functional and sectoral layers illustrate the legislative system's diverse and multidimensional nature, reflecting its adaptability to societal needs and governance structures.

10.7 International Law as a Special Legal Phenomenon

International law, or the law of nations, constitutes a distinct body of legal norms governing the relationships between sovereign States. It establishes the rights and obligations of these States in their mutual interactions, forming a framework for coexistence and cooperation at the international level. Although its scope has expanded to include non-State entities such as international organizations, the system of international law fundamentally arises from the existence of independent sovereign States. Public international law governs inter-State relations, while private international law addresses conflicts of laws within national legal systems that involve a foreign element, such as cross-border residency, property, or marital relations. This dual dimension highlights the unique breadth of international law, bridging public and private spheres in ways that distinguish it from purely domestic legal frameworks.

The uniqueness of international law lies in its nature as a **system of legal norms that transcends national boundaries** while lacking the centralized legislative and enforcement mechanisms typical of domestic legal systems. Unlike national systems, where a sovereign authority enacts laws and enforces compliance, international law operates on the basis of **mutual consent** and **recognition** among sovereign States. Treaties, customary practices, and principles of general international law constitute its primary sources, creating a decentralized system where compliance depends largely on the willingness of States to honor their commitments. Despite these differences, international law maintains a systematic and coherent structure, capable of regulating a wide array of international interactions, from peace and security to trade and environmental protection.

One of the most notable challenges of international law is its **lack of a centralized enforcement mechanism**. While national legal systems rely on courts, police, and other institutions to ensure compliance, international law must rely on mechanisms such as diplomacy, economic sanctions, and the collective actions of States through international organizations. The International Court of Justice, the International Criminal Court, and similar international bodies provide avenues for dispute resolution and accountability, but their jurisdiction often depends on the voluntary acceptance of States. This reliance on consent underscores the structural differences between international and national legal systems and is frequently cited as a limitation of international law. Nevertheless, this decentralized system does not undermine its legitimacy as a legal order but rather reflects the realities of a world composed of sovereign and equal States.

International law is best understood as a "**horizontal law of coordination**" rather than a "vertical law of subordination". In national systems, laws are imposed from above, with clear hierarchies and subordinate relationships between citizens and the state. In contrast, international law functions on the principle of equality among States, each of which retains its sovereignty while agreeing to adhere to shared rules. This horizontal structure fosters cooperation and coordination, facilitating agreements and resolving disputes without subordinating one State to another. It reflects a legal order that prioritizes mutual respect and collaboration over coercion, embodying a fundamentally different paradigm of legal regulation.

Despite its deficiencies when compared to national legal systems, international law fulfills a critical role in maintaining global order and addressing issues that transcend national boundaries. Its capacity to adapt to changing circumstances and accommodate diverse interests has allowed it to evolve into a comprehensive system that regulates complex international relations. The flexibility and resilience of international law demonstrate its enduring relevance as a legal phenomenon, capable of integrating disparate legal traditions and principles into a coherent framework that supports the peaceful coexistence and cooperation of the global community.

10.8 Operation (Implementation) of the Law

The purpose of law lies in regulating social relations and guiding human behavior. However, legal norms and regulatory acts, no matter how carefully crafted, remain ineffective unless they are implemented—realized in the behavior and interactions of society's members. Without this realization, the law remains dormant, unable to fulfill its intended purpose.

The implementation of law refers to the process through which the prescriptions of legal norms are translated into life through the **lawful behavior of participants** in social relations, including government bodies, officials, public associations, and individuals. This implementation is essential for the law to achieve its regulatory objectives. Closely related to the concept of implementation is the action of law. While implementation involves the direct legal mechanisms that enforce or embody legal norms, the action of law is a broader concept. It encompasses not only the legal regulation of social relations but also the informational, psychological, and social impacts that law exerts within society. The action of law thus reflects both its formal mechanisms and its broader influence on human behavior and societal dynamics.

At its core, the action of law is predicated on the law's ability to influence the actions and behavior of individuals, thereby shaping social relations. This influence extends beyond mere compliance with legal norms, as it embodies the transformation of abstract legal models into concrete actions and activities. Law exists insofar as it acts, i.e., its essence is realized through its dynamic impact on participants in social relations. This dynamic nature captures the transformation of abstract norms into tangible realities, reflecting the state's authoritative imposition of legal obligations and their realization in the lived experiences of society's members.

The concept of the action of law can be understood as encompassing all forms of its legal force. In practical terms, it signifies the concretization of abstract legal norms within the real behavior of individuals and institutions. More broadly, it involves an informational, motivational, and regulatory impact on social relations, operating within specific spatial, temporal, and personal contexts. The action of law is, therefore, a multidimensional process that exists at various levels—affecting individuals, groups, and society as a whole. It demonstrates the integration of law into everyday life, fostering a dynamic interplay between abstract legal values and their manifestation in practice.

Law becomes effective through its implementation, which occurs via compliance, execution, use, and application, ensuring legal norms shape social behavior

Several key processes underline the operation of law. First, the *development of tools* for legal regulation provides society with mechanisms to influence its various spheres of life. Second, the *actual use of these tools* within lawful activities ensures the rule of law in social relations, achieving tangible results. The action of law is not confined to its implementation but extends to the materialization of its inherent principles—justice, freedom, and equality—within the conduct of individuals, the operations of institutions, and the collective life of society. This translation of abstract values into real-world practices underscores the central role of law as a dynamic force in shaping and sustaining the social order.

The implementation of law exhibits several defining characteristics that underline its essential role in translating legal norms into practical reality. First and foremost, implementation is inherently tied to **lawful behavior**. This includes both active engagement in legal actions and passive compliance, such as refraining from unlawful conduct. Only lawful behavior fulfills the prescriptions of legal norms, whereas unlawful behavior represents their violation, standing outside the scope of proper legal implementation.

Legal norms, as articulated in normative legal acts, achieve their actual realization through the process of implementation. This process ensures that the instructions, regulations, and prescribed rules of conduct established by law are brought into effect **within society**. As such, the implementation of law serves as a fundamental mechanism for maintaining law and order, reinforcing the stability and predictability necessary for societal cohesion.

The process of implementation is inherently linked to the interests of the subjects to whom legal rights and obligations apply. Those who hold subjective rights have a vested interest in seeing the law implemented, as it is through this process that their rights are protected and realized. At the same time, implementation takes diverse forms, reflecting the variety of social relations it governs. Differences in the content of legal norms, the means of influencing behavior, the roles of subjects within the legal system, and the mechanisms available for enforcing the law all contribute to this diversity. The multiplicity of factors shaping legal implementation underscores its complexity and adaptability to varying circumstances.

Based on the nature and degree of activity involved, the implementation of law is generally categorized into four distinct forms: **compliance**, **execution**, **use**, and **application**. Compliance involves adherence to prohibitive norms by refraining from forbidden acts, while execution entails the active performance of duties imposed by law. The use of law refers to the voluntary exercise of subjective rights by legal subjects, and the application of law involves authoritative action by competent bodies to resolve disputes, enforce obligations, or protect rights. Each of these forms highlights a different aspect of the implementation process, collectively illustrating the multifaceted nature of law's operation within society.

Compliance with the law involves refraining from actions prohibited by legal norms. This form primarily implements prohibitive norms, such as those found in areas like criminal, administrative, and tax law. As a passive form of legal operation, compliance often occurs without recognition or formal acknowledgment, reflecting the everyday adherence of individuals and organizations to established societal rules and expectations.

The **execution** of the law encompasses active efforts to fulfill obligations imposed by legal norms. This form reflects the operation of binding norms, such as those requiring the fulfillment of contracts, the payment of taxes, or the provision of alimony to minor children. By actively engaging in these duties, individuals and entities contribute to the structured functioning of social relations and the maintenance of legal order.

The **use** of the law is demonstrated in the exercise of rights granted by legal norms. Empowering norms operate in this form, enabling individuals to take advantage of opportunities such as the right to vote, the right to housing, or the right to own private property. The exercise of these rights is discretionary, meaning that individuals are not obligated to use them. However, this principle applies predominantly to individuals; when societal institutions or officials fail to exercise their assigned powers, it can undermine legal and social frameworks, as their roles often carry inherent responsibilities.

Most legal norms are realized through these three forms: compliance, execution, and use. These forms rely on the voluntary or obligatory actions and inactions of participants in societal relations, reflecting a decentralized approach to legal operation. In some instances, however, specialized mechanisms are required to ensure the proper **application** of the law to specific circumstances. This process, often referred to as *law enforcement*, involves the structured activities of competent societal bodies, local authorities, or community representatives acting within the framework of established rules. These activities may include creating new legal facts, granting specific rights, imposing obligations, or facilitating the resolution of disputes and the development of relations. By doing so, the legal system integrates both individual actions and collective responsibilities, ensuring the coherent operation of law within society.

Questions for Students

1. *What are the key elements of the system of law, and how do they interact to regulate social relations?*
2. *How is a legal norm structured, and what roles do hypothesis, disposition, and sanction play in its operation?*
3. *What is the function of legal institutions, and how do they contribute to the broader legal framework?*
4. *How do substantive and procedural branches of law differ in their roles and objectives?*
5. *What distinguishes public law from private law, and how do they balance collective and individual interests?*
6. *How does the legislative system relate to the legal system, and why is alignment between the two important?*
7. *What are the four forms of law implementation, and how do they ensure that legal norms influence real-world behavior?*

References

Morozova L (2021) Theory of State and Law (in Russian), 6th edn. Norma, Moscow
Nersesyants V (2016) Common Theory of Law and State (in Russian). Norma INFRA-M, Moscow

Chapter 11
Interpretation of Law

Contents

Abstract This chapter explores the concept, methods, and types of legal interpretation, emphasizing its central role in the implementation and correct application of legal norms. Interpretation is defined as the process of clarifying and explaining the true meaning of legal rules in specific contexts, bridging the gap between abstract legal texts and concrete social realities. The chapter outlines the structure of interpretation through its object (normative text), method (legal-logical analysis), and subject (actual meaning), and explains how these interact to derive regulatory significance. It presents key interpretive methods such as grammatical, logical, systematic, historical-political, teleological, special-legal, and functional, each contributing uniquely to uncovering legislative intent. Types of interpretation are classified as official (normative and case-specific) and unofficial (ordinary, professional, and doctrinal), with differing authority and legal effect. The chapter also distinguishes between literal, expansive, and restrictive interpretation, cautioning against unjustified extensions or contractions of legal meaning. Ultimately, it reinforces that interpretation ensures legal certainty, harmonizes the "letter" and "spirit" of law, and is vital for sound legal reasoning and consistent application across legal systems.

Keywords Legal interpretation · Methods of interpretation · Official vs. unofficial interpretation · Literal, expansive, and restrictive meaning · Legislative intent · Legal certainty · Doctrinal interpretation

R. Atadjanov, *A Common Theory of Law*, https://doi.org/10.1007/978-94-6265-711-3_11

11.1 The Object and Subject of Legal Interpretation

Interpretation of a legal norm involves **clarifying and explaining its true content, tailored to the specific conditions under which it operates**. This process encompasses all forms of implementation, including the application of legal norms. As a distinct legal concept, the interpretation of law holds a unique significance and serves a pivotal role within the framework of categories that define and characterize the operation of law.[1]

In its abstract and general form, the normative content of a legal rule is captured in the text of the relevant source of positive law. However, the implementation of law, including its enforcement, inherently requires a specific and contextualized approach. The abstract and general provisions of a static legal norm become concretized during its application to particular circumstances, relationships, and contexts—taking into account specific facts, locations, and times.

Interpretation of law entails accurately clarifying and explaining the regulatory significance of this concretization. **Clarification** is a legal-cognitive process that involves identifying, comprehending, and substantiating the intended meaning of the norm being interpreted. Every interpretation includes this essential step, which allows the interpreter to discern the true content of the norm, often as a preliminary understanding for themselves.

Explanation, on the other hand, refers to the various external, public expressions of the results of clarification. These may take formal or informal forms and are intended for broader use. Given the distinctions between these activities, it is crucial not to conflate clarification (interpretation-clarification) with explanation (interpretation-clarification). For proper interpretation of a legal norm, it is essential to identify its object, method, and subject.

Legal interpretation is the process of clarifying and explaining the meaning of legal norms to ensure their correct application in specific contexts

The object of legal interpretation is the **text of the normative-legal (or law-establishing) act** that corresponds to a specific regulatory case or situation in which the interpreted norm is expressed. The method of interpreting a legal norm involves a **coherent, legal-logical analysis** of the text of the norm's source and its application to the specific situation. This process emphasizes their mutual alignment, interrelation, and unity to identify and define the structural elements and overall framework of the norm, along with its regulatory significance in the context of the specific situation. The subject of interpretation is the **actual, current regulatory-legal meaning** of the legal norm that is intended to be applied in the specific situation under consideration.

[1] The main ideas and descriptions in this chapter are mostly based on the reworked conclusions and useful progressive explanations from *passim* Nersesyants 2016, as well as from *passim* Morozova 2021.

The connection between the object, method, and subject of legal interpretation can be understood as follows: the legal-logical interpretation (method) of the normative text (object), when analyzed in relation to a specific regulatory case or situation, reveals, formulates, substantiates, and determines the actual regulatory-legal meaning (subject) of the legal norm applicable to the case. Thus, understanding the object of interpretation through the method of interpretation results in identifying the subject of interpretation—where the subject represents a methodically analyzed object.

This process reflects the cognitive essence of interpreting the true content of the legal norm: determining its actual regulatory-legal meaning for the given regulatory case or specific situation. This situationally specific and relevant regulatory-legal meaning, as uncovered and substantiated through interpretation/clarification, represents the true essence of the legal norm being sought for implementation in the specific case.

11.2 Means of Legal Interpretation

When interpreting a legal norm, the analysis goes beyond its direct content to include its legal connections with other regulations, internal structural elements, and its broader relationship with social phenomena. The clarification of a legal norm is achieved through specific techniques, commonly referred to as **means, or methods, of interpretation**, which serve as tools for determining the norm's content and the legislative intent embedded within it. Legal scholarship identifies several methods of interpretation, including **grammatical**, **logical**, **systematic**, **historical-political**, **teleological**, **special-legal**, and **functional** approaches.

The **grammatical** method (also known as the **philological** or **textual** method) focuses on the analysis of individual words and their lexical relationships within the text. This includes the examination of punctuation, conjunctions, introductory words, and other linguistic elements that influence the meaning of the legal provision.

The **logical** method involves analyzing the logical relationships between different provisions of a legal norm or legal act. This method is grounded in the principles of formal logic, recognizing that the intended meaning of a legal provision may not always align precisely with its literal wording. Instead of focusing on individual words, this approach examines the concepts, phenomena, and interrelations that the legal text conveys.

The **systematic** method is based on the premise that every legal norm exists within a broader legal system and interacts with other norms. Under this approach, the meaning of a legal provision is clarified by analyzing its position within a particular legal institution, branch, or sub-branch of law. This method also identifies the legal interconnections between the interpreted norm and other related norms, helping to define its scope, the subjects to whom it applies, and any inconsistencies or conflicts within the legal framework. Additionally, it facilitates the examination of the interplay between the General Part and the Special Part of legal codes, thereby enabling a more comprehensive understanding of the legal norm's content and significance.

Interpretation methods include grammatical, logical, systematic, historical-political, teleological, special-legal, and functional approaches, each focusing on different aspects of the legal text

The **historical and political** method of interpretation involves identifying the specific conditions and circumstances—economic, political, social, and others—that led to the creation of a particular legal norm. This includes analyzing the goals and objectives that society aimed to achieve when regulating a given sphere of public relations. Failing to consider the historical and political context in which a legal norm or act was adopted may lead to formally correct but substantively flawed decisions that contradict the original objectives of legal regulation.

The **teleological** (or, alternatively, **purpose-oriented**) interpretation ensures the correct, precise, and consistent understanding and application of legal norms. It focuses on uncovering the intended goals behind the enactment of a legal act, both its immediate and long-term objectives. This method is particularly essential when significant changes occur in the socio-political landscape or when there are fundamental shifts in the legal regulation of public relations.

The **special-legal** method of interpreting law involves analyzing the technical and legal mechanisms used to express the intent of the legislator. In other words, this method is grounded in the principles of legal technique. Through the examination of legal terms, concepts, and structures, the content of legal norms is clarified. Special-legal interpretation generally includes the following techniques:

a. *Normative interpretation*: determining the normativity of a rule of conduct;
b. *Clarification of legal constructions*: analyzing the structural features of legal formulations;
c. *Determination of the legal field*: identifying the branch of law to which the norm belongs;
d. *Terminological interpretation*: defining legal terms precisely;
e. *Comparative analysis*: contrasting the content of the norm with annotations, exceptions, and other interpretative tools.

The **functional** method of interpretation considers the specific conditions and factors influencing the implementation of a legal norm, including contextual elements such as time, place, and other relevant circumstances. For example, when determining the appropriate amount of alimony for minor children, a court must assess the financial and family status of the parties, along with other significant considerations.

To ascertain the precise meaning of a legal norm and the intent behind it, not all methods are applied simultaneously—typically, only one or two are used. However, in particularly complex cases, a comprehensive approach involving multiple interpretative methods may be necessary.

11.3 Types of Interpretation: Understanding of the Law and Clarification of the Law

Interpretation and explanation of legal norms differ depending on the entities providing them. Based on this criterion, legal interpretation is classified into **official** and **unofficial** types. **Official** interpretation is provided by authorized bodies or officials whose powers to interpret legal norms are established through specific legal acts. This type of interpretation is binding on other subjects, holds legal significance, and carries legal consequences by ensuring a uniform understanding and application of legal norms. In contrast, **unofficial** interpretation is given by individuals or entities that do not hold official status and lack the authority to provide legally binding interpretations. Such interpretations take the form of recommendations or advisory opinions and do not produce legal consequences or possess authoritative force.

Official interpretation is further categorized into **normative** and **case-specific** (or **casual**) interpretation. **Normative** interpretation involves explanations of a general nature that apply to all future cases where the legal norm may be enforced. It is often required when the legal text is ambiguous, the legislator's intent is inadequately expressed, or law enforcement agencies and officials misinterpret the provision. As a result, normative official interpretation serves as a general legal guideline, ensuring consistency in law enforcement and applying to an unlimited number of cases, much like normative legal regulation.

Normative interpretation is divided into **authentic** (i.e., author's) and **legal** (permitted, or delegated) types. **Authentic** official interpretation originates from the body that issued the given act. In other words, all law-making bodies have the authority to provide an authentic interpretation, but only in relation to their own acts. For example, the legislator can interpret all legislative acts, while the Government may only interpret its own regulations. The legislative body may also authorize the relevant executive bodies to explain a particular law, but such an explanation would constitute an act of legal interpretation rather than an authentic one.

Interpretation can be official (normative or case-specific) or unofficial (ordinary, professional, or doctrinal), with each type differing in authority and applicability

Legal interpretation, being subordinate, is carried out either by instruction from the body that issued the legal act or by a body that has been granted this authority by the legislator. For instance, the Supreme Court, when generalizing judicial practice, provides courts with explanations on how to apply the law in specific categories of cases. These explanations are binding on all courts. Another example of official normative legal interpretation is the decisions of the Constitutional Court (if applicable, meaning, if it exists), particularly when it interprets the Constitution.

Casual interpretation is also a form of official interpretation. It is provided by a competent authority for a specific case, addressing a particular legal matter, and is binding only in that instance. The need for such interpretation typically arises when current legislation is misapplied in a given legal dispute. Although casuistic interpretation is mandatory only for the case in question, it often serves as a precedent or guidance for other bodies dealing with similar cases or applying the same legal norm.

Unofficial interpretation can be either oral or written and is generally classified into three types: **ordinary**, **professional**, and **doctrinal** (or **scientific**). **Ordinary** interpretation of a legal norm may be provided by any individual in everyday life, including during discussions on draft laws. **Professional**, or **competent**, interpretation is offered by individuals with specialized legal education, such as lawyers, prosecutors, notaries, and legal advisers. **Doctrinal** interpretation is carried out by specialized research institutes, individual scholars, or groups of scientists in academic articles, legal literature, commentaries, and legal reviews of draft laws. While this type of interpretation is not legally binding, its influence is derived from the authority of the scientific institution or the credibility of the scholar providing it. It plays a significant role in shaping both lawmaking and law enforcement. Commentaries on legal codes and key laws are widely used in judicial and legal practice. Although they cannot be cited as direct justification for legal decisions, they serve as essential reference materials and contribute to reinforcing the rule of law.

As is well known and as is believed by this author, the outcome of interpreting a legal norm should result in complete clarity and precision, eliminating any ambiguity or multiple meanings. Ideally, there should be no discrepancies between the "spirit" and the "letter" of the law, meaning that the intended meaning of the norm should align perfectly with its textual expression.

Based on the results of interpretation, three types can be distinguished: **literal** (or **adequate**), **expansive** (or **broad**), and **restrictive**. **Literal**: in most cases, the legislator's intent is understood exactly as it is expressed in the text of the norm. In other words, the wording of the legal provision and its actual meaning are fully aligned. When this occurs, it is said that the "spirit" and "letter" of the law do not diverge but coincide.

Expansive interpretation, also referred to as broad interpretation, occurs when the verbal expression of the norm is narrower than its actual meaning. In such cases, the "spirit" of the law extends beyond its "letter", requiring an interpretation that captures its broader intent rather than its strictly literal wording.

Restrictive interpretation is applied in cases where the textual expression of a norm is broader than its actual substantive meaning. For instance, circumstances that aggravate punishment, as listed in the Criminal Code or other relevant legislation, are always interpreted restrictively or literally and can never be given a broad interpretation. Both broad and restrictive interpretations are considered exceptional approaches, while literal interpretation remains the standard method. It is generally accepted that legal norms imposing restrictions, stricter liability, or sanctions should not be interpreted broadly. However, if the text of a norm includes phrases such as "and other conditions or circumstances", "other", "etc.", or "and so on", a broad interpretation is implied.

The interpretation of legal norms and regulatory acts is closely linked to their specification. The refinement of regulatory provisions most commonly occurs during subordinate lawmaking, but legal norms may also be specified in the course of their interpretation. This is particularly characteristic of constitutional court decisions, where legal provisions are clarified and given precise meaning within the framework of judicial review.

Questions for Students

1. *What is the main purpose of legal interpretation, and how does it contribute to the implementation of legal norms?*
2. *How do the methods of interpretation, such as grammatical and logical, differ in their approaches to clarifying legal norms?*
3. *What distinguishes official interpretation from unofficial interpretation, and what are some examples of each?*
4. *How can expansive and restrictive interpretations impact the application of a legal norm in specific cases?*

References

Morozova L (2021) Theory of State and Law (in Russian), 6th edn. Norma, Moscow
Nersesyants V (2016) Common Theory of Law and State (in Russian). Norma INFRA-M, Moscow

Chapter 12
Lawful Behavior and Legal Responsibility

Contents

Abstract This chapter explores the dual concepts of lawful behavior and legal responsibility as central elements in the regulation of social relations. It begins by defining lawful behavior as conduct aligned with legal norms and examines its types such as marginal, conformist, habitual, and socially active, based on motivation and internalization of legal values. The chapter stresses the role of legal culture and conscious engagement in fostering stable, socially beneficial conduct. The second part analyzes unlawful behavior (offenses), outlining its legal characteristics and structural elements: subject, subjective side (guilt), object, and objective side (harm and causality). It categorizes offenses into criminal, administrative, civil, disciplinary, procedural, and international violations. The final section presents legal responsibility as the coercive response to offenses, detailing its key features, goals, and principles: legality, justice, inevitability, expediency, individualization, guilt-based responsibility, and protection against double jeopardy. Different forms of legal responsibility (criminal, administrative, civil, disciplinary, material) are distinguished by their enforcement mechanisms and legal consequences. The chapter emphasizes that balanced, principled legal responsibility reinforces legal order and encourages voluntary compliance in post-Soviet societies.

Keywords Lawful behavior types · Legal responsibility · Offense structure (corpus delicti) · Criminal and civil liability · Principles of legal responsibility · Legal consciousness and motivation · Post-Soviet legal culture

R. Atadjanov, *A Common Theory of Law*, https://doi.org/10.1007/978-94-6265-711-3_12

12.1 Lawful Behavior and Its Types

The primary objective of legal regulation within society is the establishment of **lawful behavior** among all participants in legal interactions. Legislative efforts are directed precisely toward achieving this outcome, ensuring that individuals conduct themselves in accordance with established legal norms. Consequently, the study of the patterns of lawful behavior formation, its underlying motives, and the mechanisms that facilitate compliance with legal prescriptions holds significant theoretical and practical value. A fundamental aspect of legal assessment involves comparing an individual's actions with the requirements set forth by the legal system. Post-Soviet systems are no exception here. Such a comparison makes it possible to differentiate between lawful conduct, unlawful acts, and behavior that remains legally neutral. The latter category encompasses actions that either do not necessitate legal intervention or have been intentionally left within the sphere of individual discretion, allowing persons the **freedom to choose** their course of action in alignment with their interests.[1]

The evaluation of lawful behavior is grounded in its correlation with legal norms. Conduct that aligns with legal requirements or does not conflict with them is regarded as appropriate, desirable, preferable, and legally endorsed. Within legal scholarship, lawful behavior is typically defined by three principal characteristics: (a) *full compliance with legal norms*, reflecting strict adherence to prescribed legal obligations; (b) *absence of contradiction with the legal order*, meaning that the conduct remains within the established legal boundaries; (c) *the absence of explicit legal prohibition*, signifying that such behavior, while not necessarily mandated, remains permissible within the framework of legal regulation.

In defining the concept of lawful behavior and its typology, one of the most comprehensive and precise formulations characterizes it as **an activity within the realm of law's social influence, shaped by an individual's cultural and moral values as well as their life experience, and founded on the conscious fulfillment of legal goals and requirements**. This definition underscores several fundamental aspects: first, that lawful behavior is a *deliberate and volitional manifestation*; second, that its evaluation is conducted through a *comparison with the objectives and mandates of the law*; and third, that its internal regulators, or motivational determinants, are rooted in an individual's *moral and cultural orientations*, as well as their personal life experience.

Several key characteristics are inherent in lawful behavior: **social utility**, **prevalence**, **consciousness**, and **active compliance with legal requirements**. The **social utility** of lawful behavior reflects the fundamental interest of society in maintaining legal order, ensuring respect for law, and upholding its provisions. Its **prevalence** is determined by the fact that lawful conduct is characteristic of a significant portion of the population; without it, society would be unable to function in an orderly and stable

[1] The major ideas and descriptions in this chapter are mostly based on the reworked conclusions and useful progressive explanations from *passim* Nersesyants 2016, but also from *passim* Morozova 2021.

manner. **Consciousness** manifests in the ability of individuals to make an informed choice between lawful and unlawful behavior, as this choice is made freely and deliberately, guided by personal interests and needs, and shaped within the framework of a consciously developed model of conduct. **Activity in lawful behavior** entails an independent civic and moral stance, an awareness of the social consequences of one's actions, and the ability to weigh personal interests against those of other individuals and of society as a whole.

Lawful behavior manifests in a variety of forms, making it possible to classify its types according to different criteria. One of the most significant classifications is based on *motivation*, that is, the internal regulation of human conduct. From this perspective, four primary types of lawful behavior can be distinguished: **marginal**, **conformist**, **stereotypical** (or **habitual**, or **positive**), and **socially active**.

Marginal behavior, derived from the term meaning "borderline" or "on the edge", is motivated primarily by fear—whether of legal responsibility, punishment, or social condemnation. It reflects a state of internal conflict, characteristic of individuals who have a predisposition toward unlawful conduct but refrain from engaging in it solely due to the perceived risk of sanctions or disapproval from their immediate environment. This type of lawful behavior is exhibited by individuals who do not accept the law or its prescriptions on an internal, value-based level but nonetheless comply out of personal calculation or fear of negative consequences. The defining feature of marginal behavior is its transitional and unstable nature, positioned between lawful and unlawful conduct. Such individuals may be inclined to violate legal norms when convinced of impunity, yet adhere to them when punishment appears unavoidable. Despite formal compliance with the law, there is an underlying disapproval of its provisions, making this type of lawful behavior particularly precarious and dependent on external enforcement mechanisms.

Lawful behavior is conduct that complies with legal norms, reflecting individual and societal alignment with legal standards

Marginal individuals are distinguished by a distortion of traditions, value systems, and both social and legal orientations. Within this category, two primary subgroups can be identified. The first is the risk group, which includes refugees and neglected minors—individuals whose marginal status results from adverse external circumstances rather than deliberate rejection of social norms. The second is the asocial group, encompassing vagrants, beggars, homeless individuals, prostitutes, former prisoners struggling to reintegrate into society, persons suffering from alcohol or drug dependence, and street children. This group is often characterized by asocial tendencies and unlawful conduct, necessitating not only the legal responsibility of these individuals but also comprehensive measures aimed at overcoming their marginalization and facilitating their reintegration into society.

Conformist behavior, by contrast, arises from adaptation to external conditions and is expressed through passive compliance with legal norms. It results from an individual's subordination of personal actions (or inaction) to the prevailing behavior of their social environment. In other words, a person observes legal norms primarily because those around them—family, colleagues, and acquaintances—do so as well. Conformism is marked by adaptability to external circumstances, the absence of independent positions, and uncritical acceptance of the existing social and legal order without any attempt to influence it. While this form of behavior ensures compliance with the law, it is often purely external, as the individual does not necessarily internalize legal or moral values but rather conforms to the expectations of the group to which they belong in an effort to secure social approval and avoid disapproval.

Stereotypical (habitual, or positive) behavior is characterized by the consistent adherence to legal norms as a result of an ingrained habit of acting lawfully. For individuals exhibiting this type of behavior, compliance with legal requirements becomes second nature, requiring no conscious effort or deliberation. They act in accordance with the law automatically, as lawful conduct is deeply embedded in their behavioral patterns. This habit is rooted in a stable and internalized attitude toward legal norms, supported by a firm belief in their necessity and social utility. Such stability, in turn, arises from a conscious and profound assimilation of legal values, which reinforces the individual's unwavering commitment to lawful conduct.

Socially active behavior represents the highest form of lawful conduct, as it is motivated not merely by habit or external influences but by a genuine internalized agreement with the law and its underlying principles. Individuals who exhibit this form of behavior demonstrate solidarity with legal norms, consciously choosing to be guided by them not out of compulsion or routine but out of moral conviction. This form of behavior is not only socially beneficial but also reflects a proactive and engaged approach to legal compliance, where individuals do not merely observe legal prescriptions but actively contribute to their realization in practice. It is characterized by a deep perception of legal ideas, a strong personal commitment to justice, and an inclination toward initiative and creativity in the implementation of legal norms. Socially active behavior is most commonly found among individuals with a high level of legal culture and consciousness/awareness, who impose strict ethical and legal standards upon themselves and expect the same from others.

This author is convinced that society cannot remain indifferent to the motives that drive lawful behavior. As previously noted, socially active and habitual behavior are considered the most desirable forms of compliance, as they contribute to legal stability and social cohesion. The classification of lawful behavior holds particular significance for legislators, who must take into account different motivational factors when establishing legal rules. To promote preferred types of behavior, appropriate incentives and rewards must be devised, while targeted sanctions should be established to deter individuals with unstable legal orientations from potential violations. Additionally, scientifically grounded predictions regarding the likelihood of unlawful conduct among certain individuals are essential for the timely development of preventive measures aimed at addressing deficiencies in legal consciousness before they manifest in unlawful actions.

12.2 Unlawful Conduct (Offense), Its Basic Characteristics, Elements and Forms

An offense represents the social and legal antithesis of lawful behavior, with the two exhibiting fundamentally opposing characteristics. As a form of antisocial and unlawful conduct, an offense stands in direct contradiction to established legal norms. From a social perspective, such behavior either directly violates or has the potential to harm the rights and interests of individuals, groups, and society as a whole. It disrupts the stability of social relations, hinders their orderly development, and contributes to disorganization within the legal and social framework.

The concept of an offense is one of the fundamental categories in legal science. Each branch of law defines offenses within its domain, including criminal, administrative, disciplinary, environmental, and other types of legal violations. Despite the diversity of offenses, all share common characteristics that distinguish them as legally significant wrongful acts. The following key features of any offense are most commonly identified.

First, an offense is always an act, which may take the form of an **action** or **inaction**. It represents **conscious and deliberate behavior** by an individual capable of controlling their actions. Mere thoughts, emotions, or intentions hold no legal significance unless they materialize in concrete acts.

Second, an offense is characterized by its **illegality**, meaning that it contradicts an established legal norm and exceeds its permissible boundaries. The scope of illegality is typically determined by legal frameworks, which take into account historical conditions, national traditions, public sentiment, and patterns of antisocial behavior.

Third, any offense carries **social harm or social danger**, as it disrupts public order and causes damage to legally protected interests—whether public, private, or individual. The severity of this harm varies. In legal science, the term social danger is traditionally applied to crimes and certain administrative offenses, while other categories, such as civil, disciplinary, or procedural offenses, are often described in terms of social harm. The impact of an offense can take multiple forms, including material or moral harm, compensable or irreparable damage, and consequences that are physical, psychological, or social in nature. Harm to public relations does not necessarily require tangible destruction; it may arise from actions such as the formation of a criminal group that has not yet committed a crime or the production of a forged document that remains unused. Thus, an offense is present not only when an unlawful act results in concrete harm but also when it possesses the potential to lead to harmful consequences.

Fourth, an offense requires the **guilt of the person committing the act**. The individual must have acted with **free will**, meaning they had the ability to choose between lawful and unlawful conduct. If a person was deprived of this ability due to physical or psychological coercion, guilt is absent, and consequently, no offense can be attributed to them.

Finally, an offense must be committed by a **legally responsible subject**, which may be either an individual or a legal entity. This capacity for legal responsibility, or tortious capacity, is determined by specific criteria. For individuals, it depends on factors such as age and mental state, while for legal entities, it is defined by their legal status. The determination of tortious capacity involves both socio-legal and medical-legal considerations, which form the basis for deciding whether a subject can be held accountable under the law.

The defining features outlined above make it possible to conceptualize an offense as **an unlawful and culpable act (whether an action or inaction) that either causes or has the potential to cause harm to society, individuals, or legal entities and is committed by a subject with legal capacity**. Another widely accepted definition describes an offense as a culpable and unlawful act committed by a legally capable person or persons, resulting in harm to society and leading to legal liability.

All of these features are essential, and the absence of any one of them prevents an act from being classified as an offense. To systematically identify all necessary characteristics of an offense, legal science employs an abstract conceptual framework known as the legal composition of an offense. This framework serves as a model for typical offenses, encapsulating the essential elements that distinguish different types of violations. It also provides the basis for imposing legal responsibility, as an act cannot be recognized as an offense—and legal liability cannot be assigned—unless all its defining elements are present.

The legal composition of an offense (otherwise known as *corpus delicti*, or elements of offence/crime) consists of four fundamental elements: **subject**, **subjective side**, **object**, and **objective side**.

The **subject** of an offense may be either an individual or a legal entity. Individuals can be held responsible for nearly all types of offenses and are the exclusive subjects of crimes. As previously mentioned, individuals must possess tort capacity, which varies depending on the type of offense and the legal framework of a given jurisdiction. In many post-Soviet legal systems, criminal liability begins at 16 years of age, while for certain serious crimes—such as murder, theft, robbery, extortion, terrorism, and hostage-taking—liability applies from 14 years of age. Administrative liability typically applies from 16 years of age, while full civil liability is established at 18 years of age, though it may be granted earlier in cases of marriage or emancipation (from 16 years of age).

An offense is an unlawful and culpable act that causes or has the potential to cause harm to individuals, society, or legally protected interests

Legal entities, in turn, are recognized as subjects of civil offenses and certain administrative violations, such as those related to environmental protection, taxation, and construction regulations. Just as individuals must meet the requirements for tort capacity, legal entities must also possess legal responsibility, which is established from the moment of their official registration.

The **subjective side** of an offense (also known as *mens rea*) is defined by the presence of guilt, which is typically understood as an individual's mental attitude toward their behavior and its consequences. Guilt manifests in two primary forms: intent and negligence. Intent, in turn, is divided into direct and indirect, while negligence is classified as recklessness or carelessness. These categories originate from the field of criminal law and are determined by three key factors: an individual's awareness of the illegality of their actions, their anticipation of potential harmful consequences, and their attitude toward those consequences.

If a person is aware of the unlawful nature of their conduct, foresees the harmful consequences, and actively desires their occurrence, guilt takes the form of direct intent. If the individual acknowledges the illegality of their behavior, foresees the harmful consequences, and does not wish for them to occur but nevertheless allows them to happen, guilt is classified as indirect intent. A person's actions are considered reckless negligence when they are aware of the illegality of their behavior, foresee possible harmful consequences, but carelessly presume they will be able to prevent them. If a person fails to foresee the harmful or dangerous consequences of their actions but, given the circumstances, should have and could have foreseen them, their guilt is in the form of carelessness due to negligence. These distinctions primarily apply to individual offenders.

In civil offenses, legal entities are most frequently the liable subjects. Within civil law, guilt is generally defined as the failure of a legal entity to exercise the level of care and prudence required by the nature of its obligations and the conditions in which it operates. In this context, guilt consists of an omission or failure to take due care and diligence in fulfilling legal duties. Civil law also recognizes intent and negligence, with negligence being further divided into gross and slight. However, distinguishing slight negligence from an absence of guilt can be difficult. Notably, in civil law, the specific form of guilt rarely has a qualifying impact on liability, meaning that the degree of intent or negligence does not significantly alter the extent of legal responsibility. This remains a subject of debate within civil law scholarship and is typically examined in greater detail within specialized legal studies.

In the broadest sense, the **object** of an offense consists of social relations that are or may be harmed and that are protected by law. Beyond this general object, legal doctrine also identifies a generic object, which refers to a category of homogeneous social relations that are affected by the offense, such as public safety, environmental protection, or administrative order. Additionally, each offense has a specific object, which may include individual rights or tangible assets, such as a person's life, health, dignity, or property. Every offense, therefore, simultaneously affects general, generic, and specific legal objects. In other words, the object of an offense refers to what the wrongful act is directed against, specifically the **values** and **interests** that suffer harm as a result of the offense. These may include property, life, health, public order, and other **legally protected interests**. Like the subject of an offense, the object is clearly defined within legal norms, ensuring that the law identifies and safeguards the rights and interests that offenses threaten.

The **objective side** of an offense, also known as *actus reus*, is defined by three key elements: an externally manifested act, its socially harmful consequences, and the necessary causal link between them. Like other components of an offense, the objective side is clearly established in legal norms. For instance, in the case of bodily injury, the law distinguishes between serious, less serious, and minor harm, each of which constitutes a distinct legal classification of an offense as outlined in criminal law/legislation. The objective side of an offense is thus characterized by several essential elements: (a) the unlawfulness of the act; (b) the harmful or socially dangerous consequences that result from it; (c) a direct and immediate causal link between the act and its consequences, which must not be incidental or accidental; (d) the place, time, conditions, and other relevant circumstances surrounding the offense, as well as the method and means by which it was committed.

While these circumstances serve primarily as additional factors influencing liability measures, they do not fundamentally determine whether an offense has occurred. However, if all four elements of the legal composition of an offense are present, the act is legally recognized as an offense and consequently gives rise to legal liability.

In the common theory of law, offenses are primarily classified according to their branch of law. One of the most widely used classifications is based on the degree of social danger or harm, dividing offenses into crimes and other offenses (misdemeanors), which include administrative, civil, disciplinary, and procedural violations.

Crimes represent the most socially dangerous category of offenses, as they threaten the most fundamental social relations and values. The defining characteristics of a crime include social danger, guilt, illegality as established by criminal law, and punishability. Criminal legislation classifies crimes into different categories based on the maximum severity of the punishment, particularly in terms of imprisonment, as well as the form of guilt. Crimes are generally categorized as minor, medium, serious, and especially serious. The authority to determine whether an act constitutes a crime and to impose a corresponding criminal penalty rests exclusively with the court.

Administrative offenses involve violations that affect individual rights and freedoms, public health and sanitation, moral standards, public order and safety, property, legitimate economic interests, and the proper functioning of government institutions. An administrative offense is defined as an unlawful and culpable act or omission by an individual or legal entity that carries administrative liability under administrative law. A key characteristic of administrative offenses is that the offender does not have an employment or service relationship with the authorities or officials imposing administrative penalties. In many cases, administrative offenses differ from crimes only in the degree of public danger they pose. Unlike criminal penalties, which can only be imposed by a court, administrative penalties may be issued by designated authorities and officials through administrative proceedings.

Civil offenses, or torts, occur within property and non-property relations and involve violations of civil legislation, contractual obligations, and general business practices, resulting in harm to an individual or their property. In this context, harm is understood as any reduction in personal or material benefits. Unlike other types of offenses, civil liability may arise even in the absence of guilt, as in cases of strict liability, where a debtor may be held accountable for damages regardless of fault. Civil offenses typically require the compensation of damages and other financial losses, the restoration of violated rights, the fulfillment of unfulfilled obligations, or the annulment of unlawful transactions. Consequently, the sanctions for civil offenses are primarily restorative and compensatory rather than punitive in nature. Civil offenses may arise from contractual obligations, occurring when one party fails to fulfill its duties under a contract, or they may result from non-contractual violations, such as breaches of civil law norms.

Disciplinary offenses involve violations of labor legislation, including an employee's failure to perform assigned work duties or breaches of workplace discipline, such as absenteeism, tardiness, or noncompliance with orders from the administration. These offenses typically disrupt internal organizational regulations, as well as discipline within educational, service, and other institutional settings. Sanctions for disciplinary offenses are determined by labor legislation, internal workplace rules, departmental charters, regulations, instructions, and other local legal acts.

Procedural violations occur when legally established procedures are not followed in court proceedings, constitutional justice, criminal procedural law, arbitration, or administrative processes. Such violations may include the failure of a witness, defendant, or expert to appear in court, the failure to meet deadlines for reviewing citizens' complaints in administrative bodies, or the improper filing of legal claims. Sanctions for procedural violations range from fines to the invalidation of legal acts adopted as a result of such violations, such as the annulment of improperly registered marriages.

International violations are characterized by unlawful actions that cause harm to the legally protected interests of other states or the values of international community as a whole. The most serious international crimes, or the so-called core crimes, include genocide, crimes against humanity, war crimes, and the crime of aggression. The prosecution of these offenses involves international tribunals and courts, and such crimes are not subject to a statute of limitations or amnesty. Less severe internationally wrongful acts often involve failures to protect diplomatic representatives, violations of trade obligations, and similar infractions. These violations typically do not provoke an international response but are instead addressed through internal measures or diplomatic negotiations.

The **causes** and **conditions** leading to offenses remain a complex issue that has yet to be fully resolved by legal science or other social disciplines. In legal science, there is an ongoing debate regarding the social and biological causes of offenses. While some scholars emphasize social factors as the primary determinants, there is growing recognition of the need to consider psychophysical and biological characteristics that influence an individual's legal attitudes and behavior. However, as this author believes, a comprehensive explanation of the causes of offenses should be based on the *interrelation of social and biological factors in human behavior*, particularly in the process of choosing a course of action. A thorough study of both general patterns of offenses and the specific causes of individual types of crimes is essential in developing effective strategies for addressing them.

It is also important to distinguish between the causes and conditions of offenses. Legal scholarship generally defines a cause as being in a direct and natural connection with its effect, meaning that it directly brings about an offense. A condition, on the other hand, does not necessarily cause an offense on its own but, in combination with other circumstances, may contribute to its occurrence by either intensifying or weakening the effect of a particular cause.

Among the commonly identified conditions that contribute to the commission of offenses are low standards of living and economic hardship, low levels of general and legal culture, deficiencies in legislation, inefficiency in law enforcement, a mismatch between the interests and goals set forth in legal norms and those pursued by the offender, and lifestyle deformations such as alcoholism and drug addiction, particularly prevalent among certain groups, including youth. Other causes and conditions of offenses may emerge at different points in time, requiring a combination of economic, legal, and organizational measures to address them effectively.

Additionally, some immediate situational factors may serve as direct triggers for offenses. These include emotional and psychological states such as resentment, jealousy, personal trauma, or a profound sense of humiliation, all of which may act as motivating impulses that contribute to an individual's decision to commit an offense.

In recent years, legal scholars have increasingly acknowledged the objective inevitability of offenses, arguing that the idea of completely eradicating crime and offenses is utopian. Instead, the focus should be on reducing offenses to a manageable level, ensuring they do not pose a significant threat to social stability. In this regard, particular emphasis is placed on preventive and educational measures, including legal awareness and legal education, which are key to fostering lawful behavior within society.

12.3 The Concept of Legal Responsibility

There is no unified interpretation of legal responsibility in legal science. Various perspectives and approaches exist, reflecting the complexity and multifaceted nature of this phenomenon. When analyzing legal responsibility, the following premises should be considered:

1. Legal responsibility embodies the defining characteristics of all legal phenomena—formal certainty and a structured procedural framework for implementation.
2. Legal responsibility is inseparable from the offense and arises as its direct consequence.
3. Legal responsibility is linked to the enforcement of sanctions established by legal norms.
4. Legal responsibility is associated with authoritative enforcement measures and legal coercion.

Thus, legal responsibility involves the **application of legally prescribed coercive measures against an offender, resulting in deprivations of a personal, organizational, or property nature**.

The key characteristics of legal responsibility include:

- It necessarily involves *legal coercion.*
- It is not coercion in a general sense but rather a *structured measure* of coercion, with a clearly defined scope and quantitative limits.
- It is directly connected to an *offense*, follows its commission, and is directed at the offender.
- It entails *negative consequences for the offender*, including restrictions on rights (such as deprivation of liberty or parental rights) or the imposition of new obligations (such as financial payments or mandatory actions). The nature and extent of these deprivations are determined by the sanctions specified in legal norms.

Legal responsibility is the application of legally prescribed measures against an offender, involving sanctions for violations of legal norms

The enforcement of such deprivations and coercive measures occurs within law enforcement activities, carried out by competent legal authorities in strict accordance with procedural regulations. Legal responsibility cannot exist outside a clearly defined procedural framework.

The interpretation of legal responsibility as an applied measure follows from the content of legal norms. The mere commission of an act prohibited by criminal law does not, in itself, constitute or cause legal responsibility. Furthermore, until a formal judicial decision (such as a court sentence) is issued, the person is presumed innocent and is therefore not subject to criminal responsibility. In certain cases, an individual who has committed an offense may be exempted from responsibility, meaning that the law enforcement process is not initiated. In other instances, responsibility may be imposed, but the offender may be exempted from punishment, thereby avoiding specific deprivations while still being legally recognized as responsible for the offense.

The goals of legal responsibility represent a specific manifestation of the broader objectives of law, which include the consolidation, regulation, and protection of social relations. These goals shape both the regulatory and protective functions of law. Since legal responsibility plays a role in the implementation of the protective function, its general purpose can be defined as ensuring the stability of the existing legal order and maintaining public order.

When legal responsibility is applied to a specific offender, its function extends beyond the general protection of social relations to include the punishment of the guilty party. At the same time, the application of coercive measures also serves the broader aim of preventing future offenses. In addition to these protective and preventive objectives, legal responsibility has distinct legal goals that contribute to the proper functioning of the legal system. These goals ensure the enforcement of subjective rights and legal obligations, reinforcing compliance with legal norms and serving as a fundamental safeguard of legality.

12.4 Types and Principles of Legal Responsibility

Legal responsibility cannot exist in an abstract or generalized form. In practice, it is always specific, with its general features manifesting differently depending on the type of responsibility. This variation determines the distinctive characteristics of its regulation and implementation. Legal science classifies types of legal responsibility based on various criteria, such as the authority enforcing it, the nature of sanctions, and its functional role. The most common classification, however, is based on the branch of law to which it belongs. According to this approach, legal responsibility is divided into **criminal**, **administrative**, **civil**, **disciplinary**, and **material** responsibility. Each type has a specific legal basis, a distinct procedure for enforcement, and unique coercive measures.

Criminal responsibility is the most severe form of legal responsibility. It arises from the commission of crimes and, unlike other types, is established exclusively by law. No other legal instruments can define acts as crimes or establish responsibility for them. In the legal systems of former Soviet countries, criminal codes contain an exhaustive list of offenses recognized as crimes. The process of imposing criminal responsibility is regulated by criminal procedural legislation, and only a court has the authority to determine criminal responsibility. No individual can be found guilty of a crime or subjected to criminal punishment except through a court decision and in strict compliance with legal procedures. Criminal penalties represent the most severe forms of coercion, primarily affecting the individual responsible for the offense. Such measures include imprisonment, correctional labor, confiscation of property, and other sanctions. The presumption of innocence, as previously noted, serves as the foundation of the procedural framework governing criminal responsibility.

Administrative responsibility applies to administrative offenses as defined by administrative law. Unlike criminal responsibility, administrative responsibility can also be established through various other legal acts and sources. Cases involving administrative offenses are handled by specialized legal and regulatory bodies, such as administrative commissions, commissions on minors, law enforcement agencies, customs authorities, and supervisory bodies responsible for public safety and regulatory compliance. Measures of administrative coercion typically include warnings, fines, deprivation of certain rights, administrative arrest, and other legally sanctioned penalties.

Civil responsibility arises from the violation of contractual obligations related to property matters or from causing property damage outside of a contractual relationship, meaning it applies in cases of civil torts. Its fundamental principle is the imposition of negative property-related consequences on the responsible party. The key principle of civil responsibility is full compensation for damages. In some cases, this compensation is supplemented by additional penalties, such as the payment of fines or penalties specified in the contract or law. Civil responsibility is enforced through judicial proceedings, either in general courts or arbitration courts, as well as through administrative bodies. In these cases, the plaintiff may be either a state authority or the individual or entity whose rights have been violated.

Disciplinary responsibility arises from the commission of disciplinary offenses. Unlike other types of legal violations, disciplinary offenses involve the breach of a positive legal obligation rather than a prohibitive norm. Specifically, they pertain to an employee's failure to fulfill his/her assigned labor duties. The enforcement of disciplinary responsibility falls within the authority of a person who has administrative and disciplinary power over the employee in question. This type of responsibility is divided into three categories: based on internal work regulations, within the framework of hierarchical subordination, and according to disciplinary charters and regulations. Sanctions for disciplinary responsibility include reprimand, severe reprimand, dismissal, and other measures outlined by relevant labor laws and internal regulations.

Material responsibility applies to workers and employees who have caused damage to an enterprise or institution. It entails the obligation to compensate for financial losses incurred by the organization due to an employee's actions performed in the course of their work. This responsibility is based on the existence of an employment relationship between the worker and the enterprise and is regulated by specific legal provisions that define the procedures for assessing and recovering damages.

For a comprehensive understanding of legal responsibility, it is essential to define the **principles** upon which it is based. The principles of any legal phenomenon reflect fundamental, stable, and lawful connections that ensure its existence. Recognizing the principles of responsibility allows for the correct application of protective legal norms, the resolution of cases where legal provisions are insufficient, and the enhancement of the effectiveness of legal coercion. Legal science identifies the following principles of legal responsibility: **legality**, **justice (fairness)**, **inevitability**, **expediency**, **individualization of punishment**, **responsibility for guilt**, and **the inadmissibility of double punishment**.

Legality requires the strict and precise application of legal norms.[2] In the context of legal responsibility, this means that only competent authorities may impose it, following a procedure strictly established by law and based on legally defined grounds. The actual basis for legal responsibility is the commission of an offense that meets all its legally defined elements. If even one element is absent, there is no legal basis for imposing responsibility. No external factors—such as nationality or ethnicity, political affiliation, education, gender, or ideological views—can serve as grounds for legal responsibility. Any deviation from these principles constitutes arbitrariness rather than law. Moreover, legality extends to procedural requirements. Any departure from the legally prescribed procedure, even if justified by the desire for efficiency, simplification, or acceleration, is impermissible.

Justice in the application of legal responsibility means that punishment must not only comply with legality but also reflect the principles of social justice. It is a fundamental requirement of law and fairness. A.F. Koni emphasized that justice must be reflected in legislation, which is most effective when it aligns with human needs and possibilities, and in judicial practice, which is at its highest when it considers the human dimension rather than applying rigid formalism. The same applies to legal

---

[2] See Chap. 5 for a description of the notion of the rule of law.

responsibility.[3] J.P. Marat stated that to punish the guilty without violating justice means to restrain wrongdoing, protect the innocent, shield the weak from oppression, prevent tyranny, and maintain social order and public peace. No legal objective could be more rational, noble, or significant for human well-being.[4]

One thing need to be emphasized: the fairness of legal responsibility is not an abstract moral or psychological notion but is reflected in a formalized system of legal requirements: (1) criminal punishment cannot be imposed for non-criminal offenses; (2) a law that introduces or increases legal responsibility cannot have retroactive effect; (3) if the harm caused by an offense is reversible, legal responsibility must provide for its compensation; (4) only one punishment can be imposed for a single violation; (5) responsibility must be borne exclusively by the individual who committed the offense; (6) the type and extent of punishment must correspond to the severity of the offense, with both aggravating and mitigating circumstances taken into account. In certain legally defined cases, it is possible to impose a punishment below the prescribed minimum or even to exempt an individual from punishment altogether, ensuring that legal responsibility remains just and proportionate.

Legal responsibility is guided by certain principles such as legality, justice, inevitability, expediency, and individualization to ensure fairness and consistency

Inevitability of occurrence signifies that legal responsibility is inseparable from the offense. The principle of the inevitability of responsibility means that for every offense committed, the corresponding legal consequences must follow. If legal coercion is required for a particular act, then without legal grounds, no one can be exempted from responsibility or punishment under any pretext, including social status, political affiliation, or personal connections. Failure to impose responsibility for an offense undermines the authority of the law, damages public trust in legality, and weakens the perception of justice among citizens and officials. Instilling in society the idea that an offense inevitably leads to punishment serves as a key factor in reducing the overall level of offenses.

The inevitability of responsibility implies its **expediency**. Responsibility occurs inevitably because it serves a necessary and justified legal purpose. It is impermissible to release an offender from responsibility without legal grounds under the pretext of severity, political considerations, ideological motives, or any other non-legal justification. At the same time, it is important to distinguish between the expediency of responsibility as a legal concept and the role of expediency in law enforcement, particularly in determining an appropriate penalty for a specific offender. In this context, expediency refers to the suitability of the chosen legal measure in achieving the objectives of legal responsibility. It requires a careful assessment of both the

[3] Koni 1966.

[4] Marat 2003.

seriousness of the offense and the individual characteristics of the offender, as well as the specific circumstances under which the act was committed. If the goals of legal responsibility can be achieved without formal punishment, the law may allow for the exemption of the guilty party from responsibility. However, the principle of expediency must not contradict the principle of legality. Expediency does not justify arbitrary or subjective decisions by legal authorities, nor can it be used as a pretext for violating legal norms. Instead, the law itself provides mechanisms for making reasonable and justified legal decisions. For example, the flexible structure of criminal law sanctions allows judicial authorities to select the most appropriate penalty based on the specific circumstances of each case.

The principle of **individualization** of punishment dictates that responsibility must be borne by the offender personally and cannot be transferred to another party. Assigning responsibility to someone other than the guilty party is inadmissible. For example, holding an enterprise accountable for the wrongful actions of its manager or assigning responsibility to parents or teachers for offenses committed by adolescents contradicts this principle. To ensure its proper application, legislation must clearly define the responsibilities of each individual and establish the corresponding measures of responsibility for failing to fulfill them. Legal responsibility is effective only when its subject is precisely identified, eliminating any possibility of collective or indirect responsibility. No person should be held legally accountable merely because of their association with the actual offender.

Responsibility for guilt arises only when the offender is actually guilty, meaning that the person was aware of the illegality of their actions and the consequences resulting from them. If a person is not guilty, then regardless of the severity of the act, they cannot be held responsible. However, in exceptional cases, civil law allows for responsibility without guilt, meaning that liability is imposed solely based on the occurrence of an unlawful or harmful event. For example, an individual or organization that owns a source of increased danger is obligated to compensate for any damage caused by it, even if they are not personally at fault. A common example is the responsibility of a vehicle owner for damages caused by the operation of their car, regardless of direct wrongdoing.

The determination of guilt and the burden of proof vary across different branches of law. In criminal law, the presumption of innocence applies, meaning that a person is considered innocent until proven guilty. The responsibility for proving guilt lies with the prosecuting legal authority, and the accused is not required to prove their own innocence. In civil law, however, the presumption of guilt applies to the party that caused harm. If the objective elements of an offense are present, the responsible party is presumed guilty unless they can prove otherwise. Both legal presumptions serve to protect individual rights—criminal law prioritizes the personal rights of the accused, while civil law focuses on protecting the rights of those who have suffered harm.

The **inadmissibility of double responsibility and punishment** (or *double jeopardy*) ensures that a person cannot be subjected to multiple types of legal responsibility for the same offense. This does not mean that both primary and additional penalties cannot be imposed—for instance, a court may sentence an individual to imprisonment along with the confiscation of property. However, for a single offense, a person can be punished only once, preventing excessive or unjustified legal sanctions.

Questions for Students

1. *What are the main characteristics that define lawful behavior, and why is it essential for societal order?*
2. *How is an offense categorized, and what elements must be present for an act to be considered unlawful?*
3. *What are the key features of legal responsibility, and how does it connect to offenses?*
4. *How do principles like justice and individualization shape the application of legal responsibility?*
5. *Why is it important to distinguish between lawful and unlawful behavior, and how does this distinction affect the implementation of law?*

References

Koni AF (1966) Selected Judicial Speeches and Writings (in Russian). Moscow
Marat JP (2003) Chains of Slavery (originally 1774). Dover Publications, Mineola
Morozova L (2021) Theory of State and Law (in Russian), 6th edn. Norma, Moscow
Nersesyants V (2016) Common Theory of Law and State (in Russian). Norma INFRA-M, Moscow

Chapter 13
Major Contemporary Legal Systems

Contents

Abstract This chapter presents a comparative overview of the world's major legal systems, classifying them into distinct legal families based on their historical roots, core principles, and structural features. It begins by distinguishing between national legal systems and broader legal traditions, introducing six primary families: Romano-Germanic (continental), Anglo-American (common law), socialist, Islamic, Hindu, and African customary law. The chapter analyzes the Romano-Germanic system as codified and norm-based, rooted in abstract legislation and hierarchical legal codes. In contrast, common law relies on judicial precedent and the doctrine of stare decisis to ensure consistency and adaptability through case law. The socialist legal system, influenced by Marxist-Leninist ideology, prioritizes public ownership, centralized planning, and state interests over individual rights. Islamic law (Sharia) blends legal and religious norms grounded in divine revelation, emphasizing obligations over rights. Hindu law derives from ancient religious texts and caste-based duties, while African customary law reflects unwritten traditions, focusing on communal harmony over individual legal claims. The chapter emphasizes the coexistence and interaction of these systems, especially in pluralistic post-colonial and post-socialist societies.

Keywords Legal systems and families · Comparative legal traditions · Romano-Germanic law · Common law and precedent · Socialist legal tradition · Islamic (Sharia) law · Hindu legal tradition · African customary law

R. Atadjanov, *A Common Theory of Law*, https://doi.org/10.1007/978-94-6265-711-3_13

13.1 Introduction

National legal systems vary across different states, shaped by distinct historical trajectories, cultural particularities, religious traditions, customary practices, and unique doctrinal foundations. In the contemporary international order, the existence of 195 sovereign states implies the presence of 195 distinct national legal systems, each reflecting its own legal tradition and normative structure. However, the notion of a "legal system" should not be conflated with that of a "system of law". The latter pertains specifically to the internal organization of law within a given jurisdiction, encompassing the interrelation of legal branches, institutions, and norms.[1] In contrast, the legal system represents a broader and more complex construct, integrating not only the institutional and doctrinal aspects of law but also the socio-legal environment within which legal norms operate. Typically, a legal system is understood as a historically determined amalgamation of legislative frameworks, judicial and administrative practice, and the predominant legal ideology within a particular state.[2]

A legal system encompasses laws, institutions, and ideologies within a state, while legal families group national legal systems with shared characteristics like sources of law and historical foundations

The concepts of a "legal family" or "legal tradition" are employed alongside that of a "legal system", serving to classify multiple national legal systems that exhibit shared characteristics. This classification is based on a set of common features, including the sources of law, the structural organization of legal norms, the historical trajectory of legal development, and, in many cases, the prevailing conception of the rule of law. These criteria provide a methodological basis for distinguishing and categorizing legal families/traditions, thereby facilitating a comparative analysis of different legal traditions across jurisdictions.

13.2 Continental Law/Roman Germanic Tradition

The Romano-Germanic legal tradition emerged in the twelfth and thirteenth centuries as a consequence of the reception of Roman law by continental European states. This process was largely driven by economic transformations, including the expansion of trade, the rise of craftsmanship, and the growth of urban centers. The feudal legal norms, which were deeply rooted in the principles of vassalage and patrimonial

---

[1] See Chap. 10.

[2] The major ideas and descriptions in this chapter are mostly based on the reworked conclusions and useful progressive explanations from *passim* Nersesyants 2016, but also from *passim* Alekseyev 2008.

jurisdiction characteristic of rural society, proved inadequate for the evolving self-governance structures of free cities. These urban centers required a legal framework grounded in the principles of formal equality and the autonomy of participants in market relations. Roman law, with its systematic and rational approach to legal regulation, provided the most suitable foundation for meeting these demands.

A Romano-Germanic legal norm is a general rule of conduct established by the legislator or an authorized legal body. Unlike the Anglo-Saxon legal precedent, which is case-specific and evolves through judicial decisions, the Romano-Germanic norm is characterized by its generalized and abstract formulation. It is typically conceived as a model of social behavior, defining permissible boundaries ("from" and "to") rather than enumerating specific cases or variations of conduct. Even when a legal provision originates from a particular case, its resolution is expressed in an abstract and generalized form. The use of such normative models enables legislators to efficiently regulate social relations and adapt legal frameworks to changing societal conditions, making this system particularly effective in maintaining legal consistency and predictability.

This system relies on codified laws enacted by legislatures, with a focus on abstract and general norms supported by hierarchical codifications

The Romano-Germanic legal norms exhibit a systemic and hierarchical structure, forming interconnected sets of provisions that are differentiated by their legal force and societal significance. Within this framework, primary legal rules are distinguished from secondary, less significant norms. This hierarchical organization significantly facilitates legal professionals in identifying and applying current legislation. However, the abstract nature of these norms also presents practical challenges. The broader and more generalized a norm is, the more complex its application in concrete legal situations becomes, necessitating precise interpretation and specification. To address these challenges, various interpretative techniques and methodologies are employed to clarify legislative intent. As a result, judicial, arbitration, and other legal bodies contribute to the development of numerous secondary provisions that elaborate upon and refine statutory regulations, ensuring their effective implementation in practice.

The primary source of Romano-Germanic law is statutory law, which holds the highest legal authority within this legal tradition. Laws are enacted by the parliaments of the respective states and possess supreme legal force, applying uniformly across the entire territory and to all citizens. From the perspective of contemporary legal doctrine, legislation must reflect the will of the majority of society while upholding fundamental human rights and principles of social justice. As the dominant source of law, statutes take precedence over all other legal sources, including custom, judicial precedents, and doctrinal interpretations. The law has the capacity to either prohibit or incorporate customary practices, specific provisions of judicial precedent, or domestic treaties. When customs or legal doctrines are codified within statutory texts, they are assimilated into the body of law, becoming part of its substantive content. In modern legal systems adhering to the Romano-Germanic tradition, statutory law regulates all essential aspects of social life, defining the legal status of individuals, property rights, and the relationships among legal subjects.

Codification plays a particularly significant role within the Romano-Germanic legal system. Unlike the Anglo-Saxon tradition, which emphasizes the external organization and systematization of legal norms through incorporation, the Romano-Germanic approach seeks substantive, internal unification through comprehensive legal refinement. This codification process involves a structured division of legislative provisions and their integration into coherent, hierarchical frameworks. Legal codes typically govern distinct areas of law—such as civil, criminal, commercial, and family law—serving as focal points around which other legal norms within their respective domains are organized.

A secondary but historically significant source of Romano-Germanic law is custom. Many customary norms have been incorporated into legislation over time, becoming part of statutory law. However, as an independent source, custom has largely diminished in significance, now playing a subsidiary role by supplementing statutory provisions where necessary.

Another defining characteristic of the Romano-Germanic legal system is the classical distinction between public and private law, a division that dates back to the Roman Empire. Public law is characterized by the pursuit of collective state interests, encompassing areas such as constitutional, criminal, administrative, financial, public international law, and procedural law, as well as key aspects of labor law. This domain is dominated by imperative norms, which are binding and cannot be altered by the parties involved. In contrast, private law governs relations among independent and legally equal entities, operating within a framework of dispositive norms—rules that apply only insofar as they have not been modified or excluded by the parties. The primary branches of private law include civil, family, commercial, and private international law, along with select provisions of labor law.

A further structural feature of the Romano-Germanic legal tradition is the consistent classification of legal norms within specific branches of law and legal institutions. Each normative provision, upon enactment, is assigned a designated sector of law, taking into account the subject matter of its regulation as well as the methods and mechanisms of legal influence. This systematic organization reflects the rational and academically grounded nature of the Romano-Germanic legal family, a tradition deeply influenced by its historical development within university-based legal scholarship.

The Romano-Germanic, or continental, legal family encompasses the national legal systems of countries in continental Europe, including France, Germany, Italy, Spain, and the Scandinavian states, among others. Additionally, this legal tradition extends beyond Europe, as numerous non-European legal systems have developed in accordance with the fundamental principles and structural frameworks of the Romano-Germanic legal family, integrating its core doctrinal and institutional elements into their respective legal orders.

13.3 Common Law/Anglo-American Tradition

The evolution of Anglo-Saxon law, universally known as "common law", has been influenced by a multitude of historical, geographical, national, political, and economic factors. A unified legal system for England began to emerge following the Norman Conquest in 1066 under William I, known as William the Conqueror. Judicial decisions during this period served as precedents for other courts in analogous cases, leading to the development of a cohesive system of precedents referred to as "common law". Juries, composed of free citizens from local communities, played a role in resolving legal disputes. While these jurors may not have been well-versed in legal precedents or royal edicts, they were familiar with local customs and traditions, which significantly influenced the substance of court decisions. In this context, English common law can be seen as customary, traditional law.

Over time, two distinct legal systems developed in England: common law and equity. Equity emerged to address the rigidities and limitations of common law by providing remedies based on principles of fairness and justice. Initially, equity was administered by the Court of Chancery, which operated separately from common law courts. However, by the nineteenth century, equity had evolved into a system of precedent-based law, diminishing the differences between the two systems. The Judicature Acts of 1873–1875 unified the administration of common law and equity, merging their courts and streamlining legal procedures.

The common law system of England has profoundly influenced the legal development of numerous countries, including the United States, Canada, Australia, India, and New Zealand. Within the United Kingdom, however, the application of common law is not uniform. It is predominantly applied in England and Wales, while Scotland and Northern Ireland maintain distinct legal systems. Constructive legal cooperation among countries within the common law tradition has led to the cross-fertilization of precedents, with decisions from English courts informing those of other jurisdictions and vice versa.

In Anglo-Saxon law, there are two primary types of norms: legislative and precedent. Legislative norms, as in the Romano-Germanic system, are general rules of conduct established through statutes. Precedents, on the other hand, are specific components of judicial decisions in particular cases. The binding element of a precedent, known as *ratio decidendi*, comprises the legal reasoning and principles underlying the decision. Other observations made by judges, referred to as *obiter dictum*, are considered persuasive but are not obligatory for other courts. In practice, distinguishing between ratio decidendi and obiter dictum can be challenging.

Judicial precedent has historically been the most significant source of Anglo-Saxon law. Precedents are established by higher judicial authorities, including the Supreme Court (formerly the House of Lords), the Court of Appeal, and the High Court. Lower courts are generally expected to follow precedents set by higher courts, adhering to the doctrine of *stare decisis*, which mandates that cases should be decided in accordance with established precedents. This doctrine ensures consistency and predictability in the legal system.

Common law emphasizes judicial precedents, with decisions based on the doctrine of stare decisis, ensuring consistency and adaptability

Statutory law, or legislation, emerged later than judicial precedent but has become increasingly significant in regulating social relations. English statutes are categorized based on their scope of application: public statutes apply to the general populace and operate throughout the United Kingdom, while private statutes pertain to specific individuals or localized areas. The interplay between statutory law and judicial precedent continues to shape the dynamic landscape of Anglo-Saxon law.

It is important to note that the highest judicial authority in the United Kingdom is the Supreme Court, which replaced the appellate jurisdiction of the House of Lords in 2009. The Court of Appeal is divided into two divisions: Civil and Criminal. The High Court consists of three divisions: the King's Bench Division, the Chancery Division, and the Family Division. The Crown Court handles serious criminal cases, while Magistrates' Courts deal with minor criminal matters and some civil cases. County Courts primarily address civil disputes. This hierarchical structure ensures the orderly administration of justice across England and Wales.

13.4 Socialist Law System

The socialist legal system emerged in Russia following the October Revolution of 1917. Unlike traditional legal families, which developed in response to historical, cultural, and doctrinal factors, the formation of the socialist legal system was primarily driven by Marxist-Leninist ideology and its principles regarding the political and economic organization of society. Consequently, the fundamental distinctions between this legal system and other established legal traditions lie in the substantive content of legal norms rather than in their sources, structure, or doctrinal foundations.

In the Soviet Union and other socialist legal systems, key ideological tenets were legally codified, including:

- The centralized management of the economy, which necessitated the widespread application of imperative legal norms, state planning mechanisms, strict regulation of civil contracts, and detailed legal provisions governing property relations and the powers of legal subjects;
- The socialization of property, whereby state and "public" ownership became the foundation of the economic system;
- The nationalization of enterprises, financial institutions, and economic assets, and, in some jurisdictions, the expropriation of land and other real estate holdings;

– The regulation of labor and consumption, leading to the establishment of social and legal institutions responsible for standardizing labor relations and distributing material resources in accordance with state planning objectives.

Rooted in Marxist-Leninist ideology, the socialist system prioritizes state ownership and centralized planning, diminishing the role of private law

Comprehensive state control over all spheres of economic and social life resulted in the gradual erosion of private law and the dominance of public law institutions. This transformation was ideologically justified by Vladimir Lenin's assertion that the Soviet state did not recognize private ownership as a legal category. Many civil law institutions, including property law, were redefined within a public law framework. The most significant types of commercial contracts were concluded and executed in accordance with administrative and planning directives rather than private negotiations.

In the fields of criminal and administrative law, state property was accorded paramount legal protection, while private entrepreneurship, foreign exchange transactions, and commercial mediation were strictly prohibited. Severe legal sanctions were imposed for offenses such as "anti-Soviet agitation and propaganda", the dissemination of information deemed detrimental to the socialist state, and actions considered contrary to communist moral principles. Procedural law was characterized by simplified judicial processes, restrictions on the rights of the accused and defendants, and a pronounced prosecutorial bias. The judicial system became highly ideologized, with a marked emphasis on state interests over individual rights. Trial by jury, a feature of earlier legal traditions, was abolished in favor of a more controlled adjudicative process.

At present, the socialist legal tradition continues to exist in several states, including China, Vietnam, North Korea (DPRK), and Cuba, where legal institutions remain fundamentally shaped by Marxist-Leninist principles and state-centric regulatory frameworks.

13.5 Islamic Law Tradition (Sharia)

Muslim law developed as an integral part of Sharia, a comprehensive system of religious and legal norms governing the conduct of individuals who adhere to Islam. As one of the most fundamental components of the Islamic faith, Sharia encompasses not only legal provisions but also ethical and religious obligations. The historical development of Muslim law, often referred to as *fiqh*, traces back to the teachings and actions of the Prophet Muhammad (570 or 571–632 CE). Acting as the messenger of Allah, Muhammad conveyed fundamental rules of conduct to the

Muslim community, primarily through public sermons. Additionally, certain legal norms were derived from the Prophet's personal life and behavior, which became exemplary for subsequent legal interpretation.

Since the latter half of the nineteenth century, various Muslim-majority states have actively incorporated elements of European law, particularly Romano-Germanic legal principles, into their legal frameworks. In some countries, such as Turkey, this process has resulted in the near-complete displacement of traditional Islamic legal norms. In contrast, in states such as Algeria, Egypt, and Syria, Islamic law continues to regulate specific domains of social life, particularly matters pertaining to personal status, including marriage, divorce, inheritance, and family relations. In jurisdictions where Islamic fundamentalist ideology exerts a dominant influence—such as Iran, Pakistan, Yemen, Libya, and Sudan—Muslim law extends to multiple branches of law, including civil, criminal, constitutional, and administrative law. This trend reflects a broader resurgence of Islamic legal culture, marked by a renewed emphasis on traditional Islamic values and an expansion of the scope of Sharia-based legal regulation.

Based on divine guidance from the Qur'an and Sunnah, Islamic law integrates religious and legal norms, emphasizing duties over rights

The Muslim legal system is distinct from other legal traditions due to the unique nature of its sources, structure, terminology, legal constructs, and concept of the legal norm. In contrast to continental European legal thought, where legal norms are understood as commands issued by a historically specific legislator, Islamic jurisprudence perceives the norm as a divine directive communicated by Allah to the Muslim *ummah* (community of believers). Unlike laws formulated through logical reasoning and legal codification, Islamic legal norms are grounded in religious doctrine and faith, rendering them immutable, absolute, and beyond human revision or repeal. Consequently, compliance with these norms is seen as a matter of religious duty rather than legal discretion.

The supra-social and dogmatic nature of Muslim legal norms necessitates special mechanisms for their adaptation to contemporary social realities. A significant aspect of legal practice in Muslim jurisdictions involves the ability of judges and legal scholars to navigate and interpret Islamic law in a manner that achieves pragmatic legal outcomes without overtly contravening specific textual provisions. This approach frequently relies on legal fictions, interpretative techniques, and juristic reasoning to reconcile religious doctrine with practical governance needs.

The content of Muslim legal norms also differs significantly from that of European legal systems. Unlike Western legal provisions, which typically grant rights or impose prohibitions, Islamic legal norms are primarily structured around obligations—they prescribe duties that individuals must fulfill. This obligatory nature reflects the religious foundations of Islamic law, wherein compliance is both a legal and spiritual imperative.

Here are the sources of Muslim law. The primary and most authoritative source is the Qur'an, the sacred scripture of Islam. Structurally, the Qur'an consists of 114 *surahs* (chapters) and over 4000 poetic verses, which are not systematically organized under a unifying legal framework. The Qur'anic texts, dating from 610 to 631 CE, primarily comprise religious and moral guidance, while legal provisions constitute only a minor portion. The legal norms contained in the Qur'an primarily address interpersonal relations, ethical conduct, and certain aspects of legal interaction between Muslims and non-Muslims. Due to its fragmentary and theological nature, the Qur'an did not evolve into a codified legal document akin to a constitution or civil code. Nevertheless, it remains the most authoritative source of Islamic jurisprudence, serving as the foundation upon which Islamic legal scholars base their interpretations.

The second fundamental source of Muslim law is the Sunnah, a collection of hadiths, which are narrations detailing the sayings, actions, and practices of the Prophet Muhammad. The Sunnah is closely linked to the Qur'an and provides additional legal and ethical guidance based on the Prophet's personal example. However, like the Qur'an, the Sunnah contains few explicit legal norms, with the majority of its content revolving around moral, religious, and ethical precepts. The legal prescriptions found within the Sunnah primarily consist of case-specific rulings derived from Muhammad's life experiences, rather than generalized legal principles.

The third source of Muslim law is *ijma*, which refers to the consensus of authoritative Islamic legal scholars on a given legal issue. The legitimacy of *ijma* is derived from the belief, articulated by Muhammad, that the collective judgment of the Muslim community cannot be erroneous. In practice, *ijma* represents the scholarly consensus of Islamic jurists and theologians, who interpret and apply Islamic legal principles in response to contemporary legal questions. Over time, *ijma* has played a crucial role in shaping the evolution of Muslim law, particularly in matters where neither the Qur'an nor the Sunnah provides clear guidance.

The fourth source of Muslim law is *qiyas*, or reasoning by analogy, which serves as a customary method of legal decision-making. In Western legal systems, analogy is not considered an independent source of law but rather a tool that facilitates the application of existing legal norms within statutory or precedent-based regulation. In Islamic jurisprudence, however, *qiyas* holds a unique and significant status because the object of legal reasoning is not the rational will of a human legislator but rather a religious doctrine that is regarded as absolute, eternal, and unquestionable. Unlike in Western traditions, where analogy is viewed as an extension or interpretation of an existing norm, *qiyas* is treated as a distinct and autonomous source of law.

The structure of Muslim law also possesses specific characteristics that distinguish it from other legal systems. It does not follow the division between public and private law that characterizes the Romano-Germanic tradition, nor does it reflect the bifurcation between common law and equity found in Anglo-Saxon legal systems. Instead, the classification and organization of legal norms in Islamic law are based on different principles of integration and structural unity. Legal norms and principles are often grouped in accordance with the major sectarian traditions within Islam, particularly the Sunni schools (Hanafi, Maliki, Shafi'i, Hanbali) and the non-Sunni branches (Shi'a, Wahhabi, Zaydi, Ibadi). The existence of multiple Islamic sects has resulted in corresponding differences in legal interpretation, with legal norms aligning themselves with specific theological doctrines. Each sect, in turn, tends to develop and adhere to a distinct body of legal norms shaped by its doctrinal foundations. Despite this sectarian differentiation, the classification of legal norms into functional legal sectors is maintained, though with certain distinctive features.

All human actions under Muslim law are classified into five fundamental categories: obligatory, recommended, permitted, reprehensible, and prohibited. This classification is derived from the religious and moral evaluation of particular forms of conduct, emphasizing their ethical and theological significance. Additionally, Muslim legal norms can be further categorized based on their level of generality. Some are formulated as norms-principles, which take the form of broad theoretical generalizations, while others exist as casuistic norms, which have typically developed empirically, such as those found in the Sunnah.

13.6 Hindu Law Tradition

Hindu law is rooted in the Hindu (Brahman) religious tradition and serves as the regulatory framework governing the behavior of individuals within the Hindu community. It should not be conflated with the Indian legal system, as Hindu law is not limited to India but is also observed in various Hindu communities across Southeast Asia, including Pakistan, Malaysia, Singapore, Nepal, and Sri Lanka, as well as in East African countries such as Kenya, Tanzania, and Uganda.

The foundational ideas of Hinduism (Brahmanism) are reflected in the ancient Indian scriptures of the second millennium BCE, collectively known as the "Vedas". These texts provide the ideological basis for the division of society into four varnas, or social estates: the *Brahmins* (priests), *Kshatriyas* (warriors), *Vaishyas* (farmers, artisans, and traders), and *Shudras* (the lower social class). Within this hierarchical caste system, the highest social status is accorded to members of the first two varnas, particularly the Brahmins, who are regarded as the custodians of religious and legal wisdom. According to the Vedas and other Brahmanic texts, individuals belonging to different varnas are required to adhere to *dharma*, a divinely ordained code of law, duty, custom, and ethical conduct specific to their social status.

Various Brahmanic schools undertook the interpretation, systematization, and compilation of dharmic rules, producing authoritative legal treatises known as the *dharma shastras*. Among the most significant *dharma shastras*, compiled between the second century BCE and the third century CE, are the "Laws of Manu", the "Laws of Yajnavalkya", and the "Laws of Narada". The "Laws of Manu" emphasize that all members of society, including the king, must abide by the guidance and rulings of the Brahmins concerning matters of *dharma*. Failure to observe *dharma* was believed to result not only in severe earthly punishments but also in consequences in the afterlife. All dharma shastras are considered integral components of a unified Hindu legal tradition.

Another significant source of Hindu law, alongside the *dharma shastras*, is the body of commentaries known as *nibandhas*, compiled between the twelfth and seventeenth centuries. Both the *dharma shastras* and their commentaries place great emphasis on "good custom", which is understood as a reflection of *dharma*'s divine truth and eternal order. Consequently, custom is recognized as a fundamental source of Hindu law. Each Hindu community, caste, subcaste, and even individual families possess their own customary laws. Disputes arising within these groups are traditionally resolved through assemblies of caste or subcaste members, who adjudicate based on their respective customs. In cases where no pre-established rules exist, Hindu law advises that individuals and judges rely on reason, conscience, and the principles of justice in rendering their decisions.

Hindu law does not recognize state legislation or judicial precedent as sources of law. During the Muslim conquest of India in the sixteenth century, the application of Hindu law in judicial and administrative institutions was prohibited. Under English colonial rule, beginning in the seventeenth century, this prohibition was lifted, and a legal framework was introduced that provided for the application of "the law of the Quran in relation to Muslims and the law of the Shastras in relation to Hindus". The subsequent development of Hindu law was significantly influenced by the legislative policies of the British administration and the principles of common law. As a result, various traditional provisions of Hindu law were abolished, including those related to caste-based discrimination and the legal incapacity of women. Additionally, the practice of widow self-immolation (sati) was officially prohibited.

Following India's independence in 1947, the country pursued a policy of legal modernization, both in relation to Hindu law and the national legal system as a whole. The Indian Constitution of 1950 explicitly prohibited discrimination on the basis of caste. The Hindu Marriage Act of 1955 introduced substantial reforms concerning marriage and divorce, while the Hindu Succession Act of 1956 strengthened the inheritance rights of women, formally recognizing them as legal heirs. The earlier regime of joint family property was revised, and multiple categories of property were legally designated as personal property. In 1984, a law was enacted establishing "family courts", which were tasked with adjudicating family and matrimonial disputes without regard to the religious affiliation of the parties involved.

Many provisions of modernized Hindu law, which are currently in force in India, do not extend to Hindu communities outside the country, where traditional Hindu legal norms continue to govern social and familial relations. The Indian national legal system itself has been significantly shaped by the influence of English law and is now classified as part of the common law legal family.

13.7 African Customary Law

The system of customary, or traditional, law refers to the regulatory framework governing social relations in equatorial and southern Africa, as well as in Madagascar. It is based on the formal recognition by the state of social norms and customs that have developed organically over time and have become ingrained in the daily lives of the population. Custom is the oldest known source of law, present in all legal systems. However, while it plays only a supplementary role in Romano-Germanic and Anglo-Saxon legal traditions (see the sections above), in Africa it has historically been, and continues to be, a primary regulator of social relations, particularly in rural areas outside major urban centers.

African customary law governs through traditions and social norms, focusing on community reconciliation rather than individual rights

The diverse ethnic groups of Africa maintain their own distinct customs, which serve to reinforce the unity and cohesion of their respective social structures, including tribes, clans, and villages. These customs often emphasize respect for ancestors, a deep spiritual connection to nature, and belief in supernatural forces. The mythical and pluralistic nature of these customs, along with their informal and decentralized character, presents challenges for their codification into national legal systems similar to those found in Europe. The colonial period facilitated the introduction of modern legislative frameworks and judicial institutions, yet it did not fundamentally alter the legal consciousness of the rural population, which continues to adhere to traditional values and customary norms. In contemporary African states, efforts are being made to systematize existing customs by incorporating them into sectoral legal codes and other legislative acts. However, this process often overlooks the customs of certain ethnic and social groups, leading to legal inconsistencies and tensions within pluralistic societies.

Similar challenges arise in the establishment of judicial institutions and the administration of justice. The European legal tradition conceives of courts as bodies designed to adjudicate disputes between legally equal and independent parties. However, this concept is foreign to many African societies, where individuals are regarded primarily as members of a collective social unit, rather than as autonomous legal subjects. Within tribal and clan structures, internal conflicts are not typically resolved through the formal recognition of individual rights but rather through mechanisms aimed at achieving reconciliation and restoring harmony within the community. As a result, the current phase of legal development in Africa can be characterized as a complex transitional period, in which states seek to define the appropriate methods for integrating two distinct legal cultures—the European legislative-precedent system and the indigenous customary-legal tradition.

Questions for Students

1. *What distinguishes a legal system from a legal family, and why is this distinction important for comparative legal studies?*

2. *How does the reliance on codification shape the application of law in the continental legal tradition?*
3. *What role does the doctrine of stare decisis play in ensuring consistency in common law systems?*
4. *How does the socialist legal system reflect Marxist-Leninist principles in its approach to law and governance?*
5. *In what ways do Islamic legal norms differ from Western legal norms in their foundations and applications?*
6. *What are the challenges of integrating African customary law into modern legislative frameworks, and how do they affect legal pluralism?*

References

Alekseyev S (2008) Theory of State and Law, 3rd edn. Norma, Moscow
Nersesyants V (2016) Common Theory of Law and State (in Russian). Norma INFRA-M, Moscow

Chapter 14
Conclusion

Contents

Abstract This chapter summarizes the core arguments and overarching vision of the textbook, emphasizing the need for a reimagined legal theory in post-Soviet states—one that views law not merely as a tool of state power but as a societal institution grounded in values, justice, and pluralism. It revisits each chapter's contribution to this framework, from the theoretical foundations to the practical mechanisms of legal interpretation, behavior, and responsibility. The chapter reinforces the central thesis: that legal reform in the region requires both a critical break from statist-positivist legacies and a forward-looking embrace of legal culture, civil society, and rule-of-law principles. The author calls on academics, educators, and legal practitioners to engage with these ideas, not as final answers but as starting points for further dialogue and transformation. The book closes with the hope that it will serve as both a teaching resource and a catalyst for meaningful legal development across post-Soviet societies.

Keywords Legal theory reform · Post-Soviet legal systems · Rule of law · Legal pluralism · Legal education · Civil society and law

14.1 Introduction

The "Common Theory of Law for Post-Soviet States" represents an effort to engage deeply with the theoretical and practical challenges that continue to shape the legal systems and cultures of the region. In doing so, I sincerely aspired to offer a comprehensive framework for understanding law not merely as an instrument of governance but as a societal phenomenon integral to and necessary for public life. By synthesizing insights from diverse legal theories and examining their relevance to the post-Soviet

R. Atadjanov, *A Common Theory of Law*, https://doi.org/10.1007/978-94-6265-711-3_14

context, my book addresses a pressing need for a holistic and accessible approach to legal education in this part of the world.

The overarching theme of this work has been the rethinking of legal theory within a region where law has traditionally been subordinated to state interests and statist ideologies. As explored throughout the chapters, law must be understood as more than a set of rigid rules or an apparatus for state control. Instead, it is an evolving and dynamic phenomenon that reflects and shapes societal values, norms, and aspirations. This perspective challenges entrenched doctrines that prioritize state power, offering an alternative vision in which law serves as a unifying, constructive force within society.

14.2 The Structure of the Book and the Particulars of the Chapters

The book begins by setting out its conceptual framework in the introductory chapter, Chap. 1, which underscores the urgency of reforming legal education and thought in the post-Soviet region. This theme runs through all the chapters, each of which contributes to a broader understanding of law's role and significance. In Chap. 2, the foundations of the common theory of law are laid, defining its scope, subject matter, and methodology. By treating law as an autonomous science with interdisciplinary dimensions, this chapter provides readers with the tools necessary for engaging critically with legal phenomena.

The subsequent chapters delve into the multifaceted relationships between law and society. Chapter 3 explores society as a legal phenomenon, highlighting the interplay between legal norms and societal values. This chapter emphasizes the reciprocal nature of law and society, with each shaping and influencing the other. Chapter 4, in turn, examines the concepts of power and state, critiquing the statist approaches that have dominated the region while advocating for a more balanced understanding of law's autonomy from political authority.

The theoretical insights introduced in these early chapters are further developed in discussions on the *Rechtsstaat*, civil society, human rights, and the notion of law itself. Chapter 5 examines the principles of the rule of law and the role of civil society in fostering accountable and transparent governance. It situates these concepts within the post-Soviet context, where their implementation has often been undermined by systemic challenges. Chapter 6 offers a nuanced exploration of law's nature, including its dual character as both a social regulator and a value in its own right. These chapters collectively build a compelling case for viewing law as a cornerstone of societal progress and cohesion.

Chapter 7 provides a detailed overview of the main theories of law's origin and nature, tracing their evolution from mythological and religious perspectives to contemporary libertarian and psychological theories. By presenting these diverse viewpoints, the book highlights the richness of legal thought and its relevance to addressing modern challenges. This thematic diversity is complemented by Chap. 8's analysis of law's principles and functions, which underscores its regulatory and protective roles within society.

The latter chapters turn to the practical dimensions of law's operation. Chapter 9 examines the sources of law, offering a comprehensive overview of legal norms and their development in the region. Chapter 10 addresses the system and structure of law, providing insights into the organization of legal systems and their practical implications. Chapters 11 and 12 explore the processes of legal interpretation and the relationship between lawful behavior and legal responsibility, respectively, emphasizing the importance of clarity, predictability, and accountability in legal practice. Finally, Chap. 13 situates the post-Soviet legal experience within a global context, comparing it to major contemporary legal systems and identifying opportunities for integration and innovation.

14.3 Conclusions

The lessons distilled from all these chapters (whose quantity turned out to be more than I had initially expected and foreseen) converge in this conclusion, synthesizing the book's key insights and reflects on their broader implications. Thus, central to the argument of this work is the conviction that the legal systems of the post-Soviet region must embrace a more inclusive and pluralistic approach to legal theory. The author views such a key aspect as a progressive one. This includes recognizing law's potential to serve as a bridge between diverse social interests and as a foundation for achieving societal cohesion and justice. By drawing on the strengths of various legal traditions while addressing the specific challenges of the region, the proposed common theory of law offers a pathway, as I think, toward more effective and equitable legal systems.

The textbook does not claim to provide definitive answers to the complex questions it raises. Rather, it seeks to provoke critical reflection and dialogue among scholars, educators, and practitioners. The recommendations presented here—ranging from rethinking legal education to promoting legal values rooted in constitutionalism, human rights, and the rule of law, are intended as starting points for further exploration and adaptation.

Looking ahead, the future of legal theory and practice in the post-Soviet region will eventually depend on the willingness of its academic and professional communities to engage with these ideas and implement them in meaningful ways. This requires not only intellectual openness (with which all the contexts in the region have a problem) but also a commitment to fostering a culture of critical inquiry and respect for legal principles. It is the hope of this author that this textbook will serve as a catalyst for such change, providing readers with the knowledge and tools they need to contribute to this endeavor.

As this book concludes, it is my humble hope that it will not go unnoticed by my colleagues—scholars, professors of law, legal experts, researchers, and law students alike. I wish for this work to be actively used in both theoretical and practical settings, contributing to the generation and dissemination of knowledge on legal theory. If the book can play even a small role in instilling and securing proper legal values within this important region, then its mission will have been fulfilled.

Bibliography

Adams J (1971) A Defence of the Constitutions of Government of the United States of America. Da Capo Press, New York

Alekseyev S (2008) Theory of State and Law, 3rd edn. Norma, Moscow

Amos S (1874) The Science of Law. John Murray, London

Aquinas T (1947) Summa Theologica (transl. Fathers of the English Dominican Province). Benziger Bros., New York

Aristotle (1908) Aristotle's Ethics (in Russian). Saint-Petersburg

Aristotle (1984) The Athenian Constitution (transl. Rhodes P). Oxford University Press, Oxford

Aristotle (1996) Constitution of the Athenians (in Russian). Moscow

Atadjanov R (2019) Humanness as a Protected Legal Interest of Crimes against Humanity – Conceptual and Normative Aspects. International Criminal Justice Series, vol 22. TMC Asser Press, The Hague

Auer A (1971) Autonome Moral und christlicher Glaube [Autonomous Morality and Christian Faith]. Matthias-Grünewald-Verlag, Mainz

Austin J (1998) The Province of Jurisprudence Determined (ed. Campbell R). Hackett Publishing, Indianapolis

Ávila H (2007) Theory of Legal Principles. Springer

Baitin A (1990) General Theory of State and Law (in Russian). Moscow

Bergbohm H (1892) Jurispudenz und Rechtsphilosophie [Jurisprudence and Legal Philosophy]. Duncker & Humblot, Leipzig

Black's Law Dictionary (2009) 9th edn. Thomson Reuters

Burlatsky F, Keyzerov K (1989) Political Science: Theory and Methodology (in Russian). Moscow

Cabantou A (1900) Le pouvoir d'État: étude de droit public et de philosophie politique [State Power: A Study in Public Law and Political Philosophy]. Sirey, Paris

Chloros AG (1958) What Is Natural Law? The Modern Law Review, Vol. 21, No. 6 (Nov. 1958):609–622

Cicero (1928) On the Republic, Book I. Harvard University Press, Cambridge

Cicero (1998) On the Laws and On the Republic (transl. Zetzel J). Cambridge University Press, Cambridge

Dalpane F, Baideldinova M (eds) (2024) Animal Law Worldwide: Key Issues and Main Trends Across 27 Jurisdictions. T.M.C. Asser Press, The Hague

Dombois H (1971) Das Recht der Kirche im pluralistischen Staat [The Law of the Church in the Pluralistic State]. Vandenhoeck & Ruprecht, Göttingen

Feinberg J (1986) The Moral Limits of the Criminal Law: Harm to Self. Oxford University Press, New York

Frändberg A (2014) From Rechtsstaat to Universal Law-State. An Essay in Philosophical Jurisprudence. Springer

R. Atadjanov, *A Common Theory of Law*, https://doi.org/10.1007/978-94-6265-711-3

Friedmann W (1962) The Uses of "General Principles" in the Development of International Law. 106 Hague Recueil 1, 54
Garner BA (ed) (2004) Black's Law Dictionary. Thomson West
Golmsten VV (1901) Lectures on the Encyclopedia of Law (in Russian), 2nd edn. St. Petersburg
Gong GW (1984) The Standard of "Civilization". International Society
Grimm DN (1900) Introduction to the Science of Law (in Russian). St. Petersburg
Grotius H (2005) On the Law of War and Peace (De Jure Belli ac Pacis), 2nd edn (transl. and ed. Tuck R). Oxford University Press, Oxford
Hage J et al. (eds) (2017) Introduction to Law, 2nd edn. Springer
Hamilton A, Madison J, Jay J (1987) The Federalist Papers (ed. Isaac K). Penguin Books, London
Hart HLA (1961a) The Concept of Law. Oxford University Press, Oxford
Hart HLA (1961b) The Concept of Law, 3rd edn. Oxford University Press
Hegel GWF (2001) Lectures on the Philosophy of History. Oxford University Press, Oxford
Herodotus (2003) The Histories, Book II (transl. Waterfield R, ed. Dewald C). Penguin Books, London
Hobbes T (1996) Leviathan (ed. Tuck R). Oxford University Press, Oxford
Hurst F (1959) Naturrecht und christlicher Glaube [Natural Law and Christian Faith]. Evangelische Verlagsanstalt, Berlin
Ibrayeva A et al. (2017) Theory of State and Law (in Russian), 3rd edn. Zhety Zhargy, Almaty
Janis MW (2003) An Introduction to International Law, 4th edn. Aspen Publishers
Jefferson T (1975) The Portable Thomas Jefferson. In: Peterson M (ed). Viking Press, New York
Kant I (1996) The Metaphysics of Morals (ed. and transl. Gregor M). Cambridge University Press, Cambridge
Katkov AB (1985) Language and Jurisprudence (in Russian). Moscow
Kelsen H (1967a) Pure Theory of Law (transl. Knight M). University of California Press, Berkeley
Kelsen H (1967b) Pure Theory of Law (transl. from the 2nd German edn.). University of California Press
Khropanyuk V (2019) Theory of State and Law (in Russian), 13th edn. Omega-L, Moscow
Koni AF (1966) Selected Judicial Speeches and Writings (in Russian). Moscow
Korkunov N (1909) General Theory of Law (in Russian). St. Petersburg
Lazarev VV (1992) Theory of State and Law (in Russian). Moscow
Lazarev VV, Lipen SV, Saidov AKh (2022) Problems of the Common Theory of jus (in Russian). Norma, Moscow
Leonov I (2005) Social State of Law: Difficulties of Formation (in Russian). 2 Law and Governance: 21st Century 17
Locke J (1960) Selected Philosophical Works, Vol. II (in Russian). Moscow
Locke J (1988) Two Treatises of Government (ed. Laslett P). Cambridge University Press, Cambridge
MacKinnon CA (1989) Toward a Feminist Theory of the State. Harvard University Press, Cambridge, MA
Marat JP (2003) Chains of Slavery (originally 1774). Dover Publications, Mineola
Marchenko M (2015a) Problemy obshhej teorii gosudarstva i prava [Problems of Common Theory of State and Law], Vol. 2, 2nd edn. Prospect
Marchenko M (2015b) State of Law and Civil Society (in Russian). Prospect, Moscow
Marchenko M (2019) Theory of State and Law. An Elementary Course (in Russian), 3rd edn. Norma, Moscow
Maritain J (1951) Man and the State. University of Chicago Press, Chicago
Marx K, Engels F (1976) The German Ideology. Progress Publishers, Moscow
Montesquieu (1955) Selected Writings (in Russian). Moscow
Montesquieu (1989) The Spirit of the Laws (transl. and ed. Cohler AM, Miller BC, Stone HS). Cambridge University Press, Cambridge
Morozova LA (2021) Theory of State and Law (in Russian), 6th edn. Norma, Moscow

Neff S (2014) Justice among Nations. A History of International Law. Harvard University Press, Cambridge/London
Nersesyants V (2016) Common Theory of Law and State (in Russian). Norma INFRA-M, Moscow
Organization for Security and Co-operation in Europe (1975) Final Act of the Conference on Security and Co-Operation in Europe. OSCE
Pakhman SV (1908) Lectures on the General Part of Civil Law (in Russian). Moscow
Petrażycki L (1955) Law and Morality (transl. Solomon HJ). Harvard University Press, Cambridge
Plato (1925) Statesman (transl. Fowler HN). Harvard University Press, Cambridge
Plato (1926) Laws (transl. Bury R). Harvard University Press, Cambridge
Plato (1937a) Republic (transl. Shorey P). Harvard University Press, Cambridge
Plato (1937b) Republic, Book I (transl. Shorey P). Harvard University Press, Cambridge
Plato (1937c) Republic, Book VIII (transl. Shorey P). Harvard University Press, Cambridge
Rousseau JJ (2004) The Social Contract (transl. Cranston M). Penguin Books, London
Schäffle A (1875–1878) Bau und Leben des sozialen Körpers [Structure and Life of the Social Body], Vols. 1–4. J.G. Cotta, Stuttgart
Schmitt C (2007) The Concept of the Political (transl. Schwab G, ed. Strong T). University of Chicago Press, Chicago
Shaw M (2017) International Law, 8th edn. Cambridge University Press
Shershenevich G (1995) Common Theory of Law (in Russian), Vol. I. Moscow
Silkenat J et al. (2014) The Legal Doctrines of the Rule of Law and the Legal State (Rechtsstaat). Springer International Publishing AG
Smith A (1982) Lectures on Jurisprudence (ed. Meek RL, Raphael DD, Stein P). Liberty Fund, Indianapolis
Sokolova A (2012) Legal Education in Post-Soviet Countries: Problems and Principles of Reform. 2(5) Int'l Lawyer 46
Spengler O (1926) The Decline of the West. Oxford University Press, Oxford
Stoilov Y (2022) Principles of Law: Concept and Application. Prospekt, Moscow
The Holy Bible (1989) New Revised Standard Version. National Council of the Churches of Christ, New York
Toynbee A (1934) A Study of History. Oxford University Press, Oxford
United Nations Security Council (2004) The Rule of Law and Transitional Justice in Conflict and Post-Conflict Societies. Report of the Secretary-General, S/2004/616, 23 August 2004
van Schilfgaarde P (2019) Law and Life. Why Law? Springer
Vas'kovsky EA (1907) Public Law: General Part (in Russian). St. Petersburg
von Gerber CF (1869) Das Problem der Gesetzgebung [The Problem of Legislation]. Mohr, Tübingen
von Hayek FA (2018) The Constitution of Liberty (in Russian). New Publishing Moscow
von Jhering R (1915) The Struggle for Law (transl. Lalor J). Callaghan & Company, Chicago
von Lilienfeld P (1873) Gedanken über die Socialwissenschaft der Zukunft [Thoughts on the Social Science of the Future]. Duncker & Humblot, Leipzig
von Mohl R (1817) Encyclopedie der Staatswissenschaften. Berlin
Weber M (1978) Economy and Society: An Outline of Interpretive Sociology. University of California Press, Berkeley
Welcker CT (1813) Die letzten Gründe von Recht, Staat und Strafe: Philosophisch und nach den Gesetzen der merkwürdigsten Völker rechtshistorisch entwickelt. Heyer, Gießen
Windscheid B (1906) Lehrbuch des Pandektenrechts [Textbook on the Pandects], 9th edn. De Gruyter, Berlin
Wolf E (1961) Gesetz und Gesetzlichkeit in der Theologie und im Recht [Law and Legality in Theology and Law]. Mohr Siebeck, Tübingen
Worms R (1896) Organisme et société [Organism and Society]. Félix Alcan, Paris
Zitelmann E (1880) Die juristische Konstruktion [The Legal Construction]. Duncker & Humblot, Leipzig

MIX
Papier aus verantwortungsvollen Quellen
Paper from responsible sources
FSC® C105338

If you have any concerns about our products,
you can contact us on
ProductSafety@springernature.com

In case Publisher is established outside the EU,
the EU authorized representative is:
Springer Nature Customer Service Center GmbH
Europaplatz 3, 69115 Heidelberg, Germany

Printed by Libri Plureos GmbH
in Hamburg, Germany